William Pope Harrison, Annie Maria Barnes

The Gospel among the Slaves

A Short Account od Missionary Operations Among the African Slaves of the

Southen States

William Pope Harrison, Annie Maria Barnes

The Gospel among the Slaves
A Short Account od Missionary Operations Among the African Slaves of the Southen States

ISBN/EAN: 9783744738934

Printed in Europe, USA, Canada, Australia, Japan

Cover: Foto ©Lupo / pixelio.de

More available books at **www.hansebooks.com**

THE
GOSPEL AMONG THE SLAVES.

A SHORT ACCOUNT OF

MISSIONARY OPERATIONS AMONG THE AFRICAN SLAVES OF THE SOUTHERN STATES.

COMPILED FROM ORIGINAL SOURCES AND EDITED BY

W. P. HARRISON, D.D., LL.D.,
Book Editor, Methodist Episcopal Church, South.

NASHVILLE, TENN.:
PUBLISHING HOUSE OF THE M. E. CHURCH, SOUTH.
BARBEE & SMITH, AGENTS.
1893.

REV. WILLIAM CAPERS, D.D.,
ONE OF THE BISHOPS OF THE M. E. CHURCH, SOUTH.

PREFACE.

The following pages record the results of missionary enterprise among the African slaves of the Southern states. From the earliest records available, the editor has obtained the narrative of the operations of various Christian Churches, including Baptists, Presbyterians, and Episcopalians. The chief authority for this narrative was kindly forwarded to me by the Hon. Richard H. Clark, a gentleman who honors the judicial office in the city of Atlanta, Ga.

To Miss Annie Maria Barnes is due the credit of collecting the materials of this volume from contemporary sources. The work of the editor has been confined to selection, abbreviation, and arrangement of these materials. When no authority is given for a statement in the text, the editor is responsible.

That the general public will be surprised to learn some of the facts recorded in these pages the editor is firmly persuaded. Who among us realizes the fact that the people of the South expended nearly or quite *two millions of dollars* for the evangelization of the slaves on the cotton and rice plantations between the years 1829 and 1864? This amount does not express the total sum expended by Southern slave holders for the benefit of the negro slaves. "Plantation missions" are alone represented, and these comprised a minority of the slaves in most of the Southern states. Nor do we include the expenditures made by other Christian Churches. The two millions of dollars were contributed by the slave holders and their friends to forward the missions to the slaves conducted by the Methodist Episcopal Church from 1829 to 1844, and from 1844 to 1864 by the Methodist Episcopal Church, *South*. THE EDITOR.

Nashville, Tenn., January, 1893.

CONTENTS.

Chapter I.
St. Paul and the Greek Slave 7

Chapter II.
The Degradation of a Name 17

Chapter III.
Man Was Created to Have Dominion over the Earth 29

Chapter IV.
A Brief Historical Sketch 38

Chapter V.
A Brief Historical Sketch (Continued) 57

Chapter VI.
A Brief Historical Sketch (Concluded) 70

Chapter VII.
The Period of Decline: The Cause 88

Chapter VIII.
The Negro without the Gospel 96

Chapter IX.
Negro Insurrections 111

Chapter X.
Beginnings of Missionary Work 117

Chapter XI.
Mission Work (Continued) 136

Chapter XII.
The Gospel on the Plantation 149

CHAPTER XIII.
Plantation Work Continued to 1844 171

CHAPTER XIV.
Notes from the Pioneers 197

CHAPTER XV.
Plantation Missions from 1844 to 1864 297

CHAPTER XVI.
Traits of Christian Character 327

CHAPTER XVII.
Memorials of Faithful Slaves 364

CHAPTER XVIII.
Testimony of Prominent Freedmen 376

CHAPTER I.

St. Paul and the Greek Slave.

ST. PAUL was the first preacher of the gospel to slaves. It is in his writings that we have the first distinct view of slavery as it existed in New Testament times, and from the pen of this apostle to the Gentiles we have distinctly defined the attitude of the Church toward human slavery:

> Art thou called being a servant? care not for it: but if thou mayest be made free, use it rather. For he that is called in the Lord, being a servant, is the Lord's freeman: likewise also he that is called, being free, is Christ's servant. Ye are bought with a price; be not ye the servants of men. Brethren, let every man, wherein he is called, therein abide with God. (1 Cor. vii. 21–24.)

This being the attitude of the Church toward a civil institution, one with which the Church had nothing to do, in enlarging, contracting, or abolishing the relations of master and slave, it is the logical consequence that this apostle should teach as a *religious* duty the service which the state exacts solely as a political duty. St. Paul says:

> Let as many slaves as are under the yoke count their own masters [δεσπότας, despots] worthy of all honor, that the name of God and his doctrine be not blasphemed. And they that have believing masters, let them not despise them, because they are brethren: but rather do them service, because they are faithful and beloved, partakers of the benefit. These things teach and exhort. (1 Tim. vi. 1, 2.)

It will be a profitable inquiry if we look briefly

into the character of the civil institution of slavery as it existed in the lifetime of St. Paul. Prof. Becker, one of the most accomplished scholars of modern times, endeavors to account for what he calls a striking contradiction between the principles and the practice of the Greeks. He says:

> One of the most striking anomalies in the character of the Greeks is, that though they acknowledged above all other nations the value of personal freedom, and kept a jealous guard against every thing that threatened it from within, and were ready to resist to the death any encroachment made upon it from without, still they did not recognize the equal claims of all to this blessing, but withheld it from millions of their fellow-men, whom they made mere personal instruments of their will, and reduced to a condition little superior to that of domestic animals. This strange contradiction may be partly due to their assumption that the barbarians were creatures of a naturally inferior order to themselves, though there was nothing in the habits of those nations which could excuse such arrogance. But the root of slavery lies elsewhere, and must be rather sought in the general disinclination to menial labor, and that abhorrence to servitude, based on false notions of liberty, which first made the possession of slaves desirable. In process of time this grew into an imperious necessity, which refused to take into consideration the justice or injustice of the case; and as there now existed a class of men which had, by birth and education, become divested of all the habits and feelings that were regarded as the essential characteristics of an ἐλεύθερος (freeman), the notion of their belonging to a different race of mankind seemed justified and strengthened. (Chariclea, p. 356.)

In the ideal republic of Plato human slavery was an integral factor. Different laws are given for the freeman and the slave, verbal censure being the punishment for a freeman, where corporal chastisement should be inflicted upon the slave; and offenses punished by fine in the case of the freeman were visited with capital punishment when the criminal was a slave. These distinctions are perfectly in keeping with the Greek view of the *inferiority* of the slave race or races. Captured in war, and bought sometimes for only a few shillings, the ancestors of the slaves of St. Paul's day were either intellectually or morally incapable of contending for their freedom against their masters.

Aristotle does not enter into the question of the origin of slavery, or the moral right that one man has to claim property in the life and service of another. But he distinctly avows the doctrine of the inferiority of the slave race. He contrasts the works, the genius, the achievements in arms, the intellectual eminence of the ruling race with the vices and degradation of the slave, and concludes that the relative position of the two classes is the due of each, the proper reward for innate greatness and innate weakness. He declares that the slave belongs to a ἕτερον γένος, *heteron genos,* a foreign race, an outside genus; and therefore the eternal law that the strong must rule the weak is in perfect keeping with all that we know of the fitness of things in the moral government of the universe. This argument compels him to the conclusion that there is a code of laws especially adopted to the wants and necessities of the φύσει δοῦλοι, the slave natures. Here and there we find a Greek poet, as Philemon, who entered a mild protest against this view of the subject, but from the great mass of the slaves in Greece there was seldom a note of remonstrance or an attempt at self-assertion in contest with their masters for personal liberty.

With the exception of the Helots of Sparta, the Greek slaves were in a much more tolerable condition than those of Rome. The Spartans carried their barbarities to a great length, and in so doing were only giving play to the distinctive features of their character. They were a cruel people. Cruel to their children and to those whom they loved best, it could not be expected that they should be kind and benevolent to those whom they disdained and despised. The clemency of the Athenians toward their slaves does not appear to have been caused by the great preponderance of the slave over the free population. The free burghers of Attica, in the time of Demetrius Phalereus, were found by a census to be twenty-one thousand; there were of resident aliens ten thousand, and of slaves four hundred thousand. Where the physical force was twenty to one against the masters, it was not the lack of power, but the want of capacity or disposition, which prevented the uprising of the servile population against their owners. Nor does it appear that the Greeks anticipated any trouble from the practice of educating their slaves to the various forms of skilled handicraft used in those times. Elevated above the manual labor which they considered servile, the Greek gentlemen did not even employ themselves with the conduct of their own business interests, but placed these in the hands of a better and costlier class of slaves, for whom they often gave extravagant prices, but not so exorbitant as those paid for a similar class among the Romans.

There are writers who are at a loss to imagine what principle was at stake in producing the long-continued and virtually voluntary subjection of a people who outnumbered their masters in the proportion of twenty to one. These persons seem to have but little knowledge of their own times, and especially of the classes of theorists whose speculations they represent. New England has been the quarter from which the most offensive and the most fanatical of these agencies have emanated. If we are to believe Mr. J. Fenimore Cooper, "the besetting, the *degrading vice* of his section of America is the moral cowardice by which men are led to truckle to what is called public opinion." When this public opinion was supposed to be in favor of protecting the manufucturing interests of New England, an abolitionist was mobbed in Boston as freely as a patriotic citizen was threatened with the same treatment if he dared openly to purchase a United States bond in 1814, during the last war with England. Why it was that the Greek slaves, who were not lacking in either intelligence or courage, were really attached to their masters, and would even die in their defense, it is utterly impossible for such worshipers of power to understand. Even Mr. Francis A. Walker, in his recent work on the "Wages

Question," cannot resist the inborn tendency of his people to measure the consciences of others by the clearly defined defects of their own ethical system. He says: "We know, by a mass of revolting testimony, that in all countries avarice, the consuming lust of immediate gain, a passion which stands in the way of a true and enlarged view of self-interest and works unceasing despite to self-interest, has always despoiled the slave of a part of the food and clothing necessary to his highest efficiency as a laborer." (Walker's "Wages Question," p. 59.) To this very oracular statement of matters that may have passed under his own eyes, among the people of his native borough, he characteristically attaches the allegation of a universal custom, holding good in all lands, those of which he has no knowledge as well as those with which he is acquainted. To this oracular deliverance he attaches in a note an ill-grained and surly hypothesis which reveals the weakness of his brethren of the abolition propagandist school in New England. "When slavery was a political and social institution," he says, "as in the Middle States of the American Union, something of grace and kindliness might come to climb upon it." It is a bare possibility that such a thing might be, and this reluctant and ungracious acknowledgment is wrung from this man, who actually believes himself an advocate of truth, by a "mass of testimony" that is "revolting" to fanatics, because it falsifies their declarations and convicts them of uttering the foulest slanders against those who have done *them* no wrong.

But in direct antagonism with all the declarations of self-styled "philanthropists," the Greek slave was attached to his master, as a rule, and therefore the advice of St. Paul was by no means a hardship. "Art thou called being a slave?" Do not suppose that any merely outward circumstances can procure or promote the happiness of the soul. Do not sorrow over the social relation that makes you the inferior of the so-called "higher classes," but accept the grace of God, be faithful to the trusts committed to you, and make your inferior position a means of showing forth the power and glory of the gospel. Nevertheless, if your master sees proper to release you from the estate of bondage, accept the gift of freedom, and use it as wisely as you would have employed yourself in the service of a master. The calling is the same to all men, there is neither bond nor free in the kingdom of God, for all are brethren. And because all are brethren, "let every man, wherein he is called, therein abide with God." To strive against the bonds that Providence has permitted to be placed upon you is to challenge the justice of God, professedly under the influence of the saving grace of the gospel.

The annals of the world have many records of super-serviceable people who have been dissatisfied with Providence, and, like Rebecca, have endeavored to hurry up the plans and purposes of divine wisdom. In every case such well-meant actions have involved the subjects of their interference in sorrow and disaster. Rebecca's stratagem, by which she caused Jacob to personate his elder brother, Esau, was successful in stealing a blessing that would have been rightfully and regularly bestowed upon her favorite son if she had suffered the hand of Providence to direct his own counsels.

Against this folly the apostle cautions the Greek slave. "Let as many slaves as are under the yoke count their own masters worthy of all honor, that the name of God and his doctrine be not blasphemed." The bare refusal to do honor to the master is declared to be blasphemy against the name of God and his doctrine! How utterly irreconcilable is that teaching with the anarchical declarations that pronounce the slave's master a fiend, and the slave's condition a crime, the one to be murdered by knife and bullet, and the other to be abolished by fire and sword!

"And they that have believing masters," continues St. Paul, "let them not despise them because they are brethren, but rather do them service, because they are faithful and beloved, partakers of the benefit." The caution against the abuse of the brotherhood of Christ, by making it a pretense to assert the equality of social station, and because all men are equal in the kingdom of Christ, in point of privilege, to wrest this principle by applying it to the organization of society, where all are *not* equal, never have been, and never will be, even in the millennial state; to do this, is to *despise* the master and dishonor the Lord Christ. " These things teach and exhort."

These were the doctrines that gave Christianity an open door to the Greek and Roman world. The revolutionary theories and incendiary speeches of a Clarkson, a Wilberforce, or even a Wesley, to say nothing of the heaven-daring impiety of New England fanatics, whose souls seemed in many instances to relapse into a state of positive savagery, would have doomed the early Church to extinction in the lifetime of the first preachers of the gospel.

I am aware that these utterances of mine are not popular in this generation, but popularity is not evidence of truth. When hard pressed with these writings of St. Paul, the abolitionists of forty years ago renounced St. Paul, the Bible, and the God of heaven, because it was impossible to defend their insane denunciations of Southern slaveholders by the pages of Holy Writ.

Nor was the *motive* of these crusaders the same that actuated St. Paul in his exhortations to the slaves of Greece. Paul loved the souls of these men. The abolitionists, as a class, cared nothing for the religious welfare of the negro. They were ready to move heaven and earth, and they declared that they were willing to sink the nation in the gulf of irretrievable ruin, unless they could abolish slavery. But once set free, the negro might starve for aught they cared. To do an injury to his master, in his pocket or his pride, they were ready to spend and be spent; but when the unfortunate subject of their zeal had perpetrated all the wrong against his owner that he was capable of doing, then these marvelous "philanthropists" turned the freedman out of doors to look out for himself. They did not hesitate to say that their mission was ended when the bonds of the slave were broken.

"O my soul, come not thou into their secret; unto their assembly, mine honor, be not thou united."

CHAPTER II.

The Degradation of a Name.

IT is a singular fact that the word *slave* occurs but once in the Authorized Version of the New Testament, and in that case it is not a translation of the original word employed by St. John. The fall of "Babylon the great" is vividly described in Revelation xviii., and part of the merchandise lamented as forever lost by the "merchants of the earth" are the proceeds of the sale of "wine, and oil, and fine flour, and wheat, and beasts, and sheep, and horses, and chariots, and *slaves*, and *souls* of men." In the Greek text the word translated "slaves" is σωματων, the *bodies* of men, as the *souls* of men form the counterpart in the next phrase. In Jeremiah ii. 14 our translators have supplied the term *slave*, placing the word in italic letters to show that there was nothing in the original Hebrew to answer to it. The word occurs nowhere else in the English Bible. The text in Jeremiah is one of the many cases in which our English version departs from the letter to preserve the spirit of the Hebrew text. Undoubtedly the prophet intended to ask the question, "Is Israel a slave? Is he born in the house, the property of a master? Why then is he despoiled?" So far from inferring any degradation in this question, the prophet's mind is engaged in considering the fact that as a slave, belonging to a great master, who was able and willing to defend his own property, it is an anomalous thing to find Israel "despoiled." With the usual strength of the parallel inquiry, "Is he a *homeborn* slave?" the prophet calls attention to the fact that Israel is a member of his master's household, a part of his family, entitled to the protection of the sovereign power, the head of the family. Therefore, the despoiling of Israel is a surprising fact, and the reason for it can only be found in the treachery and desertion of the favored slave who has cast away his master's shield and fallen a victim to enemies stronger than he.

But in the New Testament we can scarcely ascertain the reason that induced our translators to omit the rendering "slave" wherever the Greek word δοῦλος occurs. It is absolutely certain that a *bondman*, one bound to a master, bought with his money, or transferred to him as being *property*, is the meaning of the original word. It is a term of specific meaning. It never signifies a hired servant. The word for hired servant in Luke xv. 17, 19, is μίσθιοι, paid servants, or, as the Latin Vulgate has it, *mercenarii*, mercenaries, serving for wages. It is worthy of notice that in the process of time these words, "slave" and "hired servant," have changed places. As early as the old Itala, and later, in the days of Jerome, the latter part of the fourth and beginning of the fifth century, a *hired* servant was a *mercenary*, one in whom the employer had no other interest than the contract of service warranted. The degraded relation is further shown in the parable of the prodigal son. When the homeless wanderer "comes to himself" in the far country, finding himself reduced to share with the swine in their coarse and revolting food, he remembered not the slaves of the family, for these were nearer to his own station and place, but the *hired servants*. "How many hired servants of my father's house have bread enough and to spare!" In the progress of the world, the "hired servant" is now the honorable relation, and the "slave" is odious and infamous.

In all ages and in all countries the existence of a principle which produces a true *aristocracy* in society has been the most important factor in the progress and elevation of mankind. An aristocracy is nothing more than the organization of the *best* members of the social compact. When the tests of superiority are virtue, gentleness, refinement, education, and usefulness, there can be no possible objection to the sentiment which produces and the fidelity which preserves this distinction among men. It is the legitimate product of the world's renowned maxim, "Knowledge is power," and there can be no possible injury to society as a whole by the maintenance of such distinctions.

But when the possession of money, however obtained, whether dishonestly or righteously, by oppressing the poor, the orphan and the widow, or by diligence, frugality, and self-denial—when *wealth* is the only test of aristocratic place and position, a great good is transformed into a great evil. We can have patience with the man who lives in the past and boasts of the great deeds of his ancestors. It is a laudable pride when the descendant proves himself worthy of those who have gone before him, but not otherwise. When it is made the basis of a claim to honors and privileges not possessed by the masses of the people, and when illustrious birth is made an excuse for a debased life and degrading actions, the very reference to the honors of a noble ancestry aggravates the crimes of those who dishonor their parentage while they cover themselves with infamy.

But no man can rightly become indifferent to the sentiment that creates an aristocracy of worth. In early times, physical strength, united to courage and moral worth, designated the proper subjects for the possession of social distinctions, in titles conferred by kings, and honors pointed out by the voice of the people. The various grades of European nobility are founded upon supposed merit, not upon kingly caprice nor popular partiality. In the course of ages, here and there, instances have occurred in which the true principle of aristocracy has been overlooked, or despised, but the advancement of our race from the moral degradation of paganism to the present position of civilized society is largely due to the principle of honoring and ennobling the best members of the social compact.

The Christian Church knows nothing of antagonism to this aristocracy of merit. The estimate placed by St. Paul upon these social dignities would be sufficient to illustrate the importance of the principle. St. Paul does not disdain to mention the prominence of Tarsus, the city of his birth, as a claim that demands at least a hearing at the hands of his enemies. When under guard at Jerusalem, and accosted by the chief captain as "that Egyptian" which had gathered a mob of four thousand men and led them out into the wilderness for purposes of robbery and murder (Acts xxi.), he does not hesitate to assert his respectability, and says: "I am a man which am a Jew of Tarsus, a city in Cilicia, a citizen of no mean city." But while he shows himself to be proud of the city of his nativity, he does not expect or desire exemption from righteous punishment, or escape from just responsibility on that account. He desires to be heard, to defend himself by the highest and grandest of all the forms of logic: the logic of truth.

Prior to this time he had been imprisoned in Philippi, after having endured that most excruciating of all corporal sufferings, the chastisement of the rod. In the noise, confusion, and madness of the hour the apostle had no opportunity to make his voice heard, or he would doubtless have uttered the plea which was so effective the next day. (Acts xvi.) After the wonderful occurrences of the night, the earthquake, the open doors of the prison, the conversion of the jailer, and the sudden alarm of the magistrates of Philippi, word is brought to Paul and Silas in the morning, that the magistrates have ordered their release.

St. Paul exhibits a greatness of soul that astounds his enemies, particularly when they become aware of the cause of his refusal to depart. "They have beaten us openly uncondemned," he declares, and surely this was a charge of sufficient magnitude to cost any magistrate his official position; but Paul adds two words of fearful import to these unworthy officers: "being Romans." There was magic power in that expression, and when the guilty men heard of it, they were only too glad to humble themselves in the presence of these Jews whom they had despised a few hours before. "They came and besought them." That liberty of which they had deprived Paul and Silas was now tendered to them, with the most abject fear and the basest alarm, lest the Roman citizen, whose birthright of immunity from the lictor's rod had been grossly violated, should prosecute them in just retaliation, and bring the power of Cæsar into exercise in vindication of Roman citizenship.

Paul proceeds no further, however, than to humiliate the magistrates, while he gives to the gospel whatever there may be of more favorable consideration from the discovery of his social position. "I am a Roman citizen" was a truly noble record. It did equal honor to the giver and to the receiver. Citizenship in a state that was master of the world was a partnership with all Rome in the glories of more than seven hundred years of the most wonderful history known to men.

Once more the apostle has an opportunity to employ that magic phrase, "I am a Roman citizen," and on this occasion it protects him from the brutality of the Roman scourgers. The chief captain ordered Paul to be punished in order to find out the cause of the unreasonable madness of the mob that clamored for his life. Paul appeals to well-known principles of Roman jurisprudence. Although Cæsar is all-powerful, *the law* is Cæsar's mouthpiece. "Is it lawful for you to scourge a man that is a Roman, and uncondemned?" No Roman could be scourged, whether condemned or uncondemned. In this case, the language of St. Paul is the strongest possible statement of the outrage, indignity, and *crime* which they were about to commit. The centurion sought the chief captain and cautioned him. "Take heed what thou doest; for this man is a Roman." (Acts xxii. 26.) Fear lends celerity to the chief captain's movements. He interrogates the prisoner: "Tell me, Art thou a Roman?" "Yea." Then said the chief captain: "With a great sum obtained I this freedom." "But I," replied Paul, "was freeborn."

Whether the Roman citizenship of St. Paul was due to the honor conferred upon the city of Tarsus, or whether it was a special favor conferred upon the family of St. Paul, is a question that cannot be definitely determined. There are weighty arguments on both sides, but the legitimate inference from the conduct of the chief captain is in favor of the hypothesis of a family gift. When Paul informed his custodian that he was a native of Tarsus, "no mean city," the chief captain certainly did not infer from that statement that Paul was a Roman citizen, which must have been the case if at his birth Tarsus had conferred that privilege. It is possible, however, that this citizenship was only conferred upon a particular class, upon those, for example, who were born in the higher stations of society. The language of Paul, "but I was freeborn," may be understood to apply to the birthright of the Roman citizen, if we reject the word "free," supplied by our translators, and read, in substance, "but I am a Roman citizen by birth." This is a sufficient contrast with the man who had bought his privileges with "a great sum." However the fact may be, the greatness of the honor increased the ground of apprehension on the part of the chief captain. But this apostle, a nobleman of nature, did not seek to inflict punishment upon the petty officer who had endangered place and even life itself by dishonoring a Roman citizen. He makes no plea, utters no complaint, but, when occasion comes, tells his experience and preaches through his own past history the unsearchable riches of Christ.

What shall we think of this apostle, then, when we find him announcing himself in Romans i. 1 as "the *slave* of Jesus Christ?" Is there a special ignominy, an incurable, indelible stain imparted by the word "slave?" Why then does the apostle use it in regard to himself? Why does he make the strange contrast in Galatians i. 10: "If I yet pleased men, I should not be the *slave* of Christ?" How shall we account for the peculiar form of argument which asserts in Galatians iv. 1: "Now I say, That the heir, as long as he is a child, differeth nothing from a *slave*, though he be lord of all?" In Titus he combines the word with the apostolic function: "Paul, a *slave* of God and an *apostle* of Jesus Christ." There is nothing peculiar to St. Paul in this use of the word. St. Peter calls all Christians the "*slaves* of God" in 1 Peter ii. 16. So St. James (j. 1.) calls himself "*a slave* of God and of the Lord Jesus Christ." So also Jude i. and St. John the Divine, Revelation i. 1.

Now these are no accidental facts. The word δοῦλος never meant anything but a bondman. The very essence of the word repels the idea of *hired* service. It is a permanent, lifelong bond that unites the servant to his lord. It is so absolutely settled, fixed, determined, that the servant never looks forward to a period when it shall cease to be. Every interest of the slave is bound up in the same bundle with his master's welfare. The consequence is that the bonds are reciprocal. The slave is bound to his lord, and the master is bound to the slave. Nothing that makes for the physical and moral welfare of the slave can be overlooked or neglected by the master without blame when that master is a pagan, or without sin when that master is a Christian. By the very ties that unite them—ties that are above the sordid nature of a money interest in the labor of the slave—there is nothing that can contribute to the benefit of either that is not shared in some degree by the other.

That there were some Christian masters in Greece is evident by the story of the runaway slave, Onesimus. No refined and cultured mind can read St. Paul's letter to Philemon without feeling his estimate of the manhood of Paul enlarged and exalted. The slave Onesimus leaves his master, and in his wanderings, probably at Rome, he meets with Paul and listens to his preaching. The gospel finds its way to the heart of the fugitive, and he makes known to Paul the truth in regard to himself. He is a runaway. Perhaps he has taken the money of his master, and, like the prodigal son, has spent all, and has no means of repaying it. He cannot go to Philemon, for he is afraid of his master's righteous anger.

Paul volunteers to help him. Unlike the Garrisons, Gerritt Smiths, and Henry Ward Beechers, who cast themselves in the very teeth of human and divine law, and did all that they could to rob the Southern masters of their lawful property, St. Paul determined at once that Onesimus must return to his master. That was the first, necessary, inevitable step. But the apostle further promised to interpose in behalf of the runaway slave, in order to lessen the anger of the master, and to secure to the fugitive a kind reception.

In this spirit Paul pleads most eloquently, tenderly, and efficaciously with the injured master. He reminds him that Philemon himself belongs to Paul, as a convert to the gospel, and therefore owes him far more than he can ever repay. Nevertheless, if Onesimus has taken his master's money, and if the master holds him responsible for the loss of his time, Paul generously offers to pay the whole debt, and binds himself to do so.

Between the conduct and spirit of St. Paul and the conduct and spirit of the abolitionists of fifty years ago there is an "impassable gulf." The one is the conduct of a man who is himself the *slave* of Christ; the other is the conduct of those who are only *hired servants*, who remain in the household just so long as the wages are forthcoming and the sumptuous fare holds out.

It is impossible to read the Bible with attention without perceiving that the inherent sinfulness of human slavery is not taught in the word of God. So far from constituting even a defect in the character of the men of olden times, the most illustrious men in sacred history are recorded as the owners of slaves, and no blame is imputed to them on that account. Abraham, the father of the faithful and the friend of God, was able to raise up a considerable army among the slaves born in his own house. Nor is there a solitary instance in which the mere possession of slaves is stated as a fault, much less a crime.

It is scarcely conceivable that the case could have been otherwise. The time has been in the world's history, and the time now is in the history of many millions of human beings, that the alternative existing for these millions is either slavery or perpetual barbarism.

CHAPTER III.

Man Was Created to Have Dominion over the Earth.

THAT the aboriginal races of men, occupying the soil for thousands of years, yet failing to accomplish the object of their creation, must give place to a higher type of mankind possessing both the genius and the energy to *subdue* the earth, and to exercise dominion over it, is a truth that is illustrated by the history of every aboriginal race. In no quarter of the earth has a savage people been redeemed and civilized without bringing the penalty upon the defaulters. Within a very brief period the Australian tribes have furnished a striking proof of the operation of this law of nature. Mere tenants at will on the domain of Providence, neglecting, and stubbornly refusing to be assisted in learning and developing the powers of the soil upon which they had tented for ages, these people were incapable of obeying the terms of the Great Charter of Man as an occupant of earth. " Be fruitful, and multiply, and replenish the earth, and *subdue* it." This is the command given to the first man. The great charter of humanity, the tenure by which any race holds the earth on which they dwell, is given in the first chapter of Genesis, verse 26: "And God said, Let us make man in our image, after our likeness: *and let them have dominion over the fish of the sea, and over the fowl of the air, and over the cattle, and over all the earth, and over every creeping thing that creepeth upon the earth.''*

Dominion over the earth is the condition of man's residence upon the globe, and wherever any tribe or race shall cease to exercise that dominion in the measure possible to the opportunities of the age, that tribe or race will fade away and be no longer a cumberer of the ground. In proof of this proposition we cite the testimony of Rev. J. G. Wood, author of " The Uncivilized Races of Men: "

> This one tribe is but an example of the others, all of whom are surely, and some not slowly, approaching the end of their existence. For many reasons we cannot but regret that entire races of men, possessing many fine qualities, should be thus passing away; but it is impossible not to perceive that they are but following the order of the world, the lower race preparing a home for the higher.
>
> In the present instance, for example, the aborigines performed barely half of their duties as men. They partially exercised their dominion over the beasts and the birds, killing but not otherwise utilizing them. But, although they inhabited the earth, they did not subdue it nor replenish it. They cleared away no useless bush or forest, to replace them with fruits; and they tilled no land, leaving the earth exactly in the same condition that they found it. Living almost entirely by the chase, it required a very large hunting ground to support each man, and a single tribe gained a scanty and precarious living on a tract of land sufficient, when cultivated, to feed a thousand times their number. In fact, they occupied precisely the same relative position toward the human race as do the lion, tiger, and leopard toward the lower animals, and suffered in consequence from the same law of extinction.

In process of time white men came to introduce new arts into their country, clearing away the useless forest, and covering the rescued earth with luxuriant wheat crops, sufficient to feed the whole of the aborigines of the country; bringing also with them herds of sheep and horned cattle to feed upon the vast plains which formerly nourished but a few kangaroo, and to multiply in such numbers that they not only supplied the whole of their adopted land with food, but their flesh was exported to the mother country.

The superior knowledge of the white man thus gave to the aborigines the means of securing their supplies of food, and therefore his advent was not a curse, but a benefit to them. But they could not take advantage of the opportunites thus offered to them, and, instead of seizing upon these new means of procuring the three great necessaries of human life—food, clothing, and lodging—they not only refused to employ them, but did their best to drive them out of the country, murdering the colonists, killing their cattle, destroying their crops, and burning their houses.

The means were offered to them of infinitely bettering their social condition, and the opportunity given them, by substituting peaceful labor for perpetual feuds, and of turning professional murderers into food producers, of replenishing the land which their everlasting quarrels, irregular mode of existence, and carelessness of human life, had well-nigh depopulated. These means they could not appreciate, and, as a natural consequence, had to make way for those who could. The inferior must always make way for the superior, and such has ever been the case with the savage. I am persuaded that the coming of the white man is not the sole nor even the chief cause of the decadence of savage tribes. I have already shown that we can introduce no vice in which the savage is not profoundly versed, and feel sure that the cause of extinction lies within the savage himself, and ought not to be attributed to the white man, who comes to take the place which the savage has practically vacated. ("Uncivilized Races," Vol. II., p. 790.)

The proofs presented by Mr. Wood are such as no reasonable man can call in question. The Australians are nearly extinct; many tribes of them wholly so. The slow but steady steps that lead to the extinction of the great masses are replaced, in some instances, by an exceedingly rapid progress to oblivion. A missionary testifies as follows concerning the Barrabool tribe, the people whose history occasioned the foregoing remarks of Mr. Wood. Mr. Loyd says:

When I first landed in Geelong, in 1837, the Barrabool tribe numbered upward of three hundred sleek and healthy-looking blacks. A few months previous to my leaving that town, in May, 1853, on casually strolling up to a couple of miam-miams, or native huts, that were erected upon the banks of the Burwan River, I observed seated there nine loobras (women) and one sickly child.

Seeing so few natives, I was induced to ask after numbers of my old dark friends of early days—Ballyyang, the chief of the Barrabool tribe, the great Jaga-jaga, Panigerong, and many others, when I received the following pathetic reply: "Aha, Mitter Looyed, Ballyyang dedac [dead], Jaga-jaga dedac, Panigerong dedac," etc., naming many others; and, continuing their sorrowful tale, they chanted, in minor and funeral tones, in their own soft language, to the following effect:

"The stranger white man came in his great swimming corong [vessel], and landed at Corayio with his dedabul boulganas [large animals], and his anaki boulganas (little animals). He came with his boom-booms (double guns), his white miam-miams [tents], blankets, and tomahawks; and the dedabul ummageet [great white stranger] took away the long-inherited hunting grounds of the poor Barrabool coolies and their children," etc.

Having worked themselves into a fit of passionate and excited grief, weeping, shaking their heads, and holding up their hands in bitter sorrow, they exclaimed, in wild and frenzied tones: "Coolie! coolie! coolie! where are our coolies now? Where are our fathers, mothers, brothers, sisters? Dead! all gone! Dead." Then in broken English they said: "Nebber mind, Mitter Looyed, tir; by'm by all dem black fella come back white fella like it you." Such is the belief of the poor aborigines of Victoria; hence we may fairly infer that they possess a latent spark of hope in their minds as to another and better world.

Then, with outstretched fingers, they showed me the unhappy state of the aboriginal population. From their statement it appears that there existed of the tribe at that moment only nine women, seven men, and one child. Their rapid diminution in numbers may be traced to a variety of causes. First, the chances of obtaining their natural food were considerably lessened by the entire occupation of the best grassed parts of the country, which originally abounded in kangaroos and other animals upon which they subsisted. The greater number of these valuable creatures, as an irresistible consequence, retired into the wild, uninhabitable countries, far from the hands of the white man and his destructive dogs.

Having refused the aid of the government and the Missionary Societies' establishments on the River Burwan and Mount Rouse, the natives were, to a serious extent, deprived of animal food, so essential to a people who were ever exposed to the inclemencies of winter and the exhausting heats of summer. Influenza was one of the greatest scourges under which they suffered. Then, among other evils attending their association with the colonists, the brandy, rum, and tobacco told fearfully upon their already weakened constitutions. (*Ibid.*, p. 789.)

No proposition can be sustained by a greater amount of moral evidence than that which asserts that a mild and Christian form of domestic servitude would have preserved these tribes in the land of the living perhaps for ages. But the temper of the times was not in accord with that view of things. White men desired to have communication with these dark-skinned barbarians only as their own necessities required. The white man was not responsible if the Australian bushman chose to starve to death. There was work for him to do, and honest wages were paid to all that would work. But the accumulating energies of a thousand years found expression in the white man's "push" and "go," for all of which the Australian had neither sympathy nor toleration. Unable to adapt himself to the changed world which white immigration had created; unwilling to place himself in the position of a learner, that he might be taught how to accommodate himself to it; and utterly powerless to prevent the growth and establishment of a state of things which meant nothing but death to him, the miserable savage groaned his life away, leaving his native land in the hands of another, but superior race.

This is perfectly in accordance with all that we know of the divine policy in the government of this earth. Why has God placed in the bowels of the earth immense stores of the precious and the useful metals; inexhaustible supplies of materials that must be sought out, prepared by human skill and industry for the purposes of a civilized society of men? The same great law of design may be seen exemplified in the mineral world that we find in the animal and vegetable kingdoms. Man was born to labor, and only by labor is the highest type of human character attained. We are baffled by difficulties, but encouraged by partial successes, led on, step by step, to further and greater effort, conscious, meanwhile, that no lawful exertion can prove an utter failure. Even the life that has been devoted to noble purposes, and yet failed of actual attainment of the object of lifetime study and research, can be pronounced in no sense a lifetime of labor lost. No man toils after this sort without enriching his generation, and his race, while his own personal exaltation is the legitimate and unfailing reward of his exertions.

Will it be said that a race of human beings who have no capacity to appreciate an argument of this kind have, nevertheless, the right to prevent others from developing the resources of the soil? Has the American Indian, for example, any moral right to hold as his own ten thousand acres per capita, when multitudes of honest, hard-working men have not a yard of earth that they can call their own? Shall the unknown and unmeasured capacity of the soil be doomed to perpetual barrenness because the Indian delights in hunting buffalo and deer?

There are people mad enough to answer all of these inquiries in the affirmative, but there is an unwritten code of moral sentiment that writes its decrees in great events and answers all criticisms by the founding of empires and the creation of a nobler civilization. The horseman who carried a letterbag across the continent was compelled to give way to the driver of the stage coach, and he to the steamboat and the railroad, and these in turn to the captured forces of nature serving the pen of the ready writer with electric power, spanning a continent in a moment of time. Other undeveloped forces lie asleep in the bosom of nature, ready to be awakened whenever the superior man shall break the locks and throw off the chains that have hitherto preserved these agencies until the fullness of time should come, and the wants of mankind should call for their resurrection.

That the African race has been made a partaker in the progress of the nineteenth century is due to the institution which bound them to masters who exacted profitable labor at their hands. In no other country in the known world has the negro race increased in numbers. From 757,178 in 1790 the American negroes increased to nearly four millions and a half in seventy years. The various census reports that have been made of the West Indian negroes show a stationary and, in many places, a decreasing population. Left to themselves in the tropics, these sensual races earn a bare subsistence amid the most abundant provisions of nature.

What is there in the character of the African to make his case an exception to all others among the black tribes of men? If, in a tropical land where one day's work in seven will serve to procure food, and little clothing is required by reason of the climate—if in a land so endowed by nature we find the inhabitants absolutely destitute of the common necessities of life, what must be the condition of the same race when compelled to do battle with the forces of a superior and dominant race?

Can the negro maintain himself in the presence

of the Caucasian? So long as the ties engendered by their former history and experience endure, there will be partial progress and partial development. But the continuance of the struggle must, sooner or later, bring into the field the same moral and physical features which have removed a kindred population in every country that man has conquered from the desolation and ruin of the Adamic fall.

That the negro has many fine qualities of head and heart, and that these qualities were recognized by their masters in the days of slavery, it will be the purpose of this volume to show.

CHAPTER IV.

A Brief Historical Sketch.

IN the year 1842 Rev. C. C. Jones published in Savannah, Ga., a book on "The Religious Instruction of the Negroes in the United States." From this excellent work we copy a short summary of the missionary movements among the slaves prior to the beginning of the nineteenth century. After giving the number of slaves and free persons of color at 757,178 in the census of 1790, the author says:

Having brought distinctly to view this multitude of people introduced amongst us in the inscrutable providence of God, the *original stock* being in a state of absolute *heathenism*, we may inquire into the efforts made for their *religious instruction*.

1673. Mr. Baxter published his "Christian Directory," in which he has a chapter of "Directions to Those Masters in Foreign Plantations Who Have Negroes and Other Slaves; Being a Solution of Several Cases about Them."

The first direction calls upon masters to "understand well how far your power over your slaves extendeth and what limits God hath set thereto."

"Remember that they have immortal souls, and are equally capable of salvation with yourselves; and therefore you have no power to do anything which shall hinder their salvation. Remember that God is their absolute owner, and you have none but a derived and limited property in them; that they and you are equally under the government and laws of God; that God is their reconciled, tender father, and if they be as good doth love them as well as you, and that they are the redeemed ones of Christ. Therefore so use them as to preserve Christ's right and interest in them."

The second direction: "Remember that you are Christ's trustees, or the guardians of their souls; and that the greater your power is over them the greater your charge is of them and your duty for them. So must you exercise both your power and love to bring them to the knowledge and the faith of Christ, and to the just obedience of God's commands."

The third: "So serve your necessities by your slaves as to prefer God's interest and their spiritual and everlasting happiness. Teach them the way to heaven, and do all for their souls which I have before directed you to do for all your other servants. Though you may make some difference in their labor and diet and clothing, yet none as to the furthering of their salvation. If they be infidels, use them so as tendeth to win them to Christ and the love of religion, by showing them that Christians are less worldly, less cruel and passionate, and more wise and charitable and holy and meek than any other persons are. Woe to them that by their cruelty and covetousness do scandalize even slaves and hinder their conversion and salvation!"

The seventh and last direction: "Make it your chief end in buying and using slaves to win them to Christ and save their souls. Do not only endeavor it on the by when you have first consulted your own commodity, but make this more of your end than your commodity itself; and let their salvation be far more valued by you than their service; and carry yourself to them as those that are sensible that they are redeemed with them by Christ from the slavery of Satan, and may live with them in the liberty of the saints in glory."

The works of this eminent servant of God had an extensive circulation, and these directions may have been productive of much good on the plantations of those owners into whose hands they fell.

1630. Forty-four years after the settlement of Connecticut, the assembly forwarded answers to the inquiries of the lords of the Committee of Colonies, wherein they say: "There are but few servants and fewer slaves; not above thirty in the colony. There come sometimes three or four blacks from the Barbadoes, which are sold for £22 each. Great care is taken of the instruction of the people in the Christian religion by ministers catechising and preaching twice every Sabbath and sometimes on lecture days; and also by masters of families instructing their children and servants which the law commands them to do."

1701. "The Society for the Propagation of the Gospel in Foreign Parts" was incorporated under William III. on the 16th day of June, 1701, and the first meeting of the society under its charter was the 27th day of June of the same year. Thomas Lord Bishop, of Canterbury, Primate and Metropolitan of all England, was appointed by his Majesty the first President.

This society was formed with the view, primarily, of supplying the destitution of religious institutions and privileges among the inhabitants of the North American colonies, members of the Established Church of England; and *secondarily*, of extending the gospel to the Indians and negroes.

It had been preceded by a company incorporated by Charles II. in 1661, for "*the Propagation of the Gospel amongst Heathen Nations of New England and the Parts Adjacent in America;*" which, however, did not accomplish much; the design, for the times then present and the necessities of the colonies, being too narrow. The Honorable Robert Boyle was first President of this company, and it was his connection with this society which led him to a deeper interest in the defense and propagation of the Christian religion, and he therefore left in his will an annual salary, forever, for the support of eight sermons in the year for proving the Christian religion against notorious infidels; and he requires that the preachers employed " shall be assisting to all companies and encouraging them in any undertaking for propagating the Christian religion in foreign parts."

" The Society for the Propagation of the Gospel in Foreign Parts" entered upon its duties with zeal, being patronized by the king and all the dignitaries of the Church of England.

They instituted inquiries into the religious condition of the colonies, responded to " by the Governors and persons of the best note" (with special reference to episcopacy); and they perceived that their work "consisted of three great branches: the care and instruction of our people settled in the colonies, the conversion of the Indian savages, and the conversion of the negroes." Before appointing missionaries they sent out a traveling preacher, the Rev. George Keith, an itinerant missionary, who associated with himself the Rev. John Talbot. Mr. Keith preached between North Carolina and Piscataqua River in New England, a tract above eight hundred miles in length, and completed his mission in two years, and returned and reported his labors to the society.

The annual meetings of this society were regularly held from 1702 to 1819, and 118 sermons preached before it by bishops of the Church of England, a large number of them distinguished for piety, learning, and zeal. The society still exists.

The efforts of the society for the religious instruction of the negroes are briefly as follows:

In June, 1702, the Rev. Samuel Thomas, the first missionary, was sent to the colony of South Carolina. The society designed he should attempt the conversion of the Yemassee Indians; but the Governor, Sir Nathaniel Johnson, appointed him to the care of the people settled on the three branches of Cooper River, making Goose Creek his residence. He reported his labors to the society, and said " that he had taken much pains also in instructing the negroes and learned twenty of them to read." He died in October, 1706.

Dr. LeJeau succeeded him in 1706, and found "parents and masters indued with much good will and a ready disposition to have their children and servants taught the Christian religion." He instructed and baptized many negroes and Indian slaves. His communicants in 1714 arose to seventy English and eight negroes. Dr. LeJeau died in 1717, and was succeeded permanently by Rev. Mr. Ludlam, who began his mission with great diligence. "There were in his parish a large number of negroes, natives of the place, who understood English well. He took good pains to instruct several of them in the principles of Christian religion, and afterward admitted them to baptism. He said if the masters of them would heartily concur to forward so good a work, all those who have been born in the country might without much difficulty be instructed and received into the Church. Mr. Ludlam continued his labors among the negroes and every year taught and baptized several of them; in one year eleven, besides some *mulattoes*."

The Indian war checked the progress of the society's mission for several years. The parishes of St. Paul's (1705), St. John's (1707), St. Andrew's and St. Bartholomew's (1713), and St. Helen's (1712) received missionaries. Mr. Hasell was settled in the last-named parish, and the inhabitants were " 565 whites, 950 negroes, 60 Indian slaves, and 20 free negroes."

Rev. Gilbert Jones was appointed missionary of Christ Church Parish in 1711. He used great pains to persuade the masters and mistresses to assist in having their slaves instructed in the Christian faith, but found this good work lay under difficulties as yet insuperable. He wrote thus concerning this matter: "Though laboring in vain be very discouraging, yet (by the help of God) I will not cease my labors; and if I shall gain but one proselyte, shall not think much of all my pains." He was succeeded in 1722 by Rev. Mr. Pownal. Two years after he reported in his parish 470 free born and above 700 slaves, some of which understood the English tongue; but very few knew anything of God or religion.

In the parish of St. George, taken out of St. Andrew's, the church stands twenty-eight miles from Charleston.

1719. Mr. Peter Tustian was sent as missionary, but soon removed to Maryland. The Rev. Mr. Varnod succeeded him in 1723. A year after his arrival, at Christmas, he had nearly fifty communicants, and, what was remarkable, seventeen negroes. He baptized several grown persons, besides children and negroes belonging to Alexander Skeene, Esq. The Rev. Mr. Taylor, missionary at St. Andrew's Parish in South Carolina, reported to the society "the great interest taken in the religious instruction of their negroes by Mrs. Haige and Mrs. Edwards, and their remarkable success, fourteen of whom on examination he baptized." The clergy of South Carolina, in a joint letter, acquainted the society with the fact "that Mr. Skeene, his lady, and Mrs. Haige, his sister, did use great care to have their negroes instructed and baptized." And the Rev. Mr. Varnod, missionary, had baptized eight negro children belonging to Mr. Skeene and Mrs. Haige, and he writes to the society that "at once he had nineteen negro communicants."

Mr. Neuman was sent as a missionary to North Carolina in 1722. He reported sometime afterward that he had "baptized 269 children, 1 woman, 3 men, and 2 negroes who could say the Creed, the Lord's Prayer and Ten Commandments, and had good sureties for their further information."

The Rev. Mr. Beekett, missionary in Pennsylvania in 1723, reported that he had baptized "two negro slaves."

In 1709 Mr. Huddlestone was appointed schoolmaster in New York City. He taught forty poor children out of the society's funds, and publicly catechised in the steeple of Trinity Church every Sunday in the afternoon, "not only his own scholars, but also the children and slaves of the inhabitants, and above one hundred persons usually attended him."

The society established also a catechising school in New York City in 1704, in which city there were computed to be about 1,500 negro and Indian slaves. The society hoped their example would be generally followed in the colonies. Mr. Elias Neau, a French Protestant, was appointed catechist. He was very zealous in his duty, and many negroes were instructed and baptized. In 1712 the negroes in New York conspiring to destroy all the English discouraged the work of their instruction. The conspiracy was defeated and many negroes taken and executed. Mr. Neau's school was blamed as the main occasion of the barbarous plot. Two of Mr. Neau's school were charged with the plot; one was cleared and the other was proved to have been in the conspiracy, but guiltless of his master's murder. "Upon full trial the guilty negroes were found to be such as never came to Mr. Neau's school; and what is very observable, the persons whose negroes were found most guilty were such as were the declared opposers of making them Christians." In a short time the cry against the instruction of the negroes subsided. The Governor visited and recommended the school. Mr. Neau died in 1722, much regretted by all who knew his labors. He was succeeded by Rev. Mr. Wetmore, who afterward was appointed missionary to Rye, in New York. After his removal "the rector, church wardens, and vestry of Trinity Church, in New York City," requested another catechist, there being about 1,400 negro and Indian slaves. A considerable number of them had been instructed in the principles of Christianity by the late Mr. Neau, and had received baptism and were communicants in their Church. The society complied with this request and sent over Rev. Mr. Colgan in 1726, who conducted the school with success.

Mr. Honeyman, missionary in 1724 in Providence, R. I., had baptized in two years 80 persons, of whom 19 were grown, 3 negroes, 2 Indians, and 2 mulattoes.

In Narragansett the congregation was reported to be 160 in 1720, with twelve Indian and black servants.

At Marblehead the missionary reported (in 1725), having baptized two negroes, "a man about twenty-five years old and a girl twelve, and that a whole family in Salem had conformed to the Church."

The society looked upon the instruction and conversion of the negroes as a principal branch of their care, esteeming it a great reproach to the Christian name that so many thousands of persons should continue in the same state of pagan darkness under a Christian government and living in Christian families as they lay before under in their own heathen countries. The society immediately from their first institution strove to promote their conversion, and inasmuch as their income would not enable them to send numbers of catechists sufficient to instruct the negroes, yet they resolved to do their utmost and at least to give this work the mark of their highest approbation. They wrote, therefore, to all their missionaries that they should use their best endeavors at proper times to instruct the negroes, and should especially take occasion to recommend it zealously to the masters to order their slaves at convenient times to come to them that they might be instructed. These directions had a good effect, and some hundreds of negroes had been instructed, received baptism, and been admitted to the communion and lived very orderly lives. (Pages 6-14.)

The Bishop of London's "Letter to the Masters and Mistresses of Families in the English Plantations Abroad, exhorting them to encourage and promote the instruction of their negroes in the Christian faith," and a similar Letter to the Missionaries Engaged in Preaching the Gospel in the English Plantations," exhibit the interest of at least one bishop of the Church of England as early as 1727. The work of the "Society for the Propagation of the Gospel in Foreign Parts" receives particular mention; and the author brings down his sketch to the commencement of the work among the negroes under the direction of the Methodist Episcopal Church:

Dean Stanhope, of Canterbury, states in his sermon in 1714 that success had attended the efforts of the society, and speaks of "children, servants, and slaves catechised."

Bishop Berkeley was in the colony of Rhode Island from 1728 till late in 1730, and he also preached a sermon before the society February 18, 1731, in which he thus speaks of the negroes: "The negroes in the government of Rhode Island are about half as many more than the Indians, and both together scarcely amount to a seventh part of the whole colony. The religion of these people, as is natural to suppose, takes after that of their masters: some few are baptized; several frequent the different assemblies; and for the greater part, none at all. "An ancient antipathy to the Indians, whom, it seems, our first planters (therein as in certain other particulars affecting to imitate Jews rather than Christians) imagine they had a right to treat on the foot of Canaanites or Amalekites, together with an irrational contempt of the blacks as creatures of another species, who had no right to be instructed or admitted to the sacraments, have proved a main obstacle to the conversion of these poor people. To this may be added an erroneous notion that being baptized is inconsistent with a state of slavery. To undeceive them in this particular, which had too much weight, it seemed a proper step, if the opinion of his Majesty's Attorney and Solicitor-general could be procured. This opinion they charitably sent over, signed with their own hands, which was accordingly printed in Rhode Island and dispersed through the plantations. I heartily wish it may produce the intended effect. It must be owned that our reformed planters, with respect to the natives and the slaves, might learn from the Church of Rome how it is their interest and duty to behave. Both French and Spaniards take care to instruct both them and their negroes in the Popish religion, to the reproach of those who profess a better."

From a "Proposal to Establish a College in Bermuda," first published in 1725, the bishop remarks: "Now the clergy sent over to America have proved, too many of them, very meanly qualified, both in learning and morals, for the discharge of their office. And, indeed, little can be expected from the example or instruction of those who quit their native country on no other motive than that they are not able to procure a livelihood in it, which is known to be often the case. To this may be imputed the small care that hath been taken to convert the negroes of our plantations, who, to the infamy of England and scandal of the world, continue heathen under Christian masters and in Christian countries, which would never be if our planters were rightly instructed and made sensible that they disappointed their own baptism by denying it to those who belong to them; that it would be of advantage to their affairs to have slaves who should 'obey in all things their masters according to the flesh, not with eyeservice as men-pleasers, but in singleness of heart as fearing God;' that gospel liberty consists with temporal servitude; and that their slaves would only become better slaves by being Christians." (Berkeley's Works. Copied by Rev. W. W. Eells.)

In 1741 Archbishop Secker, after enumerating other successes, adds: "In less than forty years great multitudes, on the whole, of negroes and Indians, were brought over to the Christian faith."

Bishop Drummond in 1754 notices the negroes in his sermon before the society, and insists upon the duty and safety of giving them the gospel.

The amiable Porteus, in 1783, when Bishop of Chester (afterward Bishop of London), took a lively interest in this work, and preached a sermon before the society in support of it, which may be found in his works.

In the year 1783 and the following, soon after the separation of our colonies from the mother country, the society's operations ceased, leaving in all the colonies forty-three missionaries, two of whom were in the Southern States, one in North and one in South Carolina. The affectionate valediction of the society to them was issued in 1785. Thus terminated the connection of this noble society with our country, which, from the foregoing notices of its efforts, must have accomplished a great deal for the religious instruction of the negro population.

Thus it is perceived that the negroes were not forgotten by the Church of Christ in England. Were they remembered by the Church of Christ in the colonies themselves? We have no records of missions or of missionary stations established by or in any of the colonies in behalf, exclusively, of the negroes up to the year 1738.

1738. The Moravian or United Brethren were the first who formally attempted the establishment of missions exclusively to the negroes. A succinct account of their several efforts down to the year 1790 is given in the report of the " Society for the Propagation of the Gospel among the Heathen," at Salem, N. C., October 5, 1837, by Rev. J. Renatus Schmidt, and is as follows:

"A hundred years have now elapsed since the Renewed Church of the Brethren first attempted to communicate the gospel to the many thousand negroes of our land. In 1737 Count Zinzendorf paid a visit to London, and formed an acquaintance with Gen. Oglethorpe and the trustees of Georgia, with whom he conferred on the subject of the mission to the Indians, which the brethren had already established in that colony in 1735. Some of these gentlemen were associates under the will of Dr. Bray, who had left funds to be devoted to the conversion of the negro slaves in South Carolina; and they solicited the Count to procure them some missionaries for this purpose. On his objecting that the Church of England might hesitate to recognize the ordination of the Brethren's missionaries, they referred the question to the Archbishop of Canterbury, Dr. Potter, who gave it as his opinion 'that the Brethren, being members of an Episcopal Church whose doctrines contained nothing repugnant to the Thirty-nine Articles, ought not to be denied free access to the heathen.' This declaration not only removed all hesitation from the minds of the trustees as to the Brethren amongst the slave population of the West Indies—a great and blessed work, which has, by the gracious help of God, gone on increasing even to the present day."

The same year Brother Peter Boehler was deputed to commence the desired mission, with Brother George Schulius as his assistant. They set out by way of London in February, 1738, and repaired, in the first instance, to Georgia, hoping to be provided with means for the prosecution of their journey by the colony of the Brethren already established there. Obstacles however being interposed through the interested views of certain individuals, this mission failed, and our brethren, settling at Purisburg, took charge of the Swiss colonists and their children in that town, Georgia not being at that period a slaveholding colony. In 1739 Schulius departed this life. In 1740 Peter Bochler emigrated to Pennsylvania with the whole Georgia colony, of which he was minister, because they were required to bear arms in the war against the Spaniards, which had recently broken out. In 1747 and 1748 some Brethren belonging to Bethlehem undertook several long and difficult journeys through Maryland, Virginia, and the borders of North Carolina in order to preach the gospel to the negroes, who, generally speaking, received it with eagerness. Various proprietors, however, avowing their determination not to suffer strangers to instruct their negroes, as they had their own ministers whom they paid for that purpose, our brethren ceased from their efforts. It appears from the letters of Brother Spangenberg, who spent the greater part of the year 1749 at Philadelphia, and preached the gospel to the negroes in that city, that the labors of the Brethren amongst them were not entirely fruitless. Thus he writes in 1751: "On my arrival in Philadelphia I saw numbers of negroes still buried in all their native ignorance and darkness, and my soul was grieved for them. Soon after some of them came to me, requesting instruction, at the same time acknowledging their ignorance in the most affecting manner. They begged that a weekly sermon might be delivered expressly for their benefit. I complied with their request, and confined myself to the most essential truths of Scripture. Upward of seventy negroes attended on these occasions, several of whom were powerfully awakened, applied for further instruction and expressed a desire to be united to Christ and his Church by the sacrament of baptism, which was accordingly administered to them."

At the Provincial Synod which was held in Pennsylvania in 1747 Brother Christian Frohlich was commissioned to take charge of the negroes of New York, who had evinced a great desire for the gospel, and of whom several had been already won for the Redeemer by means of their attendance on the ministry of the word. In 1751 he visited the scattered negroes in New Jersey, by whom he was everywhere received with joy, and preached Christ crucified to a hundred of them at once with considerable effect, besides conversing with them at their work.

A painting is preserved at Bethlehem in which the eighteen firstfruits from the heathen who had been brought to Christ by the instrumentality of the brethren, and had departed in the faith prior to the year 1747, are represented, dressed in their native costume and standing before the throne of Christ with palms in their hands, with the inscription beneath: " These are redeemed from among men, being the first fruits unto God and to the Lamb." (Rev. xiv. 4.) Amongst the number are Johannes, a negro of South Carolina, and Jupiter, a negro from New York. The graves of colored Christians who have died in the Lord are also met with in several of our burial grounds in the North American congregations.

At the request of Mr. Knox, the English Secretary of State, an attempt was made to evangelize the negroes of Georgia. In 1774 the brethren, Lewis Muller, of the Academy at Niesky, and George Wagner were called to North America, and in the year following, having been joined by Brother Andrew Broesing, of North Carolina, they took up their abode at Knoxboro, a plantation so called for its proprietor, the gentleman above mentioned. They were, however, almost constant sufferers from the fevers which prevailed in these parts, and Muller finished his course in October of the same year. He had preached the gospel with acceptance to both whites and blacks, yet without any abiding results. The two remaining brethren being called upon to bear arms on the breaking out of the war of independence, Broesing repaired to Wachovia, in North Carolina, and Wagner set out in 1779 for England.

In the great Northampton revival, under the preaching of Dr. Edwards in 1735–36, when for the space of five or six weeks together the conversions averaged at least "four a day," Dr. Edwards remarks: " There are several negroes who, from what was seen in them then and what is discernible in them since, appear to have been truly born again in the late remarkable season."

At a meeting of the General Association of the colony of Connecticut in 1738 " It was inquired whether the infant slaves of Christian masters may be baptized in the right of their masters, they solemnly promising to train them in the nurture and admonition of the Lord, and whether it is the duty of such masters to offer such children and thus religiously to promise. Both questions were affirmatively answered." (Records as reported by Rev. C. Chapin, D.D.)

Of the condition of the negroes about this time in New England it has been said: "Their lot was far from being severe. They were often bought by conscientious persons, for the purpose of being well instructed in the Christian religion. They had universally the enjoyment of the Sabbath as a day of rest or of devotion."

Looking over the old records of "Entryes for Publications" (*i. e.*, for marriages) "within the town of Boston," I observed the following, among others:

"1707. Negroe.—Essex, a Negro man of Mr. William Clark, Esqre.; Gueno, a R. Wo. of Walle Winthrop, Esqre. Negro. Will, reg. serv't of Wm. Webster: Betty, reg'r serv't of Wm. Keen, March 9th.

"1710. Negroes.—Charles and Peggy, Negro Serv'ts of Sam'l Hill; Esther, Negro serv't of Robert Gutridge, Oct'r 27."

By which it would appear that the community was not indifferent to their condition, inasmuch as their marriages were public and legalized.

1747. Direct efforts for the religious instruction of negroes, continued through a series of years, were made by Presbyterians in Virginia. They commenced with the Rev. Samuel Davies, afterward President of Nassau Hall, and the Rev. John Todd, of Hanover Presbytery.

Mr. Davies began his ministry in Hanover in 1747, and left Virginia about 1773 or 1774. Mr. Davies, four or five years after his settlement in Hanover, "found it impossible to afford even a monthly supply of preaching to the congregation organized by him. Accordingly he sought an assistant in Mr. John Todd, a young preacher from Pennsylvania, who was installed in the upper part of Hanover November 12, 1752."

In a letter addressed to a friend and a member of the "Society in London for Promoting Christian Knowledge among the Poor," in the year 1755, he thus expresses himself: "The poor, neglected negroes, who are so far from having money to purchase books that they themselves are the property of others; who were originally African savages, and never heard of the name of Jesus and his gospel until they arrived at the land of their slavery in America; whom their masters generally neglect, and whose souls none care for, as though immortality were not a privilege common to them as with their masters—these poor, unhappy Africans are objects of my compassion, and I think the most proper objects of the society's charity. The inhabitants of Virginia are computed to be about 300,000 men, one-half of which number are supposed to be negroes. The number of those who attend my ministry at particular times is uncertain, but generally about three hundred who give a stated attendance; and never have I been so struck with the appearance of an assembly as when I have glanced my eye to that part of the meeting-house where they usually sit, *adorned* (for so it has appeared to me) with so many black countenances, eagerly attentive to every word they hear, and frequently bathed in tears. A considerable number of them (about a hundred) have been baptized, after a proper time for instruction, having given credible evidence not only of their acquaintance with the important doctrines of the Christian religion, but also a deep sense of them in their minds, attested by a life of strict piety and holiness. As they are not sufficiently polished to dissemble with a good grace, they express the sentiments of their souls so much in the language of simple nature and with such genuine indications of sincerity that it is impossible to suspect their professions, especially when attended with a truly Christian life and exemplary conduct. There are multitudes of them in different places who are willing and eagerly desirous to be instructed and to embrace every opportunity of acquainting themselves with the doctrines of the gospel; and though they have generally very little help to learn to read, yet to my agreeable surprise many of them, by dint of application in their leisure hours, have made such progress that they can intelligibly read a plain author, and especially their Bibles; and pity it is that any of them should be without them." Mr. Davies furnished the negroes with what books he could procure for them, and requested from the society a supply of Bibles and Watts's psalms and hymns, which enabled them to gratify their peculiar taste for psalmody. "Sundry of them have lodged all night in my kitchen, and sometimes when I have awakened about 2 or 3 o'clock in the morning a torrent of sacred harmony has poured into my chamber and carried my mind away to heaven. In this seraphic exercise some of them spend almost the whole night. I wish, sir, you and other benefactors could hear some of these sacred concerts. I am persuaded it would surprise and please you more than an oratorio or a St.

Cecilia's day." He observes: "The negroes, above all the human species that ever I knew, have an ear for music and a kind of ecstatic delight in psalmody, and there are no books they learn so soon or take so much pleasure in as those used in that heavenly part of divine worship."

On one sacramental occasion " he had the pleasure of seeing forty of them around the table of the Lord, all of whom made a creditable profession of Christianity, and several of them gave usual evidence of sincerity, and he believed that more than 1,000 negroes attended on his ministry at the different places where he alternately officiated."

Mr. Davies writes Dr. Bellamy in 1757: "What little success I have lately had has been chiefly among the extremes of gentlemen and negroes. Indeed, God has been remarkably working among the latter. I have baptized about 150 adults, and at the last sacramental solemnity I had the pleasure of seeing the table graced with about sixty black faces. They generally behave well, as far as I can hear, though there are some instances of apostasy among them." The counties in which Mr. Davies labored were Hanover, Henrico, Goochland, Carolina, and Louisa.

"The Society for Propagating the Gospel in Foreign Parts," already noticed, in 1745 established a school in Charleston, S. C., under the direction of Commissary Garden. It flourished greatly and seemed to answer their utmost wishes. It had at one time sixty scholars and sent forth annually about twenty young negroes well instructed in the English language and the Christain faith. This school was established in St. Philip's Church and some of its scholars were living in 1822, of orderly and decent characters. (Bishop Meade and Dr. Dalcho.)

The year 1747 was marked in the colony of Georgia by the authorized introduction of slaves. Twenty-three representatives from the different districts met in Savannah, and after appointing Major Horton President they entered into sundry resolutions, the substance of which was "that the owners of slaves should educate the young and use every possible means of making religious impressions upon the minds of the aged, and that all acts of inhumanity should be punished by the civil authority."

1764. The Rev. Ezra Stiles, D.D., afterward President of Yale College, and Dr. Samuel Hopkins undertook the education of two apparently promising negroes with a view to the ministry, but it was finally a failure. (Dr. Plumer's report.)

1770. While Dr. Stiles was pastor in Newport, R. I., there were many African slaves in that town. "Of eighty communicants in his Church in that town, seven were negroes. These occasionally met by his direction for religious improvement in his study."

Methodism was introduced into this country in New York in 1766, and the first missionaries were sent out by Mr. Wesley in 1769. One of these, Mr. Pilmore, in a letter to Mr. Wesley from New York in 1770, says: "The number of blacks that attend the preaching affects me much." The first regular Conference was held in Philadelphia in 1773; number of ministers ten, and of members 1,160. From this year to 1776 there was a great revival of religion in Virginia under the preaching of the Methodists in connection with Rev. Mr. Jarratt, of the Episcopal Church, which spread through fourteen counties in Virginia and two in North Carolina. One letter states "the chapel was full of white and black;" another, "hundreds of negroes were among them with tears streaming down their faces." At Roanoke another remarks: "In general the white people were within the chapel and the black people without."

1780. At the Eighth Conference in Baltimore, the following question appeared in the minutes: "Question 25. Ought not the assistant to meet the colored people himself and appoint as helpers in his absence proper white persons, and not suffer them to stay late and meet by themselves? Answer. Yes." Under the preaching of Mr. Garretson in Maryland, "hundreds both white and black expressed their love of Jesus."

1786. The first return of colored members distinct from white occurs in the minutes of this year, and then yearly afterward—white, 18,791; colored, 1,890. "It will be perceived from the above," says Dr. Bangs in his "History of the Methodist Episcopal Church," "that a considerable number of colored persons had been received into the Church, and were so returned in the minutes of the Conference." Hence it appears that at an early period of the Methodist ministry in this country it had turned its attention to this part of the population.

Mr. Rankin, writing on the general state of Methodism in the colonies at the commencement of hostilities, observes: "In

May, 1777, we had forty preachers in the different circuits and about 7,000 members in the society, besides many hundreds of negroes who were convinced of sin, and many of them happy in the love of God." ("Life of Coke," page 33.)

In the year 1786 the following case of conscience was overtured from Donegal Presbytery, in the Synod of New York and Philadelphia, namely: "Whether Christian masters or mistresses ought in duty to have such children baptized as are under their care, though born of parents not in the communion of any Christian Church?"

Upon this overture "the Synod are of opinion that Christian masters and mistresses whose religious professions and conduct are such as to give them a right to the ordinance of baptism for their own children, may and ought to dedicate the children of their household to God in that ordinance when they have no scruple of conscience to the contrary." (Minutes, page 413, and Minutes of General Assembly, page 97.)

And on the next page (414) it was overtured "whether Christian slaves having children at the entire direction of unchristian masters, and not having it in their power to instruct them in religion, are bound to have them baptized; and whether a gospel minister in this predicament ought to baptize them. The Synod determined the question in the affirmative.

1787. The minutes of the Methodist Conference for this year furnish the following question and answer, indicative of continued interest in the colored population: "Question 17. What directions shall we give for the promotion of the spiritual welfare of the colored people? Answer. We conjure all our ministers and preachers by the love of God and the salvation of souls, and do require them by all the authority that is invested in us to leave nothing undone for the spiritual benefit and salvation of them within their respective circuits or districts; and for this purpose to embrace every opportunity of inquiring into the state of their souls, and to unite in society those who appear to have a real desire of fleeing from the wrath to come; to meet such in class, and to exercise the whole Methodist discipline among them." Number of colored members, 3,893.

1790. Again: "Question. What can be done in order to instruct poor children, white and black, to read? Answer. Let us labor as the heart and soul of one man to establish Sunday schools in or near the place of public worship. Let persons be appointed by the bishops, elders, deacons, or preachers to teach gratis all that will attend and have a capacity to learn, from 6 in the morning till 10, and from 2 P.M. till 6, where it does not interfere with public worship. The council shall compile a proper schoolbook to teach them learning and piety." The experiment was made, but it proved unsuccessful and was discontinued. Number of colored members this year, 11,682.

The Methodist is the only denomination which has preserved returns of the number of colored members in its connection. I find it impossible to make any estimate of the number in connection with the other denominations. The Methodists met with more success during this period in the Middle and Southern States than in the Northern, and as they paid particular attention to the negroes large numbers were brought under their influence.

The first Baptist Church in this country was founded in Providence, R. I., by Roger Williams in 1639. Nearly one hundred years after the settlement of America "only seventeen Baptist Churches had arisen in it." The Baptist Church in Charleston, S. C., was founded in 1690. The denomination advanced slowly through the Middle and Southern States, and in 1790 they had Churches in them all. Revivals of religion were enjoyed, particularly one in Virginia, which commenced in 1785 and continued until 1791 or 1792. "Thousands were converted and baptized, besides many who joined the Methodists and Presbyterians." A large number of negroes were admitted to the Baptist Churches during the seasons of revival, as well as on ordinary occasions. They were, however, not gathered into Churches distinct from the whites south of Pennsylvania, except in Georgia. Brief notices of Churches composed exclusively of negroes will be given in the second period of this sketch. Before the Revolution the negroes in Virginia attended in crowds the Episcopal Church, there being no other denomination of Christians of consequence in the State; but upon the introduction of other denominations they went off to them. Old Robert Carter, or Counselor, or King Carter, as he was commonly called among the richest men in the State, owning some 700 or 800 slaves and large tracts of land, built Christ's Church in Lancaster County, Virginia, and reserved one-fourth for his servants and tenants. He was himself baptized, and afterward emancipated a large number of his negroes, and living fourteen or fifteen years a Baptist embraced and died in the faith of Swedenborg.

Our author proceeds to give a brief summary of the moral and religious results of the war of independence. However salutary in a political sense the struggle of the colonies with the mother country might be, the effect of a war which divided whole communities and often set brother against brother and father against son could only be disastrous to the religious welfare of the people. War carries on its front an aggregation of horrors; and leaves in its wake death, desolation, and moral corruption in every community. It might be appropriately said that the American war of the Revolution, although right and just from every point of view, undoubtedly left all moral and religious principles in a state of solution, mixed up in a turbid current of appalling wickedness. It is not our purpose to examine the methods taken to redeem and purify the newly erected states. We have in these pages to deal exclusively with the interests of the African part of the population.

CHAPTER V.

A Brief Historical Sketch (Continued).

THE author whom we quoted in the last chapter has given an impartial review of the special labors of missionaries of various evangelical churches among the negroes. We cannot condense the information he has given in smaller space, and therefore we copy from his pages:

1790. The interest awakened in Virginia by the labors of President Davies continued throughout this period, as appears by the following letter from the venerable Dr. Alexander, of Princeton:

"In addition to the efforts made by the Rev. Mr. Davies, of Hanover, I would mention the name of a faithful coadjutor in this field, the effects of whose labors are still apparent in Cub Creek congregation in Charlotte County, Virginia. The minister to whom I allude was the Rev. Robert Henry, a native of Scotland, who was for many years the pastor of Cub Creek and Briery congregations united, although their distance apart was not less than twenty miles. This gentleman possessed very humble talents as a preacher, blundered much, and sometimes lost himself, so that he had to conclude abruptly. He was so *absent* that on one occasion after preaching, finding the horse of another person hitched where he commonly left his own beast, he mounted and rode him without noticing the mistake. He was notoriously a man of prayer; for when he turned out of the public road to go to the house where he usually lodged the evening before he preached at Briery, he could be heard praying aloud long before he was in sight, and sometimes he became so much engaged that his old bald horse would come up and stop at the gate whilst he was still in earnest supplication.

"This man judiciously turned much of his attention to the negroes, and to them his ministry was attended with abundant success. Many were converted and gathered into the Church at Cub Creek. As this congregation was situated on the northern bank of Staunton River, where the land is very fertile, there were several large estates, possessing many slaves, within reach of the house of worship where he preached."

The Rev. Henry Lacy succeeded Mr. Henry, during whose ministrations at Cub Creek about two hundred were added to the Church. There were sixty belonging to the Church under the care of Mr. Cob. (Rev. W. S. Plumer's report.)

Dr. Alexander proceeds: " Many years after Mr. Henry's death I was settled for several years in this county, and preached at the same places where Mr. Henry had labored. At Cub Creek I found about seventy black communicants, twenty-four of whom belonged to one estate. They were, in general, as orderly and as constant in their attendance on the word preached as the whites. Some of them had been received in Mr. Henry's time, but others afterward. The session of the Church appointed two or three leading men among them to be a sort of overseers or superintendents of the rest, and we found that they performed their duties faithfully.

"It was in this same county, and very much to the large colored congregation at Cub Creek, that Dr. Rice labored after I left the place. He was when first settled pastor of Cub Creek and Bethesda, a new congregation which grew out of the former. As he was willing to bestow a part of his time entirely to the blacks, *the Committee on Missions of the General Assembly* appointed him for about three months in the year to labor among them, and I know that he was much encouraged in his work, had some very promising young converts, and the number of communicants was not diminished in his time. The present pastor (1840) is the Rev. Clement Read, a native of the county. He has labored there and at Bethesda for many years past. *In general the negroes were followers of the Baptists* in Virginia, and after awhile, as they permitted many colored men to preach, the great majority of them went to hear preachers of their own color, which was attended with many evils.

"In some parts of the State the *Methodists* also paid much attention to the negroes and received many of them into their society, but still professors among the Baptists were far more numerous. In many instances those who had been brought into the Presbyterian Church were swept off by one or the other of these sects, but as long as I was acquainted with the congregation at Cub Creek I never knew one of them to leave their own communion for another. We had the testimony of their masters and mistresses to their conscientiousness, fidelity, and diligence. The lady who owned twenty-five of the communicants selected all her house servants from the number, though not herself a communicant in the Presbyterian Church. And on several estates, instead of overseers, some of these pious men were appointed to superintend the labor of the other field servants."

The Rev. Henry Patillo, pastor of the Grassy Creek and Nutbush Churches, in Greenville County, North Carolina, labored successfully among the negroes about this time, the good effects of whose efforts continued to be felt for many years after. (Dr. Plumer's report to Synods of North Carolina and Virginia.)

1792. Toward the close of this year the first colored Baptist Church in the city of Savannah began to build a place of worship. The corporation of the city gave them a lot for that purpose. The origin of this Church, the parent of several others, is briefly as follows: George Leile, sometimes called George Sharp, was born in Virginia about 1750. His master sometime before the American war removed and settled in Burke County, Georgia. Mr. Sharp was a Baptist and a deacon in a Baptist Church, of which Rev. Matthew Moore was pastor. George was converted and baptized under Mr. Moore's ministry. The Church gave him liberty to preach. He began to labor with good success at different plantations. Mr. Sharp gave him his freedom not long after he began to preach. For about three years he preached at Brampton and Yamacraw, in the neighborhood of Savannah. On the evacuation of the country in 1782 and 1783 he went to Jamaica. Previous to his departure he came up from the vessel lying below the city in the river, and baptized an African woman by the name of Kate belonging to Mrs. Eunice Hogg, and Andrew, his wife Hannah, and Hagar, belonging to the venerable Mr. Jonathan Bryan.

The Baptist cause among the negroes in Jamaica owes its origin to the indefatigable and pious labors of this worthy man, George Leile. It does not come within my design to introduce an account of his efforts in that island. I shall add only that in 1784 he commenced preaching at Kingston and formed a Church, and in 1791 had gathered a company of 450 communicants and commenced the erection of a commodious meeting-house. It finally cost, with steeple and bell, £4,000. He was alive in 1810 and about *sixty* years of age.

About nine months after George Leile left Georgia, Andrew, surnamed Bryan, a man of good sense, great zeal, and some natural elocution, began to exhort his black brethren and friends. He and his followers were reprimanded and forbidden to engage further in religious exercises. He would, however, pray, sing, and encourage his fellow-worshipers to seek the Lord. Their evening assemblies were broken up and those found present were punished with stripes. Andrew Bryan and Samson, his brother, converted about a year after him, were twice imprisoned, and they with about fifty others were whipped. When publicly whipped, and bleeding under his wounds, Andrew declared that he rejoiced not only to be whipped, but would freely suffer death for the cause of Jesus Christ; and that while he had life and opportunity he would continue to preach Christ. He was faithful to his vow, and by patient continuance in *well-doing* he put to silence and shamed his adversaries, and influential advocates and patrons were raised up for him. Liberty was given Andrew by the civil authority to continue his religious meetings under certain regulations. His master gave him the use of his barn at Brampton, three miles from Savannah, where he preached for two years with little interruption.

Not long after Andrew began his ministry he was visited by the Rev. Thomas Barton, who baptized eighteen of his followers on profession of their faith. The next visit was from the Rev. Abraham Marshall, of Kioka, who was accompanied by a young colored preacher by the name of Jesse Peter, from the vicinity of Augusta. On the 20th of January, 1788, Mr. Marshall ordained Andrew Bryan, baptized forty of his hearers, and constituted them with others, sixty-nine in number, a Church, of which Andrew was pastor. Such was the origin of the first colored Baptist Church in Savannah. ("Holcombe's Letters," "Analytical Repository," and "Benedict's History of Baptists," from which the preceding account has been taken.)

Before dismissing this notice, I cannot forbear introducing the remarks of Dr. Holcombe on Andrew Bryan, written in 1812: "Andrew Bryan has, long ago, not only honorably obtained liberty, but a handsome estate. His fleecy and well-set locks have been bleached by eighty winters; and, dressed like a Bishop of London, he rides, moderately corpulent, in his chair, and with manly features, of a jetty hue, fills every person to whom he gracefully bows with pleasure and veneration, by displaying in smiles even rows of natural teeth, as white as ivory, and a pair of fine black eyes, sparkling with intelligence, benevolence, and joy. In giving daily thanks to God for his mercies, my aged friend seldom forgets to mention the favorable change that has of late years appeared through the lower parts of Georgia, as well as of South Carolina, in the treatment of servants." (Letter 17.)

1793. The African Church in Augusta, Ga., was gathered by the labors of Jesse Peter, and was constituted this year by Rev. Abraham Marshall and David Tinsley. Jesse Peter was also called Jesse Golfin on account the name of his master, who lived twelve miles below Augusta.

The number of Baptists in the United States this year was 73,471. Allowing one-fourth to be negroes, the denomination would embrace between *eighteen and nineteen thousand.*

1795. The returns of the colored members in the Methodist denomination from 1791 to 1795, inclusive, were 12,884, 13,871, 16,227, 13,814, and 12,170.

Several Annual Conferences recommended a *general fast*, to be held in March, 1796, and in the enumeration of blessings to be invoked the last mentioned was "that *Africans* and Indians may help to fill the pure Church of God." And in the matters recommended as subjects of grateful remembrance in the day of thanksgiving for the last Thursday in October, 1796, the last mentioned is: "And for African liberty; we feel grateful that many thousands of these poor people are free and pious."

1797. The Methodists reported in 1796 11,280 colored members. The recapitulation of the numbers for 1797 is given by states, and as it is a most interesting document, I insert it entire, so far as it relates to the negroes.

State.	Members.	State.	Members.
Massachusetts	8	Virginia	2,490
Rhode Island	2	North Carolina	2,071
Connecticut	15	South Carolina	890
New York	238	Georgia	148
New Jersey	127	Tennessee	42
Pennsylvania	198	Kentucky	57
Delaware	923		
Maryland	5,106	Making a total of	12,215

Nearly *one-fourth* of the whole number of members were colored. There were *three* only in Canada.

Dr. Bang adds: "It will be seen by the above enumeration that there were upward of 12,000 people of color attached to the Methodist Episcopal Church. These were chiefly in the Southern States, and had been gathered principally from the slave population. At an early period of the Methodist ministry in this country it had turned its attention and directed its efforts toward these people with the view to bring them to the enjoyment of gospel blessings. The preachers deplored with the deepest sympathy their unhappy condition, especially their enslavement to sin and Satan; and while they labored unsuccessfully by all prudent means to effect their disenthrallment from their civil bondage, they were amply rewarded for their evangelical efforts to raise them from their moral degradation, by seeing thousands of them happily converted to God. These efforts added much to the labors of the preachers, for such was the condition of the slaves that they were not permitted, on working days, to attend the public administration of the word in company with their masters; and hence the preachers devoted the evenings to their instruction after the customary labors of the day were closed. And although at first there was much aversion manifested by the masters toward these benevolent efforts to elevate the condition of the slaves, yet, witnessing the beneficial effects of the gospel upon their hearts and lives, they gradually yielded their prejudices and encouraged the preachers in their labors, assisted in providing houses to accommodate them in their worship, and otherwise protect them in their religious privileges. While, therefore, the voice of the preachers was not heard in favor of emancipation from their civil bondage, nor their remonstrances against the evils of slavery heeded, the voice of truth addressed to the understandings and consciences of the slaves themselves was often heard with believing and obedient hearts and made instrumental in their deliverance from the shackles of sin and the bondage of Satan. Those who were thus redeemed were enrolled among the people of God, and were consequently entitled to the privileges of the Church of Christ. In some of the Northern cities houses of worship were erected for their special and separate accommodation, and they were put under the pastoral charge of a white preacher, who was generally assisted by such colored local preachers as may have been raised up among themselves; for many such, from time to time, possessing gifts of edification, were licensed to preach the gospel to their colored brethren, and some of these have been eminently useful. In the more southern states, where the municipal regulations in respect to slaves are more severe, some portion of the churches where the white population assemble is usually set apart for the blacks. Their behavior has generally been such as to insure the confidence of their masters and the protection of their civil rulers, though they labored under the disabilities incident to a state of servitude."

1799. This year is memorable for the commencement of that extraordinary awakening which, taking its rise in Kentucky and spreading in various directions and with different degrees of intensity, was denominated "the great Kentucky revival." It continued for above four years, and its influence was felt over a large portion of the Southern States. Presbyterians, Methodists, and Baptists participated in this work. In this revival originated the camp meetings which gave a new impulse to Methodism. From the best estimates the number of negroes received into the different communions during this season must have been between four and five thousand.

1800. The number of members in connection with the Methodists was 13,452. The bishops of the M. E. Church were authorized to ordain African preachers, in places where there were houses of worship for their use, who might be chosen by the majority of the male members of the Society to which they belonged and could procure a recommendation from the preacher in charge and his colleagues on the circuit, to the office of local deacons. Richard Allen, of Philadelphia, was the *first* colored man who received orders under this rule.

1803. The second African Church in Savannah was formed out of the first, December 26, 1802, and Henry Cunningham elected pastor and ordained to the work of the ministry January 1, 1803. On January 2, 1803, another Church was formed out of the first, called the Ogechee Colored Baptist Church, and Henry Francis appointed to supply it. Henry Cunningham was a slave, but obtained his freedom. He is still the pastor of the Second African Church, far advanced in life, and from age unable to attend to his sacred duties, except to a very limited extent. He still enjoys, as he has always enjoyed, the confidence and esteem of all classes of the community in which he has lived so long, so virtuously, and so usefully. The Methodist Conferences reported 22,453 colored members, an increase over the last year of 3,794.

In the report of the congregation of the Moravian Brethren at Graceham, Md., for 1801, Rev. Frederick Schlegel, under date of April 19, writes: "As a number of negroes had for several Sundays successively attended our divine worship, I collected thirteen of them and, after a suitable address, prayed with them. They were very devout, and declared it to be their sincere desire to be truly converted. A few Sundays after, Brother Browne (who preached the gospel to the negroes on Staten Island), being here on a visit, preached to thirty negroes, and after the sermon baptized two children. The transaction made such an impression on two of the adult negroes that they requested that this rite might be immediately performed on them. They were however satisfied with the reasons assigned for deferring it till they had received further instruction in Christianity. A very affecting scene took place at the close of the meeting. A negro overseer, who was present, kneeled down with his people, and in an impressive prayer thanked God for what their souls had enjoyed that day. The number of negroes that attended increased almost every week. At their request a regulation was made according to which separate meetings will be held with them at stated times. Opportunities will also be offered them for private conversation on religious subjects. Some children and a few adults were in the sequel baptized. ("History of the Church of the Brethren," Vol. II., pp. 292, 293.)

1805. An African Church was formed in Boston under the ministry of Thomas Paul, a colored man. Their house of worship was finished in 1806; the lower story was fitted up for a schoolroom.

1806. The Baptist Churches in South Carolina were 130; the number of ministers, 100; and communicants, 10,500, of whom perhaps 3,500 were negroes.

1807. The Hanover Presbytery (Virginia) addressed a circular to the Churches under their care solemnly exhorting them not to neglect their duty to their servants. ("Virginia Magazine," Vol., III., p. 159.)

1809. The Abyssinian or African Church was formed in the city of New York, the house of worship in Anthony Street; also an African Church in Philadelphia, supplied for a time by Henry Cunningham, of Savannah, Ga. The estimate of colored communicants in the Baptist Churches of Virginia this year I set down at 9,000.

1810. By the reports of the state of the congregations of the Protestant Episcopal Church in South Carolina, made in the convention, there were 199 colored communicants in 3 Churches—viz., St. Philip's and St. Michael's, Charleston, 120 and 73, and Prince George's Winyaw, 6. The other reports do not distinguish between white and colored communicants.

1813. There were 40,000 negroes connected with the Baptist denomination in the states of Pennsylvania, Delaware, Virginia, North Carolina, South Carolina, and Georgia. The historian remarks that "among the African Baptists in the Southern States there are a multitude of preachers and exhorters whose names do not appear on the minutes of the Associations. They preach principally on the plantations to those of their own color, and their preaching, though broken and illiterate, is in many cases highly useful."

1816. There was a report adopted by the General Assembly of the Presbyterian Church in the United States on the question, "Ought baptism on the promise of the master to be administered to the children of slaves?" as follows:

"1. That it is the duty of the masters who are members of the Church to present the children of parents in servitude to the ordinance of baptism, provided they are in a situation to train them up in the nurture and admonition of the Lord, thus securing to them the rich advantages which the gospel promises.

"2. That it the duty of Christian ministers to inculcate this doctrine and to baptize all children when presented to them by their masters." ("Minutes of the Assembly.")

The subject of Missions to the negroes occupied the attention of the General Assembly, but no plan of Missions was carried into effect. Dr. Rice, of Virginia, was employed by the Committee on Missions in the Assembly for a part of the year, and his labors were encouraging, as already stated by Dr. Alexander in his letter, and as appears also from the Minutes of the Assembly, p. 372.

The Colonization Society was formed this year, and I notice it as furnishing an index to the feelings of many in relation to the improvement of the negro race.

The Methodists reported this year 42,304 colored members, and a decrease of 883 since 1815. Dr. Bangs says: "This was owing to a defection among the colored people in the city of Philadelphia, by which upward of 1,000 in that city withdrew from our Church and set up for themselves, with Richard Allen, a colored local preacher, and an elder in the Methodist Episcopal Church, at their head. By habits of industry and economy, though born a slave in one of the Southern States, he had not only procured his freedom, but acquired considerable wealth, and since he had exercised the office of a preacher and an elder, obtained great influence over his brethren in the Church. At the secession they organized themselves into an independent body, under the title of the "African Methodist Episcopal Church." At their first General Conference in April, 1816, Richard Allen was elected bishop. At the Conference, in 1828 Morris Brown was elected joint superintendent with Allen; and on the death of Allen, in 1836, Edward Watters was elected joint superintendent with Brown. The colored congregations in New York City followed the example. They adopted the itinerant mode of preaching and have spread themselves in different parts of Pennsylvania, New York, New Jersey, Maryland, and Delaware. There are also some in the Western States, and a few in Upper Canada. In the more southern states the Allenites could make no favorable impression, as their preachers were not recognized by the laws of the states, and the slave population who were members of our Church had the character of our white ministry pledged as a guarantee for their good behavior."

1818. Under the report of colored members for this year, the same writer remarks: "That while there was an increase of white members amounting to 9,035, there was a decrease of 4,261 of the colored members." He states that this was owing to the Allenite secession, although not all who through its influence declared themselves independent attached themselves to the Allenites.

1819. The increase of colored members this year was but 24. (1819, 39,174; 1818, 39,150.) The smallness of the increase is accounted for by the secession of the negroes in New York City, amounting to "14 local preachers and 929 private members, including class leaders, exhorters, and stewards."

A report dated June 14, 1819, of a committee of the Board of Managers of the Bible Society of Charleston, S. C., respecting the progress and present state of religion in South Carolina, will cast some light on the subject before us: "From the best information the committee have been able to obtain, they find that the gospel is now preached to about 613 congregations of Protestant Christians; that there are about 292 ordained clergymen who labor amongst them, beside a considerable number of domestic missionaries, devoted and supported by each denomination, who dispense their labors to such of the people as remain destitute of an established ministry. From actual returns, and cautious estimates where such returns have not been obtained, it appears that in the state there are about 46,000 Protestants who receive the holy communion of the Lord's Supper. In the city of Charleston upward of one-fourth of the communicants are slaves or free persons of color; and it is supposed that in the other parts of the state the proportion of such communicants may be estimated at about one-eighth. In every Church they are freely admitted to attend on divine service. In most of the Churches distinct accommodations are provided for them, and the clergy in general make it a part of their pastoral care to devote frequent and stated seasons for the religious instruction of catechumens from amongst the black population."

It may be proper to state in connection with this report that from the beginning, with scarcely an exception, the negroes applying for admission into the Churches have been under the instruction of white ministers or members; have been baptized and have partaken of the Lord's Supper at the same time with white candidates and members, and been subject to the same care and discipline; no distinction being made between the two classes of members in respect to the privileges and discipline of the Churches.

The Episcopal Church reported in part the number of colored members from 1812 to 1818, the majority in Charleston. The highest number reported was in 1817, 328. In 1818 there were 289.

1820. Bishop McKendree presented an address to the General Conference, at Baltimore, in which he took notice of "the condition of the slaves." The number of colored members, by the Minutes of the Conference, was 40,558.

The census of 1800 gave us 893,041 negro slaves and 110,555 free, making a total of 1,003,596; that of 1810 was 1,191,364 slaves and 195,643 free; total negro population, 1,387,007; that of 1820, 1,538,064 slaves and 244,020 free; total, 1,782,084.

The importation of Africans into our country ceased, by law, on January 1, 1808. The traffic was abolished by Virginia in 1778; Pennsylvania, in 1780; Massachusetts, in 1787; Connecticut and Rhode Island, in 1788. And before the year 1820 measures were taken by all the present free states, in which slavery had existed, for bringing the system to a close. What special efforts, if any, were made in these states by the Churches, or by Societies, for the religious instruction of the negroes thus obtaining their freedom, I have had no means of ascertaining with accuracy. From the best information in possession special efforts were very few and very limited.

As a nation we were scarcely reviving from the Revolution and the excitement of the formation and establishment of our Constitution when we were involved in a war with France, which, with its influences, and what was worse, the infidelity and skepticism which our previous connection with that nation introduced among us, most seriously affected the interests of religion, and the decline was perceptible in a greater or less degree over the whole Union. Not long after, our troubles with England began, which resulted in a four years' war. Notwithstanding these interruptions, the Spirit of God was poured out largely in different parts of the country. Indeed, the first quarter of the nineteenth century witnessed a remarkable revival of the missionary spirit in the American as well as English Churches. Many societies were organized on a large and liberal scale (in whose existence the world has reason to rejoice) for the spreading of the gospel, both at home and abroad, as well as by the circulation of the Scriptures and auxiliary publications, as by the living teacher.

This spirit wrought in the hearts of ministers and people generally, and a new and mighty impulse was given to religion. In the South it awakened many to see the spiritual necessities of the negroes. Many ministers began to preach particularly and more faithfully to them and to attempt a regular division of their time on the Sabbath, between the whites and blacks. Attempts were also made in some parts of the South to teach the negroes letters, so as to enable them to read the word of God for themselves. These schools were short-lived, but the fact of their existence evidences that there was considerable interest felt in their religious instruction. Houses of public worship, exclusively for the use of the negroes, were erected in many of the chief towns, and they worshiped in them under the care of white or colored teachers. In numbers of white churches space was allowed for the accommodation of the negroes, in the galleries or in the body of the house below; and within sight and hearing of the country churches, in some pleasant grove fitted up with booths, with a stand or pulpit for preaching, the negroes would ofttimes be seen assembling for worship between services or in the afternoon. There were planters also who undertook to read and explain the Scriptures, and pray with their people.

It is not too much to say that the religious and physical condition of the negroes were both improved during this period. Their increase was natural and regular, ranging every ten years between 34 and 36 per cent. As the old stock from Africa died out of the country, the grosser customs, the ignorance and paganism of Africa died with them. Their descendants, the country born, were better looking, more intelligent, more civilized, and more susceptible of religious impressions. Growing up under the eyes and in the families of owners, they became more attached to them, were identified in their households and accompanied them to church. The gospel was preached to masters and servants; servants having no religion to renounce grew up in the belief of that of their masters. On the whole, however, but a minority of the negroes, and that a small one, attended regularly the house of God, and, taking them as a class, their religious instruction was extensively and seriously neglected.

CHAPTER VI.

A Brief Historical Sketch (Concluded).

DR. JONES brings down his summary of facts to the year 1842. We quote the record as follows:

1821. The Methodist Episcopal Church reported this year 42,059 colored members in the United States, and their numbers gradually increase.

1822. The account of the labors of the Moravian Brethren by Mr. Schmidt, already referred to, brings down their labors to 1837, and is as follows:

"In January, 1822, a Female Auxiliary to the Missionary Society was formed at Salem, and at their special request an attempt was made to collect the negroes into separate congregations of their own—a plan which had, indeed, long been an object of desire. Brother Abraham Steiner was commissioned to make a commencement of the work by holding a monthly preaching on a plantation about three miles distant from Salem, where the negro communicants resided. At his first sermon there, March 24, 1822, more than fifty black and colored people were present. After a fervent prayer he discoursed on the words of our Saviour: 'The Son of man is come to seek and to save that which was lost.' With this monthly preaching, which was well attended by the negroes, catechetical instruction in the great truths of our religion was combined. On May 19th the Lord's Supper was celebrated with the three persons who were already communicants as the first fruits of this infant negro flock. Great stillness and devotion continued to mark the attendance of the negroes on divine worship, yet few sought for closer fellowship, so that this little flock has never to the present day numbered more than twenty members.

"A negro chapel was built in 1823 at the expense of the Female Auxiliary and consecrated by Brother Benade, the resident bishop, December 28, in the presence of nearly a hundred negroes and colored people and many members of the congregation at Salem. This was followed by the baptism of a married negro woman, and the solemnities of the day were closed by a cheerful love feast, at which the object of our covenant was explained and two negroes were received into the congregation. It was a day of blessing for the negroes, many of whom seemed to be deeply affected. Having now a place of worship of their own, the meetings could be better adapted to their circumstances. Several sisters offered themselves to keep a Sunday school for their benefit, and it was diligently frequented not only by children, but also by adults. This hopeful project was soon, however, painfully interrupted by a law which passed the Legislature of North Carolina forbidding any school instruction to be imparted to the negroes—a prohibition which likewise operated very injuriously on their attendance at the meetings. On May 22, 1833, the negroes were called to mourn over the loss of their faithful and much-loved pastor, Brother Abraham Steiner. His place was supplied by Brother John Renatus Schmidt. For the last year or two they have manifested a greater desire for the word of life, and visited the house of God more diligently, and our testimony to the sufferings and death of Jesus appears to find more entrance into their hearts. In the private meetings of the little negro flock, and particularly at the holy communion, the peace of God is powerfully perceptible. The company of emancipated negroes, upward of twenty in number, who sailed last year for Liberia, on the western coast of Africa, had all been diligent attendants on our meetings and former Sunday school, and one of them was a communicant member of our flock. At parting they declared with tears that nothing grieved them so much as the loss of these privileges. They promised to devote themselves to the Lord Jesus, and to remain faithful to him.

"In the fourteen years which have elapsed since their church was dedicated, 10 adults and 73 children have been baptized and 8 received into the congregation. The little flock consists at present (1837) of 17 adult members, 10 of whom are communicants.

"On the settling of the Brethren in Wachovia, N. C., it was their most cherished object to communicate the gospel both to the Indians on the borders of the Southern States and to the negro population of those states, amounting to several thousands, especially to such as resided in the neighborhood of our congregations, hoping that they might be favored to gather from among them a reward for the travail of the Redeemer's soul. Special meetings were accordingly commenced at Hope and Bethany and elsewhere in the neighborhood of Salem, and the negroes, who were numerous in these districts, were in general diligent in attending them. The various ministers stationed at Salem, the late brethren, Fritz, Kramsch, Wohfahrt, Abraham Steiner, and their wives, interested themselves with particular affection for the spiritual welfare of the negroes in their vicinity, and the Lord so blessed their labors to the hearts of many that they could be admitted to a participation of the Lord's Supper. A thankful remembrance of their faithful services is still retained by the negroes.

"In the prosecution of the Mission amongst the Cherokees, and in the attempt to establish one amongst the Creek Indians, the negroes dispersed among them were not forgotten. Our brethren at Springplace had the gratification of baptizing the firstling of these negroes July 29, 1827. He was a native African of the Tjamba tribe, and was baptized into the death of Jesus by the name of Christian Jacob, continuing faithful to his Christian profession till his happy end."

The Rev. John Mines, pastor of a Church at Leesburg, Va., published at Richmond in 1822, "The Evangelical Catechism, or a plain and easy system of the principle doctrines and duties of the Christian religion. Adapted to the use of Sabbath schools and families, with a new method of instructing those who cannot read."

His "new method" was what is called "oral instruction," the scholars repeating the answers after the teacher until committed to memory. Mr. Mines was much interested in the religious instruction of the negroes. In the preface of his catechism he states that he had several classes of them (taught by his friends). He commends the use of it to masters and mistresses as "a humble attempt" to furnish them with appropriate means for the instruction of their servants in religious knowledge; and he commends it also to his "colored friends in the United States" as a book written "especially for them," and says: "With the help of God I will attend particularly to your spiritual interest while I live."

1823. Bishop Dehon, of the Diocese of South Carolina, had all his good feelings excited in behalf of the negroes. "In his own congregation he was the laborious and patient minister of the African, and he encouraged among the masters and mistresses in his flock that best kindness toward their servants—a concern for their eternal salvation." "He endeavored to enlighten the community on this subject." "He would gladly embrace opportunities to converse with men of influence relating to it," etc. ("Life," by Dr. Gadsden.)

The Rev. Dr. Dalcho, of the Episcopal Church, Charleston, this year issued a valuable pamphlet entitled: "Practical Considerations, Founded on the Scriptures, Relative to the Slave Population of South Carolina." Its design is given in the first paragraph, namely: "To show from the scriptures of the Old and New Testament, that slavery is not forbidden by the divine law; and at the same time to prove the necessity of giving religious instruction to our negroes." Dr. Dalcho mentions that in 1822 there were 316 colored communicants in the Episcopal Churches in Charleston and 200 children in their colored Sunday schools.

A few months before this pamphlet appeared, Dr. Richard Furman, President of the Baptist State Convention of South Carolina, in the name of that convention addressed a letter to his Excellency, Governor Wilson, giving an "Exposition of the views of the Baptists relative to the colored population of the United States," in which, among other observations, we find the following: "Their religious interests claim a regard from their masters of the most serious nature, and it is indispensable."

The lamented Dr. John Holt Rice, already mentioned in this sketch, presented the subject of the religious instruction of the negroes in a strong light to the consideration of his fellow-citizens of Virginia in the *Evangelical Magazine*, Vol. VIII., pp. 613, 614. He printed a sermon on the duty of masters to educate and baptize the children of their servants. Through his influence many in Virginia were induced to give the duty of the religious instruction of the negroes serious consideration, which resulted in action. One of his objects in devoting himself to the establishment of the Prince Edward Theological Seminary was that a ministry might be educated at home and fitted for the field composed as it is of masters and servants, bond and free. This was also one prominent object in the minds of many ministers, elders, and laymen in the foundation and endowment of the Theological Seminary of the Synod of South Carolina and Georgia in Columbia, S. C.

1828. The number of colored members in the Methodist Episcopal Church was 48,096, and for 1825, 49,537; 1826, 51,334; 1827, 53,565; 1828, 58,856; showing a steady increase. In 1828 "a plain and easy catechism, designed chiefly for the benefit of the colored persons, with suitable prayers and hymns annexed," was published by Rev. B. M. Palmer, D.D., pastor of the Circular Church, Charleston, S. C." Six or eight years before this he had published a smaller work of the same kind and bearing nearly the same title. During all his ministry in Charleston, he was a firm supporter of the religious instruction of the negroes, both in word and deed.

1829. The Hon. Charles Cotesworth Pinckney, of the Episcopal Church, delivered an address before the Agricultural Society of South Carolina, in which he ably and largely insisted upon the religious instruction of the negroes. This address went through two or more editions and was extensively circulated and with the happiest effects.

1830. The historian of the Methodist Episcopal Church remarks: "This year several Missions were commenced for the special benefit of the slave population in the States of South Carolina and Georgia. This class of people had been favored with the labors of the Methodist ministry from the beginning of its labors in this country, and there were at this time 68,814 of the colored population in the several states and territories in our Church fellowship, most of whom were slaves. It was found however on a closer inspection into their condition that there were many that could not be reached by the ordinary means, and therefore preachers were selected who might devote themselves exclusively to their service."

He alludes particularly to the "Missionary Society of the South Carolina Conference, Auxiliary to the Missionary Society of the Methodist Episcopal Church," which, at least so far as its efforts respect the negro population, the Rev. Williams Capers, D.D., superintendent of these Missions to the negroes from their commencement, has spared no exertions to extend and render successful. The reports of the Board of Managers, drawn up from year to year by himself, exhibit the purity and fervor of his zeal in so good a cause, as well as the remarkable progress which it has made.

In the winter of 1830 and the spring of 1831, two Associations of planters were formed in Georgia for the special object of affording religious instruction to the negroes by their own efforts and by missionaries employed for the purpose. The first was formed by the Rev. Joseph Clay Stiles in McIntosh County, embracing the neighborhood of Harris's Neck, which continued in operation for some time, until by the withdrawment of Mr. Stiles's labors from the neighborhood and the loss of some of the inhabitants by death and removals, it ceased. The second was formed in Liberty County by the Midway Congregational Church and the Baptist Church under their respective pastors, the Rev. Robert Quarterman and the Rev. Samuel Spry Law, which Association, with one suspension from the absence of a missionary, has continued its operations to the present time.

One or more associations for the same purpose were formed in St. Luke's Parish, S. C., in which John David Mungin, Esq., took an active part.

1831. An address entitled "The Religious Instruction of the Negroes," delivered before the Associations of McIntosh and Liberty Counties, was published and circulated in newspaper and pamphlet form.

1832. Edward R. Laurens, Esq., delivered an address before the Agricultural Association of South Carolina, in which this duty in the form of oral instruction, under proper arrangements is recognized. (*Southern Agriculturist*, 1832.) "A short catechism for the use of the colored members on trial of the M. E. Church in South Carolina: by W. Capers, D.D., Charleston, 1832."

This short catechism was prepared by Dr. Capers for the use of the Methodist Missions to the negroes of the South Carolina Conferences, and it is used by all the missionaries.

1833. The Missionary Society of the South Carolina Conference, which had now fairly entered upon its work, reported that the Missions were generally in flourishing circumstances; that there were 1,395 colored members, and 490 children under catechetical instruction at the Mission stations. The Society also recommended the establishment of four or five new stations and the appointment of three or four new missionaries for stations already occupied. (Report, pp. 12–15.)

The "First Annual Report of the Liberty County Association was published and circulated in two editions.

Two essays were read before the Presbytery of Georgia, in April, 1833: one on "The Moral and Religious Condition of Our Colored Population," and the other "A Detail of a Plan for the Moral Improvement of Negroes on Plantations," by Thomas Savage Clay, Esq., of Bryan County. They were both published by order of the Presbytery. The "Detail," etc., by Mr. Clay, which was indeed the result of his own experience and observation on his own plantation for many years, was extensively circulated and received with approbation, and has done, and is still doing, much good.

In December of this year the "Report of the Committee to whom was referred the subject of the religious instruction of the negroes," of the Synod of South Carolina and Georgia was published. To this report a series of resolutions were subjoined:

"1. That to impart the gospel to the negroes of our country is a duty which God in his providence and in his word imposes on us.

"2. That in the discharge of this duty we separate entirely the civil and religious condition of the people; and while we devote ourselves to the improvement of the latter, we disclaim all interference with the former.

"3. That the plan which we shall pursue for their religious instruction shall be that permitted by the laws of the state, constituting the bond of this Synod.

"4. That we deem religious instruction to master and servant every way conducive to our interests for this world and for that which is to come.

"5. That every member of this Synod, while he endeavors to awaken others, shall set the example and begin the religious instruction of the servants of his own household, systematically and perseveringly, as God shall enable him.

"6. That we cannot longer continue to neglect this duty

without incurring the charge of inconsistency in our Christian character; of unfaithfulness in the discharge of our ministerial duty; and at the same time meeting the disapprobation of God and our consciences."

The narrative of religion of the Synod at the same session holds the following language: "The Synod continues to feel the same responsibilities and desires on this subject which they have repeatedly expressed. They rejoice to find that increasing attention is paid to it on the part of many who are largely interested as owners in this class of our population." (Minutes, pp. 24–34.)

The project of forming a Domestic Missionary Society, under the care of the Synod, with special reference to the religious instruction of the negroes, was somewhat discussed, chiefly in private, and a committee was appointed by the Synod to bring in a report at the next meeting.

The reports from the Episcopal Churches in South Carolina to the convention evidenced much attention to the negroes. The Rev. Joseph R. Walker, of Beaufort, reported 57 communicants and 234 members of the Sunday school, which was conducted by the first and best society in the place.

Bishop Ives, of North Carolina, addressed the convention "on the interesting subject of providing for our slave population a more adequate knowledge of the doctrines of Christ crucified." He stated in a letter to Bishop Meade that active efforts, in behalf of this people, were made in five or six of the Churches, and singled out the Church of St. John's, Fayetteville, embracing between three and four hundred worshipers, of whom forty were communicants.

There were several religious newspapers, conducted by different denominations, that advocated openly and efficiently about this time the religious instruction of the negroes: the *Gospel Messenger*, Episcopal, Charleston; the *Charleston Observer*, Presbyterian; the *Christian Index*, Baptist; the *Southern Christian Advocate*, Methodist; the *Western Luminary*, Kentucky; and there may be added the *New Orleans Observer* and the *Southern Churchman*, Alexandria, besides others. Through these papers, having an extensive circulation, the subject was presented to the minds of thousands of our citizens.

There was published this year (1833) "A Plain and Easy Catechism, designed for the benefit of colored children, with several verses and hymns, with an appendix; compiled by a missionary: Savannah." This missionary was a Methodist, the Rev. Samuel J. Bryan, who labored among the negroes on the Savannah River.

"The encouraging success which had attended the labors of our preachers among the slaves and free black population of the South stimulated our brethren in the Southwest to imitate their example by opening Missions for the special benefit of this class of people. Hence at the last session of the Tennessee Conference the African Mission, embracing the colored population of Nashville and its vicinity, was commenced. A regular four weeks' circuit was formed, and the good work was prosecuted with such success that in 1834 there were reported 819 Church members." (Bangs 4, p. 143.)

1834. A meeting was held in Petersburg, Va., in March, 1834, composed of representatives from the Synods of North Carolina and Virginia. After disposing of the special business for which the meeting was called, the subject of the religious instruction of the negroes was discussed, and as a result a committee was appointed, consisting of three ministers and elders in each of the states, " to bring before the Presbyteries the subject of ministers giving more religious instruction to the colored people, and to collect and publish information on the best modes of giving oral instruction to this class of our population" That committee, of which Rev. William S. Plumer, D.D., now of Richmond, was the Chairman, performed its duty and presented a report to the Synods of North Carolina and Virginia at their fall sessions in 1834. The same report, with some accompanying documents, was forwarded to the Synod of South Carolina and Georgia, and read before that body in December, 1834.

The committee of the Synods of North Carolina and Virginia reported a plan "for forming a society by the concurrence of two or more Synods for the purpose of affording religious instruction to the negroes in a manner consistent with the laws of the States and with the feelings and wishes of planters." The plan was laid before Synod of North Carolina and acceded to. It was laid over by the Synods of Virginia, South Carolina, and Georgia to their session in 1835, and then, for special reasons, indefinitely postponed. A report was presented by a committee of the Synod of South Carolina and Georgia, on this plan. The report was adverse to it, on account of the extent of the proposed organization, the excitement of the times, and the belief that each Synod could of itself conduct the work more successfully than when united with the other two. The Constitution of the proposed society, the reasons in favor of it, and Dr. Plumer's report, were all laid before the public in the columns of the *Charleston Observer.* The report has been several times referred to in this sketch.

The Synod of South Carolina and Georgia in December, 1834, passed the following resolutions:

"1. That it be enjoined upon all the Churches in the Presbyteries comprising this Synod to take order at their earliest meeting to obtain full and correct statistical information of the number of colored persons in actual attendance at our several places of worship, and the number of colored members in our several Churches, and make a full report to the Synod at its next meeting; and for this purpose that the stated clerk of this Synod furnish a copy of this resolution to the stated clerk of each presbytery.

"2. That it be enjoined on all Presbyteries in presenting their annual report to the Synod to report the state of religion in the colored part of the congregations, and also to present a statistical report of the increase of colored members, and that this be the standing rule of the Synod on this subject." The narrative states that "increasing efforts had been made to impart religious instruction to the negroes." (Minutes, pp. 22-29.)

The Synod of Mississippi and Alabama, in their narrative November 1, 1831, says: "Another very encouraging circumstance in the situation of our Church is the deep interest which is felt in behalf of our colored population, and the efforts which are made to impart to them religious instruction. All our ministers feel a deep interest in the instruction of this part of our population, and when prudently conducted we meet with no opposition. A few of us, owing to peculiar circumstances, have no opportunity of preaching to them separately and at stated times; but embrace every favorable opportunity that occurs. Others devote a portion of every Sabbath, others a half of every Sabbath, and two of our number preach exclusively to them. During the past year the condition and wants of the colored population have occupied more of our attention than at any previous period, and in future we hope to be more untiring in all our efforts to promote their happiness in this life and in that which is to come." In their resolutions this Synod enjoined all under their care directly to make "united efforts to provide means for the employment of missionaries to give oral instruction to the colored population on the plantations with the permission of those persons to whom they belong."

In this same year (1834) "the Kentucky Union, for the moral and religious improvement of the colored race" was formed, and a "circular" addressed to the ministers of the gospel in Kentucky, by the Executive Committee of that Union, to which the Constitution was appended. It was "a union of the several denominations of Christians in the state." The Rev. H. H. Kavanaugh was President; there were ten Vice Presidents, selected from different quarters of the State, and an Executive Committee of seven members, located in Danville, of which Rev. John C. Young was Chairman. President Young told me at the General Assembly of 1839 that this Union had not accomplished much.

The "second annual report" of the Liberty County Association was published, giving some good account of their operations. "An Essay on the Management of Slaves, and especially on their religious instruction," read before the Agricultural Society of St. John's, Colleton, S. C., by Whitemarsh B. Seabrook, President, was published by the Society. Mr. Seabrook reviews some former publications on the religious instruction of the negroes, and suggests his own plans and views on the subject. The Right Rev. William Meade, Assistant Bishop of Virginia, published an admirable "pastoral letter to the ministers, members, and friends of the Protestant Episcopal Church in the diocese of Virginia, on the duty of affording religious instruction to those in bondage." The bishop, in his zeal and personal efforts on this subject, demonstrates the sincerity of his published opinions.

The Missionary Society of the South Carolina Conference reported five missionaries to the blacks; one in North Carolina, the rest in South Carolina, and 2,145 members and 1,503 children under catechetical instruction.

"The Colored Man's Help; or the Planter's Catechism: Richmond, Va." was now published.

Also, in the *Charleston Observer,* "Biographies of Servants Mentioned in the Scriptures; with Questions and Answers,"

These admirable sketches were prepared by Mrs. Horace S. Pratt, then of St. Mary's, Ga., and now of Tuscaloosa, Ala. The Rev. Horace S. Pratt, previously to his appointment to a professorship in the Alabama College at Tuscaloosa, and while pastor of the St. Mary's Presbyterian Church, gave much of his attention to the religious instruction of the negroes and prepared at his own expense a comfortable and commodious house of worship for them, and which they occupy at the present time.

Also, "A Catechism for Colored Persons: by C. C. Jones," printed in Charleston.

1835. "The Third Annual Report of the Liberty County Association" was printed and more extensively circulated than the two preceding.

In the narrative of the state of religion in the Synod of South Carolina and Georgia, it is said: "Even the religious instruction of our slave population, entirely suspended in some parts of the country, through the lamentable interference of abolition fanatics, has proceeded with almost unabated diligence and steadiness of purpose through the length and breadth of our Synod." (Minutes, 1835, p. 62.)

Bishop Bowen, of the diocese of South Carolina, prepared at the request of the Convention and printed "A Pastoral Letter on the Religion of the Slaves of the Members of the Protestant Episcopal Church in the State of South Carolina," to which he appended "Scripture Lessons," for the same.

The subject had been presented to the Convention by an able report from a committee, and a portion of the report was embodied in Bishop Bowen's letter.

The Missionary Society of the South Carolina Conference reported this year 2,603 members and 1,330 children under catechetical instruction.

1836. The Rev. George W. Freeman, late rector of Christ's Church, Raleigh, N. C., published two discourses on "The Rights and Duties of Slaveholders." Mr. Freeman with pathos and energy urges upon masters and mistresses the duty of religious instruction.

The report of the Liberty County Association was prepared,

but not published this year. The operations of the Association during the year had been successful.

The bishops of the M. E. Church in the United States, in their letter of reply to the letter from the Wesleyan Methodist Conference, England, held the following language: " It may be pertinent to remark that of the colored population in the Southern and Southwestern States there are not less than 70,000 in our Church membership; and in addition to those who are mingled with our white congregations, we have several prosperous Missions, exclusively for their spiritual benefit, which have been and are still owned of God to the conversion of many precious souls. On the plantations of the South and Southwest our devoted missionaries are laboring for the salvation of the slaves, catechising their children and bringing all within their influence, as far as possible, to the saving knowledge of Jesus Christ. And we need hardly add that we shall most gladly avail ourselves, as we have ever done, of all the means in our power to promote their best interests." The total number of colored members reported for 1836 was 82,661.

1837-38. The subject of the religious instruction of the negroes was called up and attended to in the Synod of South Carolina and Georgia both these years, and many Sunday schools for children and adults reported from the different Presbyteries. It also received attention in all the Southern Synods. There appeared to be a growing conviction of the duty itself, and on the whole an increase of efforts.

The instruction of the negroes in Liberty County by the Association was carried forward as usual during the summers of these years, but in consequence of the absence of the missionary in the winters no reports were published.

The Missionary Society of the South Carolina Conference prosecuted its work with encouraging success. In an annual meeting in the town of Columbia, S. C., they collected for their Missions to the negroes between $1,200 and $1,500.

Bishop Meade collected and published " Sermons Dialogued, and Narratives for Servants, to be read to them in families: Richmond, 1836."

The second edition of the " Catechism for Colored Persons; by C. C. Jones: Savannah. T. Purse, 1837." Also, "A Catechism to be used by the teachers in the religious instruction of persons of color, etc., prepared in conformity to a resolution of the Convention, under the direction of the bishop: Charleston." The reverend gentlemen of the diocese of South Carolina, who united in preparing this catechism, were Dr. Gadsden (now bishop), Mr. T. Trapier, and Mr. William H. Barnwell.

The following resolution was passed in the Episcopal Convention of South Carolina in 1838: "*Resolved*, That it be respectfully recommended to the members of our Church, who are proprietors of slaves individually and collectively, to take measures for the support of clerical missionaries and lay catechists, who are members of our Church, for the religious instruction of their slaves."

And again: "*Resolved*, That it be urged upon the rectors and vestries of the country parishes to exert themselves to obtain the services of such missionaries and lay catechists."

1839-40. From the reports of the Liberty County Association for these years, it appears that a revival of religion commenced toward the close of the summer of 1838 among the negroes, and extended very nearly over the whole country, and continued for two years. The whole number received into the Congregational and Baptist Churches, on profession of their faith, was fully two hundred and fifty. The number of adults and children under catechetical instruction in the Sabbath schools connected with the Association and the different Churches ranged from five to seven hundred. The Missionary Society of the South Carolina Conference reported in 1839 13 Missions, 210 plantations, 19 missionaries, 5,482 Church members, and 3,769 children catechised; in 1840, 13 Missions, 232 plantations, 19 missionaries, 5,482 Church members, and 3,811 children. (Minutes.)

The Methodists returned in 1840 94,532 colored persons in their Conference.

The Rev. T. Archibald (Presbyterian) labored as a missionary to the negroes in Mississippi for several years, and in 1839, after leaving his charge in consequence of the abolition excitement, he received a call to preach to the negroes in Marengo County, Ala.

The Rev. James Smylie and Rev. William C. Blair (of the same denomination) were and still are (if our late information be correct) "engaged in this good work systematically and constantly" in Mississippi. The Rev. James Smylie is characterized as "an aged and indefatigable father; his success in enlightening the negroes has been very great. A large proportion of the negroes in his old Church can recite both Willison's and the Westminster Catechism very accurately."

The names of many other pastors in the South might be given, who have conscientiously and for a series of years devoted much time to the religious instruction of the negroes connected with their Churches.

The Rev. James Smylie and Rev. John L. Montgomery were appointed by the Synod of Mississippi in 1839 to write or compile a catechism for the instruction of the negroes. The manuscript was presented to the Synod in October, 1840, and put into the hands of a committee of revision, but it has not yet been published.

The table on the state of the Churches of the Sunbury Baptist Association, Georgia, gives six African Churches with a total of 3,987 members, as returned. One of these Churches did not return the number of communicants. Of the other Churches in the table, five have an overwhelming majority of colored members. The three African Churches in Savannah are all connected with this Association. In the Appendix to the Minutes it is said: "The committee to whom was referred Brother Sweat's letter on the subject of a Mission among the African Church reports that it is highly important that such a Mission should be established, and recommend that the subject be turned over to the Executive Committee with the instruction that the brethren engaged in that work during the past year be compensated for their services. Your committee further recommend that Brother Connor be employed as a missionary by the Association, provided he will devote half his time to the colored people."

And again: "That the table showing the state of the Churches may be more correct than the present, it is requested that at the next meeting of the Association the Church clerks will distinguish in their reports between the white and colored members, and that such Churches as send no delegates will forward a statement of their condition."

"Missions to the people of color" is noticed in the annual report of the Missionary Society of the M. E. Church in 1840.

The report thus speaks: "And surely those who devote themselves to the self-sacrificing work of preaching the gospel to these people on the rice and sugar plantations of the South and Southwest are no less deserving the patronage of the Missionary Society than those who labor for the same benevolent object in other portions of the great work. Of these there are chiefly in the Southern Conferences 12,402 members under the patronage of this Society." (Report, p. 23.)

1841. The report of the same Society for this year refers also to "Missions to the colored population." In no portion of our work are our missionaries called to endure greater privations or make greater sacrifices of health and life than in these Missions among the slaves, many of which are located in sections of the southern country which is proverbially sickly, and under the fatal influence of a climate which few white men are capable of enduring even for a single year. And yet, notwithstanding so many valuable missionaries have fallen martyrs to their toils in these Missions, year after year there are found others to take their places, who fall likewise in their work, "ceasing at once to work and live." Nor have our Superintendents any difficulty in finding missionaries ready to fill up the ranks which death has thinned in these sections of the work; for the love of Christ and the love of the souls of these poor Africans in bonds constrain our brethren in the itinerant work of the Southern Conferences to exclaim: "Here we are, send us." The Lord be praised for the zeal and success of our brethren in this self-denying and self-sacrificing work.

The Missionary Society of the South Carolina Conference reported this year of Missions exclusively to the negroes, 14; plantations served, 301; members, 6,145; children under catechetical instruction, 3,407; and missionaries, 18. The report gives an animated and cheering view of the prospects of these Missions. The great object of the Society in them is thus expressed: "So to preach this gospel that it may be believed, and being believed may prove 'the power of God unto salvation' is the great object, and we repeat it, the sole object of our ministrations among the blacks. This object attained, we find the terminus of our anxieties and toils, of our preaching and prayers." (Report, pp. 12-17.)

The total of colored communicants in the Methodist connection is given in the Minutes of the Annual Conferences for the years 1840 and 1841. For 1840, 94,532, and for 1841, 102,158. The South Carolina Conference is ahead of all, having 30,481; next comes the Baltimore Conference, 13,904; then the Georgia Conference, 9,989; Philadelphia, 8,778; Kentucky, 6,321, and so on. (Minutes, p. 156.)

The Sunbury Association reported this year seven African Churches, with 4,430 members (from one no returns); adding to this number the returns from the mixed Churches of white and black, and an estimate of some from which no returns were made, a total of 5,664 colored members is obtained. Appendix B: "*Resolved*, That the committee be authorized to offer a sum not exceeding $50 per month for one or more ordained ministers to labor among the colored people and destitute Churches within the bounds of this Association."

Bishop Meade, of Virginia, made a report to the Convention of his diocese "on the best means of promoting the religious instruction of servants," the result of his extended observation and long experience in this department of labor.

Bishop Gadsden, of South Carolina, devotes a considerable portion of his address to the Convention to the subject of the religious instruction of the negroes. He thus speaks: "Of that class peculiar to our social system, the colored people, many are members of our Church, as are the masters of a very large number of them who as yet are not converted to the gospel. To make these fellow-creatures, who share with us the precious redemption which is by Jesus Christ, good Christians is a purpose of which this Church is not and never has been regardless. The interest and efforts in this cause have increased. But the feeling ought to be much deeper, and the efforts more extended. Consider the large number who are yet almost, if not entirely, without the restraint, the incentives, the consolations, and the hopes of the gospel, under the bondage of Satan, and on the precipice of the second death. I speak more particularly of those the smoke of whose cabins is in sight of our ministers who live on the same plantations with members of our Church. Can nothing be done, ought not everything be done that can be, to bring such persons to the knowledge and obedience of Christ?"

There are thirty-one parochial reports. In twenty-two of the thirty-one Churches there are colored members, amounting to 869. In fifteen there are Sabbath schools for colored children, amounting to 1,459 scholars. Eight of the clergy preach on the plantations as well as to their colored congregations, and there are two Missions to the negroes, embracing 1,400 in the congregations. Children catechised on the plantations.

The practice of the Episcopal Church in this diocese cannot be too highly commended to those who are of similar faith in the matter referred to, which is the baptism of the infants and children of negroes who are members of the Church. When God established his visible Church on earth, he constituted the infant seed of believers members of it, and therefore commanded that the sign and seal of his gracious covenant should be applied to them. His Church has ever remained the same, the members the same, and under the same Constitution. Our practice ought to confirm to our faith, and to the plain teachings of the word of God. A recurrence to this subject will be necessary when the means and plans for the religious instruction of the negroes come under consideration in the fourth part of this work, and I therefore dismiss it in this place. There were 159 colored children baptized in the Churches of the diocese by the parochial reports. (Journal of the Fifty-second Convention, pp. 10-13 and pp. 33-48.)

From the seventh annual report of the Liberty County Association for the religious instruction of the negroes, it appears that the efforts of the Association during the year had been successful. There were 450 children and youth under catechetical instruction, and adding four schools not immediately under the care of the Association, but conducted by members of it, there were 265 more. Seven Sabbath schools in all were returned, and three stations for preaching. Congregations during the year full and attentive; general order of the people commendable.

Appended to this report is the address to the Association by the President, the Rev. Josiah Spry Law; an address which received the cordial and unanimous approbation of the Association as one which placed the religious instruction of the negroes in a clear light, as the great duty of their owners, as well as of the Churches. It was believed by the Association that the address was calculated to exert a favorable influence wherever it should be circulated in our country, and it was therefore, with the consent of the author, ordered to be printed.

CHAPTER VII.

THE PERIOD OF DECLINE: THE CAUSE.

LIVING in the midst of these missionary movements, and heartily in sympathy with them, Dr. Jones becomes an important witness in regard to the period of decline which followed the abolition propaganda of New England. He gives a statement of the tendency among the negroes to throw off all dependence upon the whites, taking the control of their own Church affairs in the so-called "Free States." Concurrently with this secession in the North, the agitation of the slavery question in New England alarmed the slaveholders of the South. The consequence was inevitable. The religious interests of the slaves suffered serious damage by the incendiary utterances of the Garrisons and other leaders of the abolition movement. Our author states the case in conservative language:

> Of late years the negroes in the free states have manifested a strong inclination to be independent of the influence and control of the whites, and to create and manage their ecclesiastical establishments in their own way; a very natural inclination, and not to be wondered at nor objected against, provided they are capable of taking care of themselves, which, however, many of their warmest friends not only seriously doubt, but wholly deny. As a specimen of this disposition I would refer to the secession of Richard Allen and his associates in Philadelphia, from the Methodist Church, which secession extended into New York

and other states. Of this secession in New York, Dr. Bangs thus writes: "It is now (1839) twenty years since this secession took place, and the degree of their prosperity may be estimated from the following statement of their number of circuits and stations, preachers and members taken from their Minutes for 1839: Circuits, 21; preachers, 32; members, 2,608. These circuits and stations are found in the states of New York, New Jersey, Connecticut, Rhode Island, and Massachusetts. In the city of New York, where the secession originated, they have a membership of 1,325, making an increase of 396 in twenty years, which is by no means in a ratio with their increase while they remained under the care of their white brethren. In the city of Boston, however, their success had been greater in proportion. In 1819 they had only 33, but now, in 1839, they have 126. As the M. E. Church never derived any temporal emolument from them, so we have sustained no other damage by the secession than what may arise from missing the opportunity of doing them all the good in our power as their pastors," etc.

In the slave states there has been action in ecclesiastical bodies on the religious instruction of the negroes, and the value of such action is that it discovers a good disposition on the part of ministers and Churches to fulfill their duty to this people.

The Episcopal Church has rather taken the lead in making efforts and in keeping up an interest in its own bosom. Bishop Meade, of Virginia, a long and unwearied advocate of this cause, Bishop Ives, of North Carolina, Bishop Bowen, of South Carolina (before his decease), and the present bishop of that state, Dr. Gadsden, have each addressed their dioceses on this subject, and commended it to the clergy and laity. The subject has been discussed in their Conventions, accompanied with some able reports. Many of the clergy devote time to the instruction of the negroes attached to their congregations, and have regular and flourishing Sabbath schools. It is a stated fact that in the Episcopal Churches generally in South Carolina there are Sabbath schools for the negroes, and some of them large and flourishing.

There are several Episcopal missionaries to this people in the state. The Churches in Charleston have always been active in the instruction of the negroes, and the present bishop, Dr. Gadsden, has been long known as an advocate of the work.

The lately elected Bishop of Georgia, Rev. Stephen Elliott, D.D., has brought the subject before his Convention in his "primary address" (1841), and urged attention to it with an energy and a zeal which promises great blessings to the negroes connected with the Churches of his new and interesting diocese. The negroes connected with the Episcopal Church have generally been noted for intelligence and fidelity.

The Methodists do not yield in interest and efforts to any denomination. From the commencement of their Church in the United States they have paid attention to the negroes, of which we have had ample proof in the progress of this sketch. In the slave states they have, next to the Baptists, the largest number of communicants. The negroes were brought under the same Church regulations as the whites, having class leaders and class meetings and exhorters, as the Church Discipline requires. The number of negro communicants is reported at their Conferences as well as labors in their behalf, and where it is necessary traveling preachers are directed to pay attention to them. In the South Carolina Conference the Missionary Society, already referred to, has a field of operations among the negroes along the seaboard, from North Carolina to the southern counties of Georgia. The missionaries of this society labor chiefly on river bottoms, and in districts where the negro population is large and the white population small, and it is understood receive most of their support from the planters themselves, whose plantations they serve. We know of no other Missionary Society in this denomination so fully devoted to this particular field, but there are Methodist missionaries for the negroes in Tennessee, Mississippi, Alabama, and other slave-holding states. Without a doubt, as the Lord has opened wide the door of usefulness to this denomination among the negroes, it will not fail to exert itself to the utmost. Bishop J. O. Andrew, whose circuit is in the Southern States, has taken up the subject in good earnest and is prosecuting it with energy and success.

The Baptists have no societies in existence expressly for evangelizing the negroes, although their Associations and Conventions do, from time to time, call up the subject and act upon it. There are more negro communicants and more Churches regularly constituted, exclusively of negroes, with their own regular houses of public worship, and with ordained negro preachers, attached to this denomination than to any other denomination in the United States.

It is difficult to collect the direct efforts of this denomination for the instruction of negroes, as the reports of the Associations are not easily obtained, they being printed and circulated chiefly within their respective bounds. If investigation were carefully made, it might be found that in many of the Associations of this denomination as much attention is paid to the instruction of the negroes as in the Sunbury Association, Georgia, already referred to. There are missionaries in destitute settlements who devote a portion of their time to this people. Perhaps in most of the chief towns in the South there are houses of public worship erected for the negroes alone. There are three, for example, in the city of Savannah. A year or two since I preached to the Baptist negroes in Petersburg, Va., in their own house of worship, crowded to suffocation.

The Presbyterians have had ecclesiastical action within the present period in the Synods of Virginia and North Carolina, South Carolina and Georgia, Kentucky, Mississippi, and Alabama, and in the Presbyteries of all these Synods. Some Presbyteries have distinguished themselves by their zeal and activity in the instruction of the negroes.

It is unnecessary to transcribe the resolutions, reports, and acts of these several bodies. Some have already met the eye of the reader. The latest and most general and satisfactory returns in our possession were gathered from the statements of members of the General Assembly of 1839, from the slaveholding states, at a meeting called by themselves for the purpose of taking into consideration the religious instruction of the negroes, and of communicating information and suggesting plans of operation. It will suffice to present the sum of the whole in a few words.

In the Synods of Kentucky, Virginia, North Carolina, Tennessee, and West Tennessee it is the practice of a number of ministers to preach to the negroes separately once on the Sabbath or during the week. There are also Sabbath schools in some of the Churches for children and adults, and in all the houses of worship, with a few exceptions, a greater or less number of colored members and negroes form a portion of every Sabbath congregation. In portions of these Synods the abolition excitement checked and in others materially retarded the work of instruction.

In the Synods of Alabama and Mississippi almost all the ministers devote a portion of the Sabbath to the negroes. There are two or three missionaries within the bounds of these Synods, and some flourishing Sabbath schools. Access, in many parts of the two states, may be had to the negroes, of unlimited extent. The abolition excitement injured the cause.

In the Synod of South Carolina and Georgia many ministers preach to the negroes separately on the Sabbath or during the week, and maintain Sabbath schools. Especially is this the fact along the seaboard of the two states. The Presbytery of Georgia has one missionary to the negroes, and in the country where he labors there are seven Sabbath schools connected with the Congregational and Baptist Churches, and upward of 600 children and youth in a course of catechetical instruction. There are three stations for missionary preaching on the Sabbath, occupied in rotation, and in addition, during the winter and spring, preaching on the plantations. There are colored members in all the Churches in this Synod, and accommodations for the negroes in the houses of public worship. The sessions conduct the discipline of the colored members in the same manner that they do the whites. They are received into the Churches under the same form and partake of the ordinances at the same time.

The ministers in the newly formed Presbytery of Florida are devoting attention to this field of labor, dispersing information and preaching as opportunity offers.

Such are the principal facts touching the religious instruction of the negroes during the third period from 1820 to 1842. And in view of them, as we close the period, we feel warranted in considering it a period of the revival of religion in respect to this particular duty, throughout the Southern States, more especially between the years 1829 and 1835.

This revival came silently, extensively, and powerfully, affecting masters, mistresses, ministers, members of the Church, and ecclesiastical bodies of all the different evangelical denominations. Some local associations of planters were formed, and societies on a large scale contemplated, and one brought to perfect organization. Sermons were preached and pamphlets published, the daily press lent its aid, and manuals of instruction were prepared and printed. Nor was there any opposition of moment to the work, conducted by responsible individuals, identified in feeling and interest with the country. Some portions of the South were in advance of others, both in respect to the acknowledgement and performance of the great duty, but the light was gradually diffusing itself everywhere.

Such was the onward course of things when the excitement in the free states on the civil condition of the negro manifested itself in petitions to Congress, in the circulation of inflammatory publications, and other measures equally and as justly obnoxious to the South, all of which had a disastrous influence on the success of the work we were attempting to do. The effect of the excitement was to turn off the attention of the South from the religious to the civil condition of the people in question, and from the salvation of the soul to the defense and preservation of political rights. The very foundations of Society were assailed, and men went forth to the defense. A tenderness was begotten in the public mind on the whole subject, and every movement touching the improvement of the negroes was watched with jealousy. Timid, ambitious, and factious men, and men hostile to religion itself, and men desirous of warding off suspicion from themselves, agitated the public mind within our own borders. The result was to arrest in many places efforts happily begun and successfully prosecuted for the religious instruction of the negroes. It was considered best to disband schools and discontinue meetings, at least for a season. The formation of societies and the action of ecclesiastical bodies in some degree ceased.

The feelings of men being excited, those who had undertaken the religious instruction of the negroes were looked upon with suspicion, and some of them were obliged to quit the field. It was not considered that a separation might be made between the religious and the civil condition and interests of a people, and that a minister could confine himself to the one without interfering at all with the other. This entire effect upon the slave states of the movement in the free states, considering all circumstances, was natural, but it was wrong; wrong because, let others act as they might, we should have gone forward and done what was obviously our duty. We could have done it; for the whole arrangement of the religious instruction of the negroes, as to teachers, times, places, matter, and manner, was in our own power. And wrong again because, admitting that the wishes of these professed friends of the negroes were to be consummated, no better could be done for the negroes, nor for ourselves, than to teach them their duty to God and man. The gospel certainly hurts no man and no body of men. Parts of the southern country took such actions as was deemed necessary (if at all), calmly and decidedly, nor were any difficulties thrown in the way of the regular course of religious instruction. A missionary in the heart of three or four thousand negroes, during the period of excitement, visited plantations during the week, and met congregations on the Sabbath, varying from 150 to 500 persons; yet it cannot be denied that the Northern movements did sensibly affect the feeling in favor of the religious instruction of the negroes throughout the whole slaveholding states, and the first prominent cause of the decline in the revival of which we speak was unquestionably those movements, and I mention the fact because the cause of that decline is sometimes inquired into.

From information obtained by correspondence and in other ways, there are favorable indications that a reaction has taken place within one or two years past, and that, taking the country throughout, more religious instruction is communicated to the negroes now than ever before. The old friends of the cause for the most part retain their integrity and labor on, while the Lord is impressing deeply the hearts and consciences of owners, and is raising up many youth in the ministry and in the Churches to carry forward the work more extensively.

The third period is now completed, and with it this historical sketch of the religious instruction of the negroes, since their first introduction into this country to the present time. I shall add in the conclusion the following general observations:

1. The negro race has existed in our country for two hundred and twenty-two years, in which time the gospel has been brought within the reach of and been communicated to multitudes, and tens of thousands of them have been converted, and have died in the hope of a blessed immortality. And there are

at the present time tens of thousands connected by a creditable profession to the Church of Christ, and the gospel is reaching them to a greater extent and in greater purity and power than ever before.

2. While there have been but few societies (and those limited in extent and influence) formed for the special object of promoting the moral and religious instruction of the negroes, and while there have been comparatively but few missionaries exclusively devoted to them, yet they have not been altogether overlooked by their owners nor neglected by the regular ministers of the various leading denominations of Christians, as the facts adduced in this sketch testify.

3. Yet it is a remarkable fact in the history of the negroes in our country that their regular, systematic religious instruction has never received in the Churches at any time that general attention and effort which it demanded, and the people have consequently been left, both in the free and in the slave states, in great numbers, in moral darkness and destitution of the means of grace.

4. The great and good work, therefore, of the thorough religious instruction of our negroes remains to be performed.

The colored population of the United States in 1830 was 2,009,043 slaves and 319,599 free, making a total of 2,328,642. By the last census, 1840, it was 2,487,113 slaves and 386,235 free, with a total of 2,873,348. This aggregate of 2,873,348 is certainly large enough to awaken our most serious attention, whether we view this people in a religious or civil point of light.

CHAPTER VIII.

THE NEGRO WITHOUT THE GOSPEL.

WE have given the foregoing sketch of missionary operations among the negroes because it was prepared by one eminently fitted for the task, and the materials gathered by him embraced all accessible means of information. The fact that Dr. Jones was not a Methodist gives additional force to his highly complimentary notices of the labors of the Methodist Episcopal Church in this important field of evangelization. But after we have given due credit to the efforts of the early missionaries of the "Society for the Propagation of the Gospel in Foreign Parts," and the occasional visits of evangelists of the Presbyterian and Baptist Churches, it must be confessed that the greatest harvest of souls has been reaped by the followers of Coke and Asbury. Methodism was an organism filled with deep and earnest piety. The fervor of the worship accorded with the impulsive and emotional nature of the negro, and thousands of the race heartily embraced the truth under the preaching that touched their hearts and filled their imaginations with the liveliest pictures of religious joy. But these negroes were, for the most part, "house negroes." They were slaves being in immediate contact with white persons.

REV. HENRY M. TURNER,
Bishop of the African M. E. Church.
(See page 870.)

From their masters and mistresses they insensibly imbibed many refining and elevating tendencies, and when these masters were professed Christians their influence helped to form a superior class of negro slaves. Many of the household servants were present at the family altar, and the daily prayers were addressed to the court of heaven in their behalf in common with the white members of the family. Lectures on the Sabbath day were given for the benefit of the negroes when there was no regular service by a Christian minister. These advantages created a favored class among the negroes, and the eye of a Southerner can almost instantly detect, by the grace of manner and the easy bearing of the person, the members of this "household of saints" belonging to the "olden time."

But the great majority of slaves were not thus favored. Living to themselves on large rice and cotton plantations, they had no social and, in the earlier times of this century, no religious facilities for development or progress. Having no standard of morals higher than their own, and coming in contact with no correcting authority, not even the reproof of well-wishing equals, we cannot be surprised at the low moral *status* of the "plantation negro." The proofs of this depravity are very numerous; and as the state of the negro previous to missionary efforts will be contrasted in these pages by the results of pioneer work among them at a subsequent period, we present the picture of the African slave without the gospel as that picture has been drawn by those who knew him in all the lights and shadows of his being.

Edwin C. Holland, Esq., published in Charleston, S. C., his "Refutations of Calumnies against the Southern and Western States in 1822." Referring to the practice of *allowancing* the negroes in the lower parts of the Atlantic States, Mr. Holland says:

> If it be asked why those in the lower country are *allowanced* while those of the interior are not, the answer is that such are the facilities of transportation to market and the disposition to thievery so innate to the blacks, that a planter's barn would in a very short time become bankrupt of its wealth, and the whole of his substance vanish like unsubstantial moonshine.

Every one acquainted with the surroundings of the rice planters in South Carolina and Georgia will readily vouch for the correctness of this statement. In almost every section of the thickly populated regions there will be found agents of Satan, who tempt the slaves in time of slavery, and the hired freedman in the time of freedom. These execrable wretches are generally foreigners, and by keeping a small stock of groceries on hand in little shops disguise the sale of ardent spirits to negroes. These tempters have no moral restraints of any kind. They induce the negroes to buy ardent spirits, and in order to pay for the indulgence the slave, having no money, carries to the gin mill his master's rice or whatever would be received as a subtitute for money. These leeches, by making enormous profits both ways, on the execrable liquors they sold and the merchandise taken in exchange, soon laid the foundations of large fortunes, acquired, in the beginning at least, by a trade but one degree below, if not indeed as infamous as the kidnapping of men and women on the shores of Africa.

Reputable merchants were always careful in their dealings with the negroes on these large plantations, but there were so many willing tools, known in the city courts as " fences," people who assisted the thief in the disposal of stolen property, that the master was often compelled to appear harsh and cruel, when a contrary course would have ended in his own financial ruin. There are traditions in all of our Atlantic seaboard territory of places, islands, swamps, dense coverts far away from civilization, where this unholy traffic has maintained large populations unknown to the takers of the census. Magnified these stories may be, but there is some foundation for them, and those who so fiercely denounced the rice planters of fifty years ago would do well to remember that all the facts have never appeared in their defense against the charge of inhuman treatment of their negroes.

But the African, as a savage, transported to America, must bring the sins and vicious nature which belong to his people and his tribe. The foolish dream of a virtuous savage, communing with nature, and rising to the highest altitudes of virtuous humanity, has long been dispelled, as nearer acquaintance revealed to the world the truth.

The fearful picture of the heathen who knows not God, as given by St. Paul in the first chapter of the Epistle to the Romans, is as true to-day as in the day in which it was written. We cannot be surprised then that these negroes, many of them born in Africa, should deserve the severe sentence of Dr. Delcho, of the Episcopal Church, in a publication issued in 1823. "Ignorant and indolent by nature," he says, "improvident and depraved by habit, and destitute of the moral principle, as they generally appear to be, ages and generations must pass away before they could be made virtuous, honest, and useful members of society." This language is too severe. "Destitute of the moral principle," they are not, as a race, for we shall have occasion to produce some of the finest specimens of moral integrity that the annals of human character can show. Nevertheless, it is not surprising that observing men, such as Dr. Delcho, should use such unqualified language. They "generally appear" to lack the foundation upon which Christianity must build if the gospel is to mold the life and habits of the negro.

The same deficiency, the absence of the moral sense, is attributed to the Chinese, as a nation, by Bayard Taylor. If we mistake not, he makes the charge without any qualifying sentence. But Mr. Taylor did not weigh his words. If the Chinaman and the negro have no moral sense, it is useless to preach the gospel to them. They have no souls according to this dark view of their condition.

But Chinamen have been converted and have testified in life and in death, witnessing a good confession under circumstances not greatly dissimilar to the trials of the apostles of the first century. So, also, we are prepared to exhibit many instances of commanding eloquence, testimonies of faithfulness not inferior to Paul's integrity and Peter's firmness. Even death itself could not break the bands of truthful allegiance, or shake the confidence of these black heroes of the cross.

Notwithstanding these instances, however, the life of the slave, removed from the influence and example of the whites, was a scene of great depravity. Gen. Thomas Pinckney, in a work published in Charleston in 1822, says:

> Everything consigned to the management of the slave, who has neither the incitement of interest nor the fear of certain punishment, is neglected or abused; horses and all inferior animals left to their charge are badly attended; their provender finds its way to the dramshop, and they are used without discretion or mercy; their carriages and harness are slightly and badly cleaned; the tools of the mechanics are broken and lost through neglect; their very clothing becomes more expensive through their carelessness arising from the knowledge that they must be supplied with all these articles, as well as their subsistence, at their master's expense, and waste, that moth of domestic establishments, universally prevails.

The Hon. Charles Cotesworth Pinckney, in an address before the Agricultural Society of South Carolina in 1829, says:

> There needs no stronger illustration of the doctrine of human depravity than the state of morals on plantations in general. Besides the mischievous tendency of bad example in parents and elders, the little negro is often taught by these his

natural instructors that he may commit any vice he can conceal from his superiors, and thus falsehood and deception are among the earliest lessons they imbibe. Their advance in years is but a progression to the higher grades of iniquity. The violation of the seventh commandment is viewed in a more venial light than in fashionable European circles. Their depredations of rice have been estimated to amount to twenty-five per cent. on the gross average of crops, and this calculation was made, after fifty years' experience, by one whose liberal provision for their wants left no excuse for their ingratitude.

Hon. Whitemarsh B. Seabrook, in an "Essay on the Management of Slaves," Charleston, 1834, says:

As human beings, however, slaves are liable to all the infirmities of our nature. Ignorant and fanatical, none are more easily excited. Incendiaries might readily embitter their enjoyments and render them a curse to themselves and the community. . . . The prominent offenses of the slave are to be traced, in most instances, to the use of intoxicating liquors. This is one of the main sources of every insurrectionary movement which has occurred in the United States. We are, therefore, bound by interest as well as the common feeling of humanity to arrest the progress of what may emphatically be called the contagious disease of our colored population. What have become of the millions of freemen who once inhabited our widely spread country? Ask the untiring votaries of Bacchus. Can there be a doubt but that the authority of the master alone prevents his slaves from experiencing the fate of the aborigines of America? . . . At one time polygamy was a common crime; it is now of rare occurrence. . . . Between slaves on the same plantation there is a deep sympathy of feeling which binds them so closely together that a crime committed by one of their number is seldom discovered through their instrumentality. This is an obstacle to the establishment of an efficient police, which the domestic legislator can with difficulty surmount.

C. W. Gooch, Esq., of Henrico County, Virginia, in a prize essay on agriculture in Virginia, says:

> The slave feels no inducement to execute work with effect. He has a particular art of slighting it, and seeming to be busy when in fact he is doing little or nothing. Nor can he be made to take proper care of stock, tools, or anything else. He will rarely take care of his clothes or his own health, much less of his companion's, when sick and requiring his aid and kindness. There is perhaps not in nature a more heedless, thoughtless human being than a Virginia field negro. With no care upon his mind, with warm clothing and plenty of food under a good master, he is far the happier man of the two. His maxim is: "Come day, go day, God send Sunday." His abhorrence of the poor white man is very great. He may sometimes feel a *reflected* respect for him, in consequence of the confidence and esteem of his master and others. But this trait is remarkable in the white, as in the black man. All despise poverty and seem to worship wealth. To the losses which arise from the *dispositions* of our slaves must be added those which are occasioned by their *habits*. *There seems to be an almost entire absence of moral principle among the mass of our colored population.* But details upon this subject would be here misplaced. To steal and not to be detected is a merit among them, as it was with certain people in ancient times, and is at this day with some unenlightened portions of mankind. And the vice which they hold in greatest abhorrence is that of telling upon one another. There are many exceptions, it is true, but this description embraces more than a majority. The numerous free negroes and worthless, dissipated whites who have no visible means of support, and who are rarely seen at work, derive their chief subsistence from the slaves. These thefts amount to a good deal in the course of the year, and operate like leeches on the fair income of agriculture. They vary, however, in every county and neighborhood in exact proportion as the market for the plunder varies. In the vicinity of towns and villages they are the most serious. Besides the actual loss of property occasioned by them, they involve the riding of our horses at night, the corruption of the habits and the injury of the health of the slaves, for whisky is the price generally received for them.

These are gloomy pictures of the moral qualities of the negro on the large plantations of the South, but those who were fully acquainted with the slave and his surroundings cannot deny the accuracy of the statements we have copied from writers of seventy years ago. It must be observed, however, that these slaves were so situated as to come under the influence of the white race to a very small extent, and these representatives of a higher civilization were by no means qualified to instruct or elevate the negro. In many instances, as Mr. Gooch says, these " poor whites " were not only the accomplices in crime in common with the negroes, but they were the instigators to petty thefts and raids upon the supplies of the planters.

If the negro slaves were thus depraved and almost destitute of moral principle, what can be said of those negroes who were set free early in this century, in the states of the North, as well as those of the South? Very many experiments were made in the South, and the conviction of conservative minds, after full and fair trial, was that the negro's condition was not improved by emancipation. The picture drawn by Dr. Jones gives the following view of the moral and religious condition of the free negro population:

> They are emphatically lovers of pleasure and show. All kinds of amusements, except those which involve labor or reflection, possess great attraction for them, and their indulgence is limited only by their means of access to them.
>
> With a passion for dress, they frequently spend all they make in fine clothes; their appearance on the Sabbath and on

public days is anything else but an index of their fortunes and comforts at home. They hire clothing for set occasions if they have none sufficiently good.

Proverbially idle, the majority work not except from necessity, and as soon as they collect a little money they must enjoy themselves upon it. They have been known to refuse employment because not exactly out of money. Their love of ease overcomes that of gain. This propensity to idleness exposes them to manifold temptations, plunges them into numerous vices, and subjects them to great privation and suffering.

They are amazingly improvident. One melting ray from a summer sun dissipates every remembrance of a long and dreary winter of suffering. The golden season of labor is passed in lounging along the streets and basking in the sun, or a lazy, bungling, and fitful attempt at work. Those that have regular trades and employment do better. Profane swearing, quarreling, fighting, and Sabbath breaking are such common vices that they require no special notice.

Drunkenness, with its attendant woes, hurries large numbers of them to sudden and untimely ends. Low, dark, secluded, and filthy dramshops are favorite resorts; often the depositories of stolen goods. I have seen them living upon a few crackers a day and as much whisky as they could procure; their life spent in idleness, nightly revels, drunkenness, and debauchery.

Theft is still with them, in a state of freedom, a characteristic vice. Their petty larcenies are without number, and they advance to burglaries and give constant employment to police officers. Let any one attend the city courts in our chief towns in the free states or read the reports of cases in the newspapers, and he will be surprised at the number of colored persons among prisoners charged with crime. Stabbing and murder have, of late years, not become infrequent.

Lewdness is without bounds. Great numbers, both in the slave and free states, not only pursue the vice, but are trained up to it as a means of living. Infanticide and the crimes and wretchedness connected with the vice are found among them. The crime of infanticide is far more common among the free negroes in the free than in the slave states. Indeed, it is by no means common among the free negroes in the slave states.

Their marriage relations, too, are subject to dissolutions from infidelity and various other causes. It is a remarkable fact that a large proportion of those of marriageable age remain single, especially in the free states, where the support of a family is difficult. This fact has a considerable bearing on their state of morals.

With a few extracts from different publications of sixty years ago, this branch of our inquiry shall be dismissed:

"The experience of the states north and east of the Susquehanna, with regard to this class of persons, is not on the whole much more encouraging—*i. e.*, than that of the Southern States, where it is bad. The number of respectable individuals is considerably greater, indeed, but the character of the mass nearly the same. Nor can it be urged that they are here debarred access to the ordinary means of moral and intellectual regeneration. On the contrary, schools are established for them, they are aided in procuring the conveniences of religious instruction and divine worship, they are united into societies adapted to produce self-respect and mental activity, exemplary attention is paid in numerous instances to the regulation of their habits and principles. They have every facility which is enjoyed by the laboring classes among the whites of acquiring a plain education and a comfortable subsistence and of making provison for their children. They have the same legal security in person and property, and generally the same political rights as the rest of the community." (Walsh's Appeal.)

"Taken as a whole, the free blacks must be considered the most worthless and indolent of the citizens of the United States. It is well known that throughout the whole extent of our Union they are looked upon as the very drones and pests of society. Nor does this character arise from their disabilities and disfranchisement, by which the law attempts to guard against them. In the nonslaveholding states, where they have been more elevated by law, this kind of population is in a worse condition and much more troublesome to society than in the slaveholding and especially in the planting states. Ohio, some years ago, formed a sort of land of promise for this deluded class, to which many have repaired from the slaveholding states; and what has been the consequence? They have been most harshly expelled from that state and forced to take refuge in a foreign land. Look through all the Northern States and mark the class upon whom the eye of the police is most steadily and constantly kept; see with what vigilance and care they are hunted down from place to place, and you cannot fail to see that idleness and improvidence are at the root of all their misfortunes. Not only does the experience of our own country illustrate the fact, but others furnish abundant testimony." (President Dew.)

"Governor Giles, upon a calculation based on the average number of convictions in the state of Virginia from the penitentiary reports up to 1829, shows that 'crimes among the free blacks are more than three times as numerous as among the whites, and four and a half times more numerous than among slaves,' and that the proportion of crime is still not as great among the free blacks in Virginia as in Massachusetts. Hence it is inferred that they are not so degraded and vicious in Virginia, a slave state, as in Massachusetts, a free state." (*Ibid.*)

"We are not to wonder that this class of citizens should be so depraved and immoral. Idleness and consequent want are of themselves sufficient to generate a catalogue of vices of the most mischievous and destructive character. Look at the penal prosecutions of every country and mark the situation of those who fall victims to the law, and what a frightful proportion do we find among the indigent and idle classes of society! Idleness generates want, want gives rise to temptation, and strong temptation makes the villain. Mr. Archer, of Virginia, well observed in his speech before the Colonization Society that the free blacks were destined by an insuperable barrier to the want of occupation, thence to the want of food, thence to the distresses which ensue that want, thence to the settled deprivation which grows out of those distresses and is nursed at their bosom." (*Ibid.*)

A colony of free blacks were expelled from Ohio in 1832 on account of their dissoluteness and dishonesty and misery, being considered in the light of vagabonds and nuisances. A college for free negroes was projected in New Haven about the same time, and the respectable citizens opposed and suppressed it, because the increase of that class of population was considered an evil.

"Few of them (the free negro population) are engaged in any trade or commerce or have any hopes of elevating themselves to that situation. Nine-tenths of them are in subordinate and menial situations, and likely thus to remain at low wages. That they labor under the most oppressive disadvantages which their freedom can by no means counterbalance is too obvious to admit of doubt."

"I waive all inquiry whether this be right or wrong. I speak of things as they are, not as they might or ought to be. They are cut off from the most remote chance of amalgamation with the white population by feelings or prejudices, call them what you will, that are ineradicable. The situation of the majority of them is more unfavorable than that of many of the slaves. With all the burdens, cares, and responsibilities of freedom, they have few or none of its substantial benefits. Their associations are and must be chiefly with slaves. Their right of suffrage gives them little, if any, political influence, and they are practically, if not theoretically, excluded from representation in our public councils. No merit, no services, no talents can ever elevate the great mass of them to a level with the whites. Occasionally an exception may arise. A colored individual of great talents, merits, and wealth may emerge from the crowd. Cases of this kind are, to the last degree, rare. The colored people are subjected to legal disabilities more or less galling and severe in every state in the Union. . . . There is no reason to expect that the lapse of centuries will make any change in this respect—*i. e.*, the jealousy with which they are regarded. They will always, unhappily, be regarded as an inferior race." ("Carey's Letters," Letter 12.)

Mr. Everett, in a speech before the Colonization Society, 1833, says: "The free blacks form in Massachusetts about one seventy-fifth part of the population. One-sixth of the convicts in our prisons are of this class."

A memorial presented to the Legislature of Connecticut in 1834 states: "Not a week, hardly a day, passes that they (the colored people) are not implicated in the violation of some law. Assaults and batteries, insolence to the whites, compelling a breach of the peace, riots in the streets, petty thefts, and continual trespasses on property are such common occurrences, resulting from the license they enjoy, that they have ceased to become subjects of remark. It is but recently that a band of negroes paraded the streets of New Haven armed with clubs and pistols and dirks with the avowed purpose of preventing the law of the land from being enforced against one of their species. Upon being accosted by an officer of justice and commanded to retire peaceably to their homes, their only reply consisted of abuse and threats of personal violence. The law was overshadowed and the officer consulted his own safety in a timely retreat." The memorial then proceeds to show that the evil complained of has so rapidly progressed that the whites have become the subjects of insult and abuse whenever they have refused to descend to familiarity with them; that themselves, their wives and children have been driven from the pavements, where they have not submitted to personal conflict; that from the licentiousness of their general habits they have invariably depreciated the value of property by their location in its neighborhood, and that from their notorious uncleanliness and filth, they have become common nuisances to the community. (Memorial.)

From the report of the warden of the Connecticut State Prison, 1838, it appears that "the number of blacks in confinement compared with the whites is ten to twelve times greater than is the proportion of the black to the white population in the state." (Journal of Commerce, May 16, 1838.)

"The records of crime in the free states show a frightful disproportion in the numbers of white and black offenders, and especially in those states where there are no disabilities or restrictions by law imposed upon the blacks."

"In Massachusetts they are 1-74th part of the population, yet they are in the proportion of 1-6 of the convicts in the state prison; in Connecticut, 1-34th part of the whole, 1-3 of the number in the penitentiary; New York, 1-35th, and 1-4 of the convicts; New Jersey, 1-13th, and 1-3; Pennsylvania, 1-35th, and 1-3. In Ohio the black population is 1 to 115 whites; convicts, 7 to 100. Vermont, by the census of 1830, contained 277,000 souls; 918 were negroes. In 1831 there were 74 convicts in the prison, and of these 24 were negroes. When compared with what is reported of the proportion of negroes in the prisons of the slaveholding states, it is shown that the proportion of negroes in the penitentiaries of the free states is in the ratio of more than ten to one in favor of the slaveholding states. The free negroes in Ohio in the aggregate are in no better condition, therefore, than the slaves in Kentucky. They are excluded from social intercourse with the whites, and whatever of education you may give them will not tend to elevate their standing to any considerable extent. (From the report of the committee on the judiciary, relative to the repeal of laws reposing restrictions and disabilities on blacks and mulattoes, by Mr. Cushing, February 21, 1835. Agreed to unanimously. Legislature of Ohio.)

These testimonies are taken from a wide range of authorities, and there is not a dissenting voice among them. The sudden emancipation of the negro race in 1820 or 1830 would have resulted in desolation and ruin to every interest of the Southern States. Can any one be surprised that the owners of slaves and those who owned none were alike interested in resisting the furious fanaticism of New England abolitionists?

CHAPTER IX.

Negro Insurrections.

IT is not an uncommon thing for the hostile writers of the North to declare that the inhumanities practiced upon the slaves were the causes of rebellion among them. Attempts at recovering their freedom were made, we are told, because Southern masters were cruel and drove their negroes to insurrection as the only remedy for their intolerable evils. The fact is that the first insurrection of note in this country, an insurrection of blacks against the whites, occurred in the city of New York in 1712. A Mr. Neau had established a school for the religious instruction of the blacks, and when the negroes, who numbered about twelve hundred, formed a conspiracy for the extermination of the whites, it was charged immediately that the school of Mr. Neau was at the bottom of all the trouble. A fearful state of excitement existed for a time, but when the calm inquiry of the judicial authorities was made, the truth became apparent. "The guilty negroes were found to be such as never came to Mr. Neau's school, and what is very observable, the persons whose negroes were found most guilty were such as were the declared opposers of making them Christians."

This is a remarkable proof of the salutary influence of the gospel among the negro race. The influence of a single school, taught by one man, prevented the entire complicity of a race in the attempt to burn a city and to murder the whole population. The dreadful massacre was to begin at the hour of midnight, and from refreshing slumbers a whole city was to be deluged with blood. Providential interference saved the city of New York in 1712, but what motives prompted the negroes of New York to insurrection?

Another insurrection is upon record, occurring in New York in 1741. It is doubtful, however, whether this was a real rebellion or only the creature of the excited imagination of the New York people. Similar "scares" were experienced by Boston, of all the places in the world. But these instances are wanting in positive proof. Nevertheless, what state of things gave rise to the *fear* of insurrection? Was it the cruel treatment of the slaves by their Northern masters? It may have been so; but one notable fact may be stated as part of the record. At no time did the black population of the North number one-half or one-third of the entire inhabitants, and in a contest of mere physical ability the negroes were never the equals to the whites. On the contrary, in the states of South Carolina and Georgia, there were large sections of the country in which the blacks outnumbered the whites by five to one. What power was it that preserved the authority of the masters, if it was not the moral power exerted by a superior race? Could this power control the thousands who were exasperated against the hundreds of whites, if there were no ties, no kindness, no respect engendered by humane treatment, and uniform justice among the masters?

There was a rebellion and an attempt at insurrection in South Carolina in 1730, and three in 1739, but these were fomented by the Spaniards of St. Augustine, and cannot be regarded as the instinctive movements of the slaves.

The insurrection of 1816 in South Carolina is the only one in which negroes hitherto religious were found to be concerned in the capacity of leaders. "Two brothers," says Mr. F. S. Deliesseline, "engaged in this rebellion could read and write, and were hitherto of unexceptionable characters. They were religious, and had always been regarded in the light of faithful servants. A few appeared to have been actuated by the instinct of the most brutal licentiousness and by the lust of plunder; but most of them by wild and fanatic ideas of the rights of man, and the misconceived injunctions of Holy Writ."

Of the insurrection of 1822 in Charleston, S. C., Mr. Benjamin Elliott writes: "This description of our population had been allowed to assemble for *religious* instruction. The designing leaders in the scheme of villainy availed themselves of these occasions to instill sentiments of ferocity by falsifying the Bible." After showing how this falsification of the Scriptures was done Mr. Elliott remarks: "Another impediment to the progress of conspiracy will be the fidelity of some of our negroes. The servant, who is false to his master, would be false to his God. One act of perfidy is but the first step in the road of corruption and of baseness, and those who on this occasion have proved ungrateful to their owners have also been hypocrites in religion."

Referring to the same affair of 1822, Mr. C. C. Pinckney says: "On investigation it appeared that all concerned in that transaction, except one, had seceded from the regular Methodist Church in 1817 and formed a separate establishment in connection with the African Methodist Society of Philadelphia, whose bishop, a colored man named Allen, had assumed that office, being himself a seceder from the Methodist Church of Pennsylvania. At this period Mr. S. Bryan, the local minister of the regular Methodist Church in Charleston, was so apprehensive of sinister designs that he addressed a letter to the city council, on file in the council chamber, dated November 8, 1817, stating at length the reasons of his suspicion."

"The South Hampton affair in Virginia in 1832 was originated by a man under color of religion, a pretender to inspiration. As far back as 1825 the Rev. Dr. J. H. Rice, in a discourse on the injury done to religion by ignorant teachers, warned the people of Virginia against the neglect of the religious instruction of the negroes, and the danger of leaving them to the control of their ignorant, fanatical, and designing preachers. His prophecy had its fulfillment in South Hampton. If we refer to the West Indies, we shall behold religion exerting a restraining influence upon the people, and particularly on one occasion all the negroes attached to the Moravian Missionary Churches to a man supported the authority of their masters against the insurgents.

"Enough has been said to satisfy reasonable and Christian men that sound religious instruction will contribute to safety. There are men who have no knowledge of religion in their own personal experience, and who have not been careful to notice its genuine effects upon servants, and they will place little or no confidence in anything that might be said in favor of it. They can place more reliance upon visible preventives of their own invention than upon principles of moral conduct wrought in the soul and maintained in supremacy by divine power, whose nature they do not understand, and whose influence, however good, is invisible, and for that very reason not to be trusted by them. Nor have they either the candor or the willingness to make a distinction between false and true religion. In their opinion the gospel is no benefit to the world. Such men we are constrained to leave to the influence of time and observation, and invoke for them the influence of the spirit of God. I shall never forget the remark of a venerable colored preacher made with reference to the South Hampton tragedy. With his eyes full of tears and his whole manner indicating the deepest emotion, he said: 'Sir, it is the gospel that we ignorant and wicked people need. If you will give us the gospel, it will do more for the obedience of servants and the peace of the community than all your guards and guns and bayonets.' This same Christian minister, on receiving a packet of inflammatory pamphlets through the post office and discovering their character and intention, immediately called upon the Mayor of the city and delivered them into his hands. Who can estimate the value, in a community, of one such man acting under the influence of the gospel of peace?"

We may append to these remarks of Dr. Jones the following inquiry: Who can measure the atrocity of the society or the individual who, in the safe shelter of a New England town, could write and print pamphlets and books designed to excite an insurrection of the slaves and the murder of their masters? Is there a more horrible act of wickedness in the whole catalogue of human crimes? Yet the time has been and now is when the writers of such pamphlets and the authors of incendiary tracts have been praised in the pulpit, and hymns to their memory chanted in the house of God by professed ministers of the gospel!

CHAPTER X.

Beginnings of Missionary Work.

IN 1758 Mr. Wesley made his first African convert, and the first African convert in the world to a Protestant religion. This was a slave woman belonging to one Mr. Nathaniel Gilbert, a rich West India planter. This conversion took place during Mr. Gilbert's sojourn in England. Of the glorious results of this conversion and also that of Mr. Gilbert every reader of Methodist history is familiar. It was the means of planting Methodism in the West India Islands.

"Slavery was introduced into Georgia in 1740. Consequently it was not there during the stay of the two Wesleys, nor at the time of the first visit of Whitefield. On the second visit of the latter, however, it had been just introduced. During his third, fourth, fifth, and sixth visits, we have the repeated record of his preaching to slaves in the congregations of the whites from Georgia to New England. In more than one instance there is the account of a happy conversion.

"On Mr. Whitefield's seventh and last visit to America he brought with him a young man, Cornelius Winter by name, who became the first missionary to the negroes.* The young man found a

---
* Smith's " History of Methodism in Georgia."

stanch friend in James Habersham, afterward Governor of the colony. He had come out the year before with Whitefield to act as teacher, but had now taken to merchandising. Winter's first post was that of catechist on the plantation of a retired Episcopal clergyman. His efforts seem to have been marked with very little success from the first. This was doubtless not owing either to the young man's inability or lack of zeal, but simply to the fact that at that early day the planters of Georgia, as elsewhere, were not in sympathy with the effort to spiritually enlighten their slaves. Still Winter kindled a little beam of light here and there that doubtless continued to shine for many a day. In a year's time, discouraged with the opposition he met, Winter returned to England.

"The year before the coming of Cornelius Winter to Georgia saw the building of the first Methodist chapel in New York, and the second in America. On the list of subscriptions raised for this building appeared the names of many African slaves. They were allowed a place in the congregation of the whites, and treated with respect and consideration within the walls of the building their zeal had helped to rear. Embury preached to them, and so did Webb. Doubtless good Mother Barbara showed many of them the way of life. Later we find Boardman, Pilmoor, Rankin, Shadford, Owens, Watters, Williams, and the other early Methodist itinerants, preaching to them here and there, as they would congregate with the whites. Asbury, from the moment of his landing on the continent, had his heart filled with plans for their spiritual amelioration.

"Almost simultaneously with the introduction of Methodism came cotton into the colonies. Now let us pause for a moment and see what relation one had to the other, and herein trace the workings of that providence which had in its hands the shaping of ends then little dreamed of by man. Before the introduction of cotton, we find indigo, rice, and tobacco the three staples of the colonies, according to geographical situation. For some years, owing to the lack of certain facilities, all three had begun to decline in marketable value, especially rice and indigo. The planters were awakening to the realization that in the end it cost as much, or almost as much, to maintain their slaves as they gained from their crops. Dissatisfaction with slavery was, therefore, rife in the colonies, and the thought of emancipation had come to be seriously entertained.

"'King Cotton' suddenly appeared upon the scene. He made his appearance at first only in a few fleecy stalks raised in flower gardens. But some one went to experimenting, and when, in 1784, eight bags of this staple arrived in Liverpool, the customhouse officers seized it on the plea that so much could not be raised in America.*

"In 1787, just four years after the last British

---

* Barnes's "United States History."

soldier had left American shores, the first cotton mill was established at Beverly, Mass. But not yet had cotton raising become profitable. One great obstacle stood in the way: to clean a pound of cotton by hand required a day's labor. On some of the plantations this work of picking the fleece from the seed used to be performed at night often by members of the planter's family. It is related of more than one of the earlier Methodist preachers, especially of Bishop Asbury, that while seated around the fireside of their host they would engage with the family and servants in picking out the cotton seed. Doubtless at such a time other seed were dropped by the way, the precious seed of immortal life.

"This slow and tedious way of picking out the cotton seed could not continue if profit was to be realized from the staple. Something must be done—some expeditious means of separating lint from seed must be found. Much was said, and much written. The question was agitated from New England to Georgia. Inventive genius was aroused. Many suggestions were made, various plans were tried. Then came the invention of the cotton gin by Eli Whitney, a Massachusetts man, while residing with the widow of Gen. Nathaniel Greene, at Mulberry Grove, Ga. But even he did not succeed at first. It was a woman, after all, who gave him his principal idea. Said Mrs. Greene: 'Crook the pins.' This he did, when lo! the result gave to the world one of the foremost inventions of the nineteenth century. The news of the wonderful invention spread from state to state. The spirits of the planters began to rise. Cotton would yet become profitable to cultivate, and the source of a great revenue. No thought now of emancipation."

The reader will be interested in the fact that the first great monopoly of inventions in the United States was the manufacture of the cotton gin. Whitney's success, by the help of Mrs. Greene, led to the construction of a machine that was absolutely indispensable to the planters. This fact promoted the cupidity and avarice of the inventor, and he attempted to extort an enormous price for the use of his cotton gin. The following extract we take from the columns of the *Louisville (Ga.) Gazette*, of November 12, 1800. It is a part of the message of his Excellency, James Jackson, Governor of the State of Georgia, addressed to the Legislature of the State:

And here I request your attention to the patent gin monopoly, under the law of the United States, entitled "An Act to extend the privilege of obtaining patents for useful discoveries and inventions to certain persons therein mentioned, and to enlarge and define the penalties for violating the rights of patentees." The operation of this law is a prevention and cramping of genius, as respects cotton machines, a manifest injury to the community, and in many respects a cruel extortion on the gin holders. The two important states of Georgia and South Carolina, where this article appears to be becoming the principal staple, are made tributary to two persons who have obtained the patent, and who demand, as I am informed, two hundred dollars for the mere liberty of using a ginning machine, in the creation of which the patentees do not expend one farthing, and which sum, as they now think their right secured, it is in their power in future licenses to raise to treble that amount, from the information given me by a respectable merchant of this town, whose letter on the subject is marked No. 6. When Miller and Whitney, the patentees, first distributed the machines of their construction, they reserved the right of property in it, as also two-thirds of the net proceeds arising from the gin; the expense of working to be joint between the patentees and the ginner. Finding, however, a defect in the law under which their patent was obtained, they determined to sell the machines, together with the right vested in them, for five hundred dollars, and for a license to authorize a person to build and work one at his own expense four hundred. But finding, as I suppose, that the defect of the law was generally understood, and that they could get no redress in the courts, they lowered the demand to the present rate of two hundred dollars. That they may raise it to the former rates is certain, and that they will do it unless public interference is had there can be little doubt. I am informed from other sources that gins have been erected by other persons who have not taken Miller and Whitney's gins for a model, but which in some small degree resemble it, and in improvement far surpass it, for it has been asserted that Miller and Whitney's gin did not on trial answer the intended purpose. The right of these improvements, however, it appears from the present act, is merged in the right of the patentees, who, it is supposed in the honest calculation, will make by it, in the two states, one hundred thousand dollars. Monopolies are odious in all countries, but more particularly so in a government like ours. The great law meteor, Coke, declared them contrary to the common and fundamental law of England. Their tendency certainly is to raise the price of the article from the exclusive privilege, to render the machine or article worse from the prevention of competition and improvement, and to impoverish poor artificers and planters who are forbidden from making, vending, or using it without license from the patentees, or in case of doing so, are made liable to penalties in a court of law. The Federal Circuit Court docket, it is said, is filled with these actions. I do not doubt the power of Congress to grant these exclusive privileges, for the Constitution has vested them with it, but in all cases where they become injurious to the community, they ought to be suppressed, or the patentees paid a moderate compensation for the discovery from the government granting the patent. The celebrated Dr. Adam Smith observes that monopolies are supported by cruel and oppressive laws. Such is the operation at present of the law on this subject. Its weight lay on the poor industrious mechanic and planter. Congress, however, did not intend it so, for when the first law on this subject was passed in February, 1793, a few individuals only cultivated cotton, and it was not dreamt of as about to become the great staple of the two Southern States—a staple, too, which, if properly encouraged, must take the decided lead of any other, bread kind excepted, in the United States. The steps proper to be taken to remedy this public grievance you will judge of; but I should suppose that our sister state of South Carolina, being so much interested, would cheerfully join Georgia in any proper application to Congress on the subject. I am likewise of the opinion that the states of North Carolina and Tennessee must be so far interested as to support such application. If you think with me, I recommend communication with all of them.

This is a very interesting paper from several points of view. It shows the rapacity with which the fortunate inventors of the day preyed upon the necessities of the planters. It exhibits also the facility with which the strong arm of the government was made tributary to private interests. There can be no question that the inventor has a property in his own work, but when public interests are involved, and the welfare of society can be advanced by a liberal reward for the inventions of men of genius, it is a cruel wrong for monopolists to extort unreasonable sums for the use of machines in which all the people are interested. We are not informed as to the measures adopted by the States mentioned by Gov. Jackson, but, as he became a Senator in Congress a few months after writing his address, we presume there must have been a compromise, one by which the inventor received a just reward and the people were allowed the use of a necessary invention.

We return to the thread of our history.

"The Methodist itinerants, having their hearts aglow with the pure missionary fire, preached to *all* alike. 'Christ came into the world to die for *every* sinner' were the broad and liberal words emblazoned upon their shields. Everywhere that Methodism went, it went in that spirit. It was the religion for the rich and the poor, for the black and the white, for master and slave; in short, for *all*. It was a noticeable fact that wherever the master obtained this religion, really and truly obtained it, he was anxious also for it to be made known to those in bondage under him. But sometimes, through influences or other irritating causes, there were exceptions to this rule. But these were rare. And there were many, very many, who, being bitterly opposed to this religion for themselves, were still more bitterly against its introduction among their servants.

"But many Christian masters, in the face of public opinion, had the courage and the will to place in the way of their servants the means of their soul's salvation. Noticeably among these was Henry Dorsey Gough. Soon after the introduction of Methodism into this country, he became a convert and built 'Perry Hall,' his elegant residence, twelve miles from the city of Baltimore, and a commodious chapel, which was designated as 'the first Methodist church in America that had a bell.' This bell rung every evening, summoning his household and his servants to family worship. These slaves were nearly one hundred in number. They filled the body of the chapel. The circuit preachers preached here regularly twice a month, and the local preachers every Sunday. Often members of the Baltimore bar, the very *elite* of the state of Maryland, beautiful, aristocratic women, and gay and handsome men, on a visit to the family, assembled in this chapel. Among them the slaves of the household always had their place. They were never excluded on any occasion. The hymns were nearly always raised by these colored servants, and often they were called on to pray, to which prayers the whites gave the utmost attention, many profiting thereby.

"Gough's own conversion, through hearing his slaves praying in their quarters on the plantation, is familiar to many Methodist readers. Even before this chapel was built and these noble efforts put forth in their behalf by their owner, Methodism had reached the slaves of this plantation. And it came in such a gladdening form that Henry Gough, on hearing them singing and praying, could not refrain from exclaiming: 'How much more blest are they than I!'

"Other masters followed the example of Henry Dorsey Gough in having their servants present when the preacher came around on his appointment. Many of these slaves were happily converted, and died a Christian death. Others lived to bear glorious witness of the power of the gospel of Jesus Christ to reach and cheer every condition of life.

"In the great revival that spread through Virginia in 1775–76, we have constant mention of blacks being in the congregations. Shadford, Lee, and Rankin often had as many as from two to three hundred blacks to hear them, filling up the doors and windows and vacant spaces about the walls. Many affecting scenes occurred among them. Rankin gives this note in his account of one of these scenes: 'Hundred of negroes were there with the tears streaming down their cheeks.' Sometimes their cries for mercy, out of the great depths of the darkness that ingulfed them, were heartrending. And all praise to these noblehearted Methodist itinerants who knew neither race nor condition in their efforts of evangelization. Through them many of these poor Africans were brought to the redeeming knowledge of life through Christ Jesus.

"One of the most useful, and consequently one of the most famous, of the early Methodist preachers was 'Black Harry.' When Dr. Thomas Coke, the newly ordained bishop of the Methodist Episcopal Church, landed in America, he found in Asbury's servant an African of remarkable gifts. This was Harry Hosier, or as he was more familiarly known, 'Black Harry.' Harry could neither read nor write, but he was one of the most powerful exhorters, white or black, then on the continent, and was taken along by Asbury in his journeys principally to preach to the blacks. Harry was not only gifted, but truly pious, and through a long and eventful life accomplished untold good to his race.

"Harry was small in stature, coal black, and with eyes of remarkable brilliance and intelligence. He had a quick mind, a most retentive memory, and such an eloquent flow of words, which he could soon put into almost faultless English, that he was pronounced by many 'the greatest orator in America.' Nor was this at all undeserved. He traveled in turn with Asbury, Coke, Whatcoat, Garrettson, Jesse Lee, and other distinguished Methodist preachers, to each of whom he acted as 'driver,' but 'excelling them all in popularity as a preacher.' The bishops were proud of Harry, and brought him out on every occasion they could, not only among the blacks, but also in the congregations of the whites. When sick or disabled, they would unhesitatingly trust their pulpit to Harry, without a single fear of his disappointing the people. Asbury was fond of openly declaring that the best way he knew to obtain a large congregation was to announce that 'Black Harry' would preach, as that never failed to bring a far more numerous concourse than if the announcement had been made for himself.

"It is related that on one occasion in Wilmington, Del., where Methodism was so long unpopular, a number of the citizens who had not been in the habit of attending the Methodist meetings came together out of curiosity to hear Bishop Asbury. The chapel was so full that they could not effect an entrance, and so were forced to remain outside. Here they stood listening as they supposed to Bishop Asbury, but in reality to 'Black Harry.' They were so much pleased that they exclaimed in honest praise: 'If all Methodist preachers can preach like the bishop, we should like to be constant hearers.' Great was their surprise to learn that it was not the bishop, but his servant, 'Black Harry.' Instead of decreasing their estimation of the bishop, however, they only raised it the higher. 'For,' said they, 'if such be the servant, what must the master be?'

"It was no wonder that such extraordinary popularity should, for a time, have turned poor Harry's head. Many a stronger one could not have withstood the alluring excitement connected with it. Harry for years bravely met the temptations aroused by his great popularity, but in one evil moment fell through a glass of wine temptingly proffered him. However, he proved the real stuff of which he was made when he showed the moral courage to cut himself loose from the fetters. He withdrew to himself and spent the solitary watches of the night under a tree wrestling in prayer until victory came. Like a true soldier Harry remained faithful to the end. He died about the year 1810, in Philadelphia, a glorious and triumphant death, and was borne to the grave by a great procession of white and black admirers, who buried him as a hero once overcome but finally victorious.

"'Black Harry Hosier' must not be confounded with 'Black Harry of St. Eustatius,' who occupied so enviable a place in the story of the founding of Methodism in the West India Islands.

"Two years after the meeting of Coke and 'Black Harry Hosier' witnessed the rather romantic meeting with the other 'Black Harry;' for it was in that year (1786) that Coke, 'driven by the winds of heaven' far out of his course, found a landing place on one of the many island worlds of the West Indies. This led to the founding of Wesleyan Missions among the blacks of these islands, and the putting into active force of an agency that contributed directly to the moral and mental improvement of the West Indian negroes.

"In the same year that witnessed the founding of the Wesleyan Missions to the slaves of the West India Islands, Freeborn Garrettson, itinerating in the bleak wilds of Novo Scotia, found there a little society of colored Methodists. They were refugee slaves from the United States, who, without the direction and aid of white pastors, had organized themselves into a Church. Garrettson formed sixty of them into a class, baptized nineteen, and administered the Lord's Supper to about forty. These African negroes to whom Garrettson came in the leadings of providence were to be the founders of Methodism in Sierra Leone, and of the whole scheme of Methodist evangelization in Africa.*

"At the Conference of 1787 the first decisive step toward the evangelization of the slaves was taken. In the rules for this year we find the following question and answer recorded: 'What direction shall we give for the promotion of the spiritual welfare of the colored people?' We conjure all our ministers and preachers by the love of God and the salvation of souls, and do require them by all the authority that is invested in us to leave nothing undone for the spiritual benefit and salvation of them within their respective circuits and districts, and for this purpose to embrace this opportunity of inquiring into the state of their souls, and to unite in society those who appear to have a real desire of fleeing the wrath to come, to meet such in class and to exercise the whole Methodist Discipline among them.'

"At this time there were reported 3,893 members in the various societies, extending from New England to South Carolina. The Methodist itinerants everywhere endeavored faithfully to follow these injunctions, and the result was a gratifying change in the spiritual condition of many a poor African throughout the various territories traveled. And it is a fact worthy of notice that during the succeeding years the numbers in societies were

---

* Stevens's "History of Methodism."

nearly doubled. Wherever the banner of Methodism went upborne by these sturdy hands, it carried life and light to *all;* to the master in his luxuriously furnished home, to the poor slave in his humble cabin.

"In that same year (1787) the Cumberland Street Methodist Church, in Charleston, S. C., was finished, with galleries for the negroes. At that time it had a colored membership of sixty-five. Other Churches followed this example, until soon it was a common sight to see white and black meeting together as one congregation.

"A few years after this Asbury, visiting Charleston, was much surprised at the religious spirit prevailing among the blacks. Indeed, he expressed himself as having stronger hopes of their steady growth in religion than of the whites, for Charleston was at that time such a gay and careless city that the good bishop was shocked by the wickedness abounding on every hand. He writes: 'Religion is reviving here among the Africans. These are poor; these are the people we are more immediately called to preach to.'

"Asbury devoted special attention to these negroes, and while in Charleston assembled them every morning at 6 o'clock for instruction and prayer. Many touching scenes occurred, which, to his zealous heart, were like the fresh, sweet oasis in the desert. Others, again, thrilled him with the keenest pain, and made him, like John Wesley, take unto himself the undying resolve to know neither rest nor cessation of zeal till poor Ethiopia lifted up her darkened eyes in glad recognition of a Saviour found.

"They were so grateful to him that they were constantly bringing him little presents, which they continued to press upon him, despite his generous refusal, seeming much hurt at this refusal, which they did not understand. One black woman, sixty years of age, who supported herself by picking oakum—being free, it is supposed—brought him a French crown, and insisted on his taking it. 'But no,' he declares, 'although I have not three dollars to travel two thousand miles, I will not take money from the poor.'

"There was always something peculiarly touching in the manner in which these negroes pressed their little gifts upon their preacher. It seemed as if they could not be grateful enough to him who had come to open the darkened chambers of their soul to the warm, sweet light of the gospel. Revs. Samuel Leard, A. M. Chreitzberg, W. W. Mood, and other former missionaries to the slaves, in writing of their labors in this connection, tell many incidents of the slaves pressing up about them after the preaching, with little offerings of eggs, pretty bird feathers, shells, or whatever else their humble resources could produce. There was always something delicate and graceful, as well as grateful, in their manner of offering these gifts. Sometimes it was: 'Here is somethin' for *my* missionary.' But often it was: 'Here is somethin' for *my* missionary's lillie [little] girl or boy,' whichever the case might be.

"In the year 1796-97, in the great revival that spread from Maine to Tennessee and from Georgia to Canada, many negroes were converted and brought into the folds of the Church. There were prayer meetings in private houses and on plantations, very few of which were not attended by the slaves. The quickening spirit extended. White and black were alike brought under its influence. In the evenings the chapels and the meetings in the private houses were crowded, while by day the harvest fields and workshops resounded with the Methodist shouts and hymns.

"It was about this time that the first Methodist Episcopal Church, exclusively for the negroes, was organized in New York City. In 1800 this society built its first house of worship, and called it Zion. Though in organization it was separate from the Methodist Episcopal Church, with which its members had been previously connected, its ministers and pastoral oversight were supplied from the parent Church for about twenty years.*

"The revival that broke forth with such power in 1796-97 continued to spread. The excitement connected with it was greatly increased through the breaking out at about the beginning of the present century of the yellow fever scourge in many parts of the Atlantic coast. The scourge spread with frightful rapidity; hundreds, both

---

* Methodist Centennial Year Book.

white and black, being cut off. News came from every direction of the great increase in the numbers joining the Methodist societies. More than a thousand colored members were added during the year 1800, and more than two thousand in 1801.

"In 1801 Senator Bassett, writing from Dover, Del., says: 'One hundred and thirty, white and black, joined the society here yesterday. Many more went away sick and sore.' For a week they had been holding daily preaching and sunrise prayer meetings. The multitude was often estimated at from seven to eight thousand a day. So great did the crowds finally become that three preachers had to be employed at once to preach to them. On Sunday the sacrament was administered to from twelve to fifteen hundred, black and white. Wilson Lee wrote of the glorious work in Maryland and Virginia, during which scores of slaves were brought to a knowledge of redeeming mercy through Christ Jesus.

"Thomas Ware, on his work in the Philadelphia division, which extended from Wilmington, Del., to Seneca Lake, N. Y., spoke of a glorious revival flame that had swept from length to breadth of his territory. This religious excitement embraced all classes—governors, judges, lawyers, statesmen, old and young, rich and poor, 'including many of the African race.'

"Similar reports continued to come from all the Churches, north and south, east and west, down to 1805. At that time there were 24,316 colored members in the bounds of the Methodist Episcopal Church, an increase of over ten thousand in five years."

The year 1792-93 was noted for the secession of James O'Kelly and his followers because the General Conference refused to incorporate a radical change in the economy of the Church. It is a little remarkable that the colored membership should exhibit the close relations of the two races in this discussion. When the white membership began to decrease, the colored membership likewise decreased, and when the white membership recovered its losses the colored membership followed the example. In 1793 the white membership was 51,416, and this aggregate was not reached again until the year 1800, when the figures were 51,442. Notwithstanding the great revivals in 1796, the white membership went down to 45,384, and the colored to 11,280, the lowest figures since 1790. In 1793 the colored membership was 16,227, and these figures were not reached again until 1802, when a large increase brought the colored membership up to 18,659.

CHAPTER XI.

Mission Work (Continued).

IN 1800 the South Carolina Conference was composed of Georgia, South Carolina, and a small part of North Carolina, forming but one ecclesiastical district, and presided over by Benjamin Blanton. In these boundaries there are now several large and flourishing Annual Conferences, which are speaking proofs of the rapid growth of Methodism. The Conferences then had 16 charges, 32 preachers, with a white membership of 4,802, and a colored membership of 1,535.

"In 1801 this Conference was divided into two districts: the Georgia, with Stith Mead as presiding elder; and the South Carolina, with James Jenkins as presiding elder. It so continued until 1830, when Georgia was made a separate Conference.

"In 1808 there appeared in the South Carolina Conference a man whose name was destined to become identified with the work of Missions to the blacks, and whose monument was to bear a prouder epitaph than that of the greatest warrior or statesman who ever lived. This was William Capers, afterward a bishop of the Methodist Episcopal Church, South, who, when a youth of eighteen was sent for his first ministerial work to the

Wateree Circuit. This charge was what might be termed a broad range, for in order to fill his twenty-four appointments once in every four weeks the young preacher had to ride a distance of three hundred miles. He had a membership of 498 whites, and 124 colored. From the first he took a deep interest in the latter, being as careful and conscientious in his ministerial duties to them as to the whites. The superstitious tendencies of many of them pained him deeply, while on the other hand his heart was greatly rejoiced at the pure religious spirit and understanding of others. No doubt on this circuit were sown the seeds of a purpose that in the heart of the young preacher were to ripen into rich fruition, and bring blessings to thousands of this race.

"In 1809 the first special efforts to evangelize the slaves were made by the South Carolina Conference. James H. Mallard was sent as a missionary to the blacks 'from Ashley to Savannah River,' and James E. Glenn as missionary to those 'from Santee to Cooper.' There were so many obstacles in the way, however, that after awhile the work was given up. But preaching to the negroes in the white charges, and taking them in as members and allowing thēm all the rights of the Church still went on zealously.

"In this year (1810) the South Carolina Conference reported 8,202 colored members, an increase of nearly two thousand from the preceding year. Of these, 1,650 were in the city of Charleston. Virginia reported a colored membership of 6,150. It is interesting to note the steady increase of the colored membership in the South Carolina Conference from 1800 to 1818: from one to three thousand yearly. But in the year 1818 occurred the noted schism in Charleston by which over five thousand negroes withdrew from the Church. From 1810, when the colored members numbered 8,208, to 1817, their numbers increased to 16,789, thus in seven years more than doubling their numbers—a ratio of increase of 104.95 per cent. Although so large a number withdrew in 1818, still there began to be a slow but steady increase in the numbers of those added up to 1828, when the first decisive measures for special missions to the slaves were inaugurated by the South Carolina Conference, at which time there were nearly nineteen thousand of them in the communion of that Conference.

"In 1810 William Capers, sent to serve the charge in Fayetteville, N. C., found there a most remarkable colored man, who, in the face of much opposition and no little persecution, had accomplished a work that deserves to be kept in undying record. This work had been not only to his own race, but also to many whites. This man was Henry Evans, whose name Methodist historians will never let sink into oblivion. But we will let Mr. Capers tell the story in his own words:

> The most remarkable man in Fayetteville, N. C., when I went there, and who died during my stay, was a negro by the

name of Henry Evans. I say the most remarkable in a view of his class, and I call him negro with unfeigned respect. He was a negro—that is, he was of that race, without any admixture of another. The name simply designates the race, and it is vulgar to regard it with opprobrium.

I have known and loved and honored not a few negroes in my life, who were probably as pure of heart as Evans, or anybody else. Such were my old friends Castile Selby and John Boquet, of Charleston; Will Campbell and Harry Merrick, of Wilmington; York Cohen, of Savannah; and others I might name. These I might call remarkable for their goodness. But I use the word in a broader sense for Henry Evans, who was confessedly the father of the Methodist Church, white and black, in Fayetteville, and the best preacher of his time in that quarter; and who was so remarkable as to have become the greatest curiosity of the town, insomuch that distinguished visitors hardly felt that they might pass a Sunday in Fayetteville without hearing him preach.

He eluded no one in private, but sought opportunities to explain himself; avowed the purity of his intentions, and even begged to be subjected to the scrutiny of any surveillance that might be thought proper to prove his inoffensiveness; anything, so that he might be allowed to preach. Happily for him and the cause of religion, his honest countenance and earnest pleadings were soon powerfully seconded by the fruits of his labors.

One after another began to suspect their servants of attending his preaching, not because they were made worse, but wonderfully better. The effect on the public morals of the negroes, too, began to be seen, particularly as regarded their habits on Sunday and drunkenness. And it was not long before the mob was called off by a change in the current of opinion, and Evans was allowed to preach in town.

At that time there was not a single church edifice in Fayetteville, and but one congregation (Presbyterian), who worshiped in what was called the Statehouse, under which was the market; and it was plainly Evans or nobody to preach to the negroes.

Now, too, of the mistresses there were not a few and some of the masters who were brought to think that the preaching which had proved so beneficial to their servants might be good for them also, and the famous negro preacher had some whites as well as blacks to hear him. Among others, and who were the first fruits, were my old friends, Mr. and Mrs. Lumsden, Mrs. Bowen (for many years Preceptress of the Female Academy), Mrs. Malsby, and, I think, Mr. and Mrs. Blake.

From these the gracious influence spread to others, and a meetinghouse was built. It was a frame of wood, weatherboarded only on the outside, without plastering, and about fifty feet long by thirty wide. Seats, distinctly separated, were at first appropriated to the whites near the pulpit. But Evans had already become famous, and these seats were insufficient. Indeed, the negroes seemed likely to lose their preacher, negro though he was; while the whites, crowded out of their appropriate seats, took possession of those in the rear.

Meanwhile Evans had represented to the preacher of Bladen Circuit how things were going, and induced him to take his meetinghouse into the circuit, and constitute a Church there. And now there was no longer room for the negroes in the house when Evans preached; and for the accommodation of both classes the weatherboards were knocked off and sheds were added to the house on either side; the whites occupying the whole of the original building and the negroes those sheds as a part of the same house. Evans's dwelling was a shed at the pulpit end of the church. And that was the identical state of the case when I was pastor.

Often was I in that shed, and much to my edification. I have known not many preachers who appeared more conversant with scripture than Evans, or whose conversation was more instructive as to the things of God. He seemed always deeply impressed with the responsibility of his position, and not even our old friend Castile was more remarkable for his humble and deferential deportment toward the whites than Evans. Nor would he allow any partiality of his friends to induce him to vary in the least degree the line of conduct or bearing which he had prescribed to himself in this respect: never speaking to a white man but with his hat under his arm, never allowing himself to be seated in their houses, and even confining himself to the kind and manner of dress proper for negroes in general, except his plain black coat for the pulpit.

"The whites are kind to me and come to hear me preach," he would say, "but I belong to my own sort, and must not spoil them." And yet Henry Evans was a Boanerges, and in his duty feared not the face of man.

I have said that he died during my stay in Fayetteville this year (1810). The death of such a man could not but be triumphant, and his was distinguishingly so. I did not witness it, but was with him before he died, and as he appeared to me triumph should express but partially the character of his feelings, as the word imports exultation at victory, or at most the victory and exultation together. It seemed to me as if the victory he had won was no longer an object, but rather as if his spirit, past the contemplation of triumph on earth, were already in communion with heaven. Yet his last breath was drawn in the act of pronouncing 1 Corinthians xv. 57: "Thanks be to God, which giveth us the victory through our Lord Jesus Christ."

It was my practice to hold a meeting with the blacks in the church directly after morning preaching every Sunday. And on the Sunday before his death, during this meeting, the little door between his humble shed and the chancel where I stood was opened and the dying man entered for a last farewell to his people. He was almost too feeble to stand at all, but, supporting himself by the railing of the chancel, he said: "I have come to say my last to you. It is this: None but Christ. Three times I have had my life in jeopardy for preaching the gospel to you. Three times I have broken the ice on the edge of the water and swam across the Cape Fear to preach the gospel to you. And now, if in my last hour I could trust to that, or to anything else but Christ crucified, for my salvation, all should be lost, and my soul perish forever." A noble testimony! worthy not of Evans only, but of St. Paul. His funeral at the church was attended by a greater concourse of persons than had been seen on any funeral occasion before. The whole community appeared to mourn his death, and the universal feeling seemed to be that in honoring the memory of Henry Evans we were paying a tribute to virtue and religion. He was buried under the chancel of the church of which he had been in so remarkable a manner the founder.

"It is perhaps not out of place at this point to make mention of the labors of Rev. William Meredith, who, as early as 1784, came to Wilmington, N. C., and began to preach there the doctrines of Methodism. His first congregations were composed solely of blacks, and he found a noble colaborer in Rev. Jesse Jennett, or 'Father Jennett,' as he was known. He was persecuted on all sides, and finally thrown into prison; but through persecutions and fiery trials he went on to victory. His church was burned; the voluntary contributions of humble but faithful negroes built another. That was the beginning of Methodism in Wilmington. Thus we see that in two of the proudest cities of the Old North State, Methodism, so great a power now, was first implanted among their humble slave population.

"Persecutions against those who undertook to preach to the negroes were now rife in every direction. The abolition sentiment had taken possession of the machinery of the Church, and had brought into existence the bitterest feelings on both sides. The Methodist preachers were everywhere looked upon as sheep in wolves' clothing, were treated accordingly, and in many instances roughly handled. In Charleston in 1801 occurred the first mob raised on the slavery question, when Rev. George Dougherty, as pure and good a man as ever lived, was dragged to a pump and nearly drowned with the water, for no other offense than that of being a Methodist preacher and preaching to the negroes and the whites. The Charleston congregations, too, came in for much of this abuse, not only because they were of the despised sect known as 'Methodists,' but because they allowed negroes in the galleries of their churches.

"About this time that pure and fearless man of God, the Rev. Samuel Dunwoody, was preaching to the negroes in the swamps around Charleston, by the light of the moon, for fear of attracting the attention of the lawless class of whites. Here he many times administered the holy sacrament of the Church as though they were 'things the daylight might not look upon.' He is said to have remained all night in the woods at the very season when the dread pestilence was abroad, baptizing and administering the Lord's Supper to a large concourse of blacks. Fully three hundred were baptized on this one night."

No apology can or ought to be made for the miscreants who resorted to violence in their treatment of the Methodist preachers, not because they cared for the slaves or their masters, but because they loved deeds of violence. But the truth of history requires it to be stated that the Methodist Episcopal Church had assumed the position of an abolitionist society. At the very beginning of our organization the subject of slavery was recognized as a fit subject for Church legislation, and the attempt was made to force slaveholders to emancipate their slaves or retire from the Church. The attempt to brand slaveholding as a crime, an offense that would exclude the offender from the kingdom of heaven failed, but it was not for lack of diligent efforts on the part of Coke and Asbury, or the majority of the traveling preachers. After reading the character given to the free negroes by statesmen and politicians, no one can wonder at the opposition offered to emancipation by the people of the South.

It was precisely the question best calculated to arouse the most intense feelings of bitterness among the holders of slaves and all who believed that the measure would fill the land with lazy and idle negroes, whose chief subsistence would come from the barns and smokehouses of the industrious whites.

Dr. Coke was indicted as an incendiary in Virginia, and no doubt, from his point of view, there was no disgrace in the fact. Yet the calm, unprejudiced mind cannot look at the subject from that point of view. He was interfering with a civil institution, lawfully established, and a stranger in England striving to overthrow monarchy was not one whit more guilty of impertinent interference with the laws of a country than Dr. Coke was in his diatribes against slavery.

The prudent observation of Bishop Asbury caused him to abate his zeal, and finally to cease all public effort in this behalf, for he saw how disastrously all of his public movements had been. But it was difficult to convince the preachers that they were not called to destroy the institution of slavery. One of the greatest provocations offered to the slaveholders of the South was an address issued by the General Conference of 1800, and published, probably, by every newspaper in the South. This address confirmed many thousands of the people in the belief that all itinerant Methodist preachers were abolition emissaries and, as a consequence, promoters of insurrection and rebellion among the negroes.

We give this address as we find it in the *Louisville Gazette*, a newspaper published in Louisville, Ga., in October, 1800:

The Address of the General Conference of the Methodist Episcopal Church to All Their Brethren and Friends in the United States.

We, the members of the General Conference of the Methodist Episcopal Church, beg leave to address you with earnestness on a subject of the first importance.

We have long lamented the great national evil of *negro slavery* which has existed for so many years, and does exist in many of these United States. We have considered it as repugnant to the inalienable rights of mankind and to the very essence of civil liberty, but more especially to the spirit of the Christian religion.

For inconsistent as is the conduct of this otherwise free, this independent nation, in respect to the slavery of the negroes, when considered in a civil and political view, it is still more so when examined in the light of the gospel. For the whole spirit of the New Testament militates in the strongest manner against the practice of slavery, and the influence of the gospel wherever it has long prevailed (except in many of these United States) has utterly abolished that most criminal part of slavery, the possessing and using the bodies of men by the arbitrary will, and with almost uncontrollable power.

The small number of adventurers from Europe who visit the West Indies for the sole purpose of amassing fortunes are hardly worth our notice, any farther than their influence reaches for the enslaving and destroying of the human race. But that so large a proportion of the inhabitants of this country, who so truly boast of the liberty they enjoy, and are so justly jealous of that inestimable blessing, should continue to deprive of every trace of liberty so many of their fellow-creatures equally capable with themselves of every social blessing and of eternal happiness is an inconsistency which is scarcely to be paralleled in the history of mankind.

Influenced by these views and feelings, we have for many years restricted ourselves by the strongest regulations from partaking of the "accursed thing," and have also laid some very mild and tender restrictions on our Society at large. But at this General Conference we wished, if possible, to give a blow at the root of this enormous evil. For this purpose we naturally weighed every regulation which could be adopted within our own society. All seemed to be insufficient. We therefore determined at least to rouse up all our influence in order to hasten to the utmost of our power the universal extirpation of this crying sin. To this end we passed the following resolution:

"That the Annual Conferences be directed to draw up addresses for the gradual emancipation of the slaves to the legislatures of the states in which no general laws have been passed for that purpose; that these addresses urge in the most respectful but pointed manner the necessity of a law for the gradual emancipation of the slaves; that proper committees be appointed out of the most respectable of our friends for the conducting of the business; and that the president elders, elders, deacons, and traveling preachers do secure as many proper signatures as possible to the address, and give all the assistance in their power in every respect to aid the committees, and to further this blessed undertaking. And that this be continued from year to year till the desired end be fully accomplished."

What now remains, dear brethren, but that you coincide with us in this great undertaking, for the sake of God, his Church, and his holy cause, for the sake of your country, and for the sake of the miserable and oppressed. Give your signatures to the addresses; hand them for signatures to all your acquaintances and all the friends of liberty; urge the justice, the ability, the necessity of the measure; persevere in this blessed work, and the Lord, we are persuaded, will finally crown your endeavors with the wished for success. O what a glorious country would be ours if equal liberty were everywhere established, and equal liberty everywhere enjoyed!

We are not ignorant that several of the Legislatures of these states have most generously stepped forth in the cause of liberty and passed laws for the emancipation of the slaves. But many of the members of our society, even in these states, may be highly serviceable to this great cause by using their influence, by writing or otherwise, with their friends in other states, whether those friends be Methodists or not.

Come then, brethren, let us join hand and heart together in this important enterprise. God is with us, and will, we doubt not, accompany with his blessing all our labors of love.

We could write to you a volume on the present subject, but we know that in general you have already weighed it, and we have great confidence that your utmost assistance will not be wanting, and we promise to aid you with zeal and diligence.

That our gracious God may bless you with all the riches of his grace, and that we may all meet where perfect liberty and perfect love shall eternally reign is the ardent prayer of your affectionate brethren.

Signed in behalf and by order of the General Conference.

THOMAS COKE,
FRANCIS ASBURY, } *Bishops.*
RICHARD WHATCOAT.

EZEKIEL COOPER,
WILLIAM MCKENDREE, } *The Committee.*
JESSE LEE.

The publication of such a pragmatic document as the foregoing was well calculated to destroy the Methodist Church in the South. At a later period it would have produced such a result. But the fact was that the antislavery sentiment was stronger at the South before the Methodist Church began to meddle with the subject than it was at any subsequent time. The effect of this "address" was injurious to the preachers, to Methodism, and to the slaves themselves.

It caused every Methodist preacher to be regarded with suspicion, as an abolitionist, and the agent of an abolition propaganda. Indiscreet men, carrying out the resolutions of the Conference, brought upon themselves the deserved condemnation of the public, and this censure naturally expressed itself in violence by the lawless elements of society.

We have in this document a reason for the riotous conduct of many of these persons who maltreated Methodist preachers in the early part of the century. The English "tough" thought he was showing zeal for "the Church" when he mobbed Mr. Wesley and his preachers. The Southern "tough" was showing his zeal for the Southern cause when he helped to "duck" a Methodist preacher who could be nothing but an abolitionist in disguise.

COLORED MEMBERS IN THE METHODIST EPISCOPAL CHURCH
Reported in the Minutes for the years 1786 to 1829.

Year.	Members.	Year.	Members.	Year.	Members.	Year.	Members.
1786	1,890	1797	12,218	1808	30,308	1819	39,174
1787	3,893	1798	12,302	1809	31,884	1820	38,753
1788	6,545	1799	12,236	1810	34,724	1821	42,059
1789	8,243	1800	13,452	1811	35,732	1822	44,377
1790	11,682	1801	15,688	1812	38,505	1823	44,792
1791	12,884	1802	18,659	1813	42,859	1824	48,040
1792	13,871	1803	22,453	1814	42,431	1825	49,435
1793	16,227	1804	23,531	1815	43,187	1826	51,084
1794	13,814	1805	24,316	1816	42,304	1827	53,542
1795	12,170	1806	27,257	1817	43,411	1828	59,056
1796	11,280	1807	29,863	1818	39,150	1829	62,814

CHAPTER XII.

THE GOSPEL ON THE PLANTATION.

THE regular organization of missionary forces to operate among the negroes on the plantations is by some attributed to an overseer, and by others to the Hon. Charles C. Pinckney. Like many other important ideas, it is doubtless true that the propriety and expediency of such a movement had been suggested to many minds before any action was taken. The prime movers in the enterprise deserve the thanks of mankind, and it is pleasing to be able to record the name of a great statesman, Charles Cotesworth Pinckney, among the benefactors of the negro race.

But without detracting anything from the merits of other persons, the Rev. George W. Moore gives the honor to Mrs. Bearfield, a pious lady who, in 1828, made earnest efforts to have the gospel preached on the plantation of Mr. Charles Baring, on Pon Pon, in South Carolina. It is certain that regular Missions to the negroes began in the South Carolina Conference, and the year 1829 is given as the date at which the movement was inaugurated.

We have already spoken of the prejudices entertained by the planters against Methodist preachers as a class. The revolutionary attempts of the early Conferences and their constant attacks made upon the institution of slavery by zealous but indiscreet men had created a feeling that required almost a whole generation of time to overcome. Where the negroes were mingled with the members of the white family, worshiping under the same roof and taught by the same minister, it was easy enough to break down this prejudice. But on the large plantations of the seaboard country in South Carolina and Georgia, where the only white persons were the overseer and his family, it was quite another matter. Who could assure the owner that under the pretense of preaching the gospel to his negroes the itinerant preacher, a stranger oftentimes, would not instill principles of rebellion in the minds of the slaves? Did not the General Conference of 1800 declare that the whole tenor of the New Testament was hostile to slavery? Did not that Conference identify emancipation with the gospel, and did they not declare perpetual hostility to a lawful institution, recognized by the state and the Constitution of the United States?

It seems to us quite natural that men of the world, generally careless about the welfare of their own souls, should care but little for the religious instruction of their slaves. If it could be made plain to them that the gospel, instead of becoming a means of creating trouble and strife, was really the best instrument to preserve peace and good conduct among the negroes, there would have been no hesitation whatever. In point of fact it was this conviction that ultimately opened the way for the gospel on the large plantations. But this result came only after the Methodist preachers had repudiated the action of 1800, and this was brought about by exchanging the fanaticism of the General Conference for the wise, conservative, and Christlike opinions and example of St. Paul. So far from breathing hostility to any civil institution, the spirit and letter of the New Testament commanded obedience to king, archon, or president, whatever the chief rulers of a nation might be, and so far from declaring one form of civil government preferable to another, the grievous national bondage of the Jews to the Romans was never alluded to in the way of censure by either our Saviour or his apostles.

Owners of large plantations, coming to the knowledge of this change in the dispositions of the Methodist preachers, and finding many of them following the example of the illustrious bishop, then Mr. Capers, and seeing the good effects produced by the preaching to the negroes on the plantations of their neighbors, ultimately gave their consent to permit their slaves to hear the gospel from the lips of capable white missionaries.

It may be proper at this point to observe that almost every Methodist preacher, in town or city, became a special missionary to the negroes prior to 1865. It was a service courted by many, for there was a peculiar *unction* that descended upon the preacher in the presence of these sable children of Africa. While they were not good judges of rhetoric, they were excellent judges of good preaching, and by their prayers and that peculiar magnetism which many have felt and none can explain the power of the Holy Ghost seemed often present in the preacher and the hearer. That sense of constraint which the minister feels when he stands in the view of hundreds of critical eyes was unknown in the pulpit of a colored Church. No learned exposition of difficult texts was needed. No exhibition of the acquirements of the preacher was provoked in that presence. He felt himself face to face with immortal souls, and indifferent to all things belonging to " delivery " and " elocution."

"God bless all the *benefit sharers*," said a negro preacher in our hearing; and who will say that he did not make a happy blunder and give a profoundly accurate definition of the word " beneficiaries " when he made it " benefit sharers?" It was this arrowlike directness, flying straight to the mark, and the simple, unadorned language of the needy soul feeling its wants—these were the conditions that made preaching to the negroes a blessing to every city pastor. The dry, decorous, and stiff congregations that too often looked like wax figures assembled in Church, and were just as often destitute of any visible evidence of interest in the preacher and his message—these were terrors to many city pastors, and from this Sahara of form and show they were glad to escape and receive a baptism from above in delivering the gospel message to appreciative hearers in a negro congregation. The chasm opened in 1865 and after by the malignant efforts of messengers of Satan who sowed the seed of mistrust and enmity in the minds of the negroes against the whites, against the preachers especially, has not been entirely closed at this day, but time will accomplish the task, and then the preachers who have never known this blessedness in the pulpit may have opportunities to understand what otherwise may seem inexplicable to them.

The condition of the negro slave had greatly improved in 1830, when South Carolina first established her Missions on the plantations. The African slave trade had legally expired in 1808, and the moral sentiment of the people of the South condemned it with great severity. There were many New England ships ready to be engaged in the traffic as of yore, and their owners were not averse to measuring arms with the feeble coast guard of the Federal Government. In nearly two thousand miles of coast line, it was simply impossible to prevent the landing of slave ships if the people on shore gave the necessary encouragement. But this stimulus was wanting. The consequence was that the negroes on the rice and cotton plantations were now natives of the soil, for the most part. Here and there a "Guinea negro" could be found, but his existence was proof of the humane treatment of his master. After twenty-two years of service, the slave captured at twenty-five or thirty becomes a source of expense, not of profit to his master. There were many of these doubtless, but they had learned English, after a fashion, and their own dialect was sufficient for their intellectual wants. The preachers who devoted their time and study to the attainment of a simple style and homely manner of address became useful in a high degree.

Among these effective preachers was the Rev. George W. Moore, of South Carolina.

"To Mr. Moore belongs the honor of having been the first plantation missionary. It is true he was not regularly appointed by the Conference, but this did not deter him from preaching to these darkened souls with all the zeal and faithfulness of a heart that counted no labor too exacting, no service too lowly in its Master's cause. In these noble efforts Mr. Moore was warmly seconded and aided by his colaborer on the circuit, the Rev. Samuel W. Capers.

"Mr. Charles Baring was so much pleased with the results of Mr. Moore's preaching to his slaves that he joined with Col. Lewis Morris, a neighboring planter, in making application to the South Carolina Conference for a missionary to be regularly sent to preach to their people. 'In the autumn of the same year,' says Dr. Shipp in his "History of Methodism in South Carolina," 'the Hon. Charles C. Pinckney, feeling a deep interest in the religious welfare of the colored people, invoked the aid of Rev. William Capers, Superintendent of Missions, in procuring the services of a Methodist exhorter in the relation of overseer for his plantation on Santee River. His attention was called to the object and aim of the Missionary Society, and he therefore made application also for a missionary.'

"As the result of these requests, the South Carolina Conference, in 1829, sent out two missionaries specially to the slaves—the Revs. John Honour and John H. Massey. The former was sent as missionary to the slaves on the plantations south of the Ashley River, and the latter to those south of the Santee. The Rev. William Capers was made superintendent of these missions. A melancholy incident marked their opening. The Rev. John Honour, although a native of the low country, and acclimated, as it was supposed, contracted the fever from exposure in the swamps, was taken seriously ill on the 11th of September, and died the week following, on September 19, 1829.

"Mr. Honour was a noble, zealous, Christian minister, not ashamed of the lowly work to which he had been called, but joyfully resigning even life itself in the cause. Through the kindness of Rev. William W. Mood, of Ridgeway, S. C., we have been permitted to make use of the following extracts from a letter written to Mr. Mood by Mr. John L. Honour, of Charleston, S. C., the grandson of Rev. John Honour:

A brief history of my grandfather can easily be furnished you, as a few months prior to the decease of my beloved father he wrote a sketch of the Honour family "for the benefit of its members who may come after me." Of his own father, the Rev. John Honour in question, he writes thus: "John, the second son of Dr. Thomas Honour, was born in St. Andrew's Parish, South Carolina, July 22, 1770. In early boyhood, having lost his father, he left Charleston in a vessel trading between that port and the West Indies on a trip to Havana. On the return passage the vessel foundered at sea, and the persons on board took to the boats and were for three days without food or water, when they fell in with a vessel bound for Philadelphia, which took them on board and carried them to that city, whence John made his way home to Charleston. Not wishing any further acquaintance with the sea, he entered into business, in which he continued for many years. In the meantime, he and his wife had become members of the Methodist Episcopal Church, and he became a local preacher, preaching every Sunday in the city and surrounding country. At length he determined to give up business and devote himself entirely to the work of the ministry, and was received into the South Carolina Conference. About the year 1829 the Conference established a mission to the blacks in the southern portion of the state, including the Sea Islands, and the Rev. John Honour was appointed first missionary. In this cause he successfully labored until the fall of 1829, when he contracted malarial fever, on the Combahee, of which he died September 19, 1829."

"The remains of the Rev. John Honour, first missionary to the slaves, were interred in the cemetery of Trinity Church, Hazel Street, Charleston, S. C. In the great conflagration of 1838, in which the church (a frame one) was burned, the tombstone was almost totally destroyed from the heat of the burning church. Mr. Honour, the grandson, writes that only a few fragments of the first monument remain. In this way the original inscription has been lost. The present monument was erected by the missionary's son, and bears the simple inscription:

FILIAL TO PARENTAL LOVE.

In Memory of
REV. JOHN HONOUR,
BORN JULY 22, 1770,
DIED SEPTEMBER 19, 1829.

"Although this first mission to the slaves had such a deplorable beginning, it continued to flourish as a tree that heaven watereth. One faithful soldier had died, but there were others ready and willing to take his place. The work went forward with healthy activity. Those noble-hearted men who were first in the movement to have the gospel preached to their people ever remained firm and helpful friends of the missionaries, giving liberally of their substance in support of the work. During the first year of these missions the faithful laborers gathered four hundred and seventeen Church members among these hitherto neglected blacks.

"The Rev. George W. Moore was deemed a fitting successor of the faithful and lamented Honour. In 1830 he was sent as missionary to the slaves on Pon Pon and Combahee, while Rev. John W. Massey was returned to those on the Santee. In the meantime another mission to the blacks had been established on the Savannah and Broad Rivers, and the Rev. James Dannelly sent to serve it. In the second year—that is, at the end of 1830—these faithful missionaries nearly trebled the work of the first year, returning a colored membership on these Missions of 1,077.

"The call for means to keep up these Missions was most urgent. Back of this was but a meagerly filled treasure-chest, for during the year 1830 the total amount collected by the Conference for Missions was only $261.* But to the credit of this grand old Conference be it said that she never once fell short of her duty because of a depleted treasury.

"In the Minutes of the South Carolina Conference of 1830, the same year in which the Georgia Conference was set off, we find record of the establishment of another mission on the Little River, in the Athens (Ga.) District.

"In 1831 there were four distinct missions to the slaves in the bounds of the South Carolina and Georgia Conferences—three in the former and one in the latter. The total number of blacks taken into the Church on these missions was 1,242, an increase of 165. In the meantime active and zealous souls had been at work, and the amount raised this year for missions in the South Carolina Conference alone more than trebled that of the previous year, being $727.67. What amount was given by the Georgia Conference for the support of her one mission the writer has been unable to find.

"The largest of these four missions was that on Combahee and Pon Pon, which had a black mem-

---

* Statistics given in 1856 by Rev. William M. Wightman.

bership of nearly 700. In addition to this there were upward of one hundred little negroes regularly receiving the benefits of a plan of catechetical instruction adopted by the Conference that year.

"In this year (1831) the Rev. Allen Turner, writing from the Little River Mission in Georgia, says that this mission grew out of a great revival among the whites and blacks that began at the Fountain camp meeting held near Warrenton.

"At the anniversary of the South Carolina Conference Missionary Society, held January 28, 1832, the cause of Missions to the slaves was declared ' one of wide and growing interest,' and that the success which had marked the enterprise proved that God had sanctioned it, and offered ' cheering argument in favor of its ultimate triumph, as well as a strong inducement for increased exertion.' This shows well the temper and zeal of the men who had this work in hand. No wonder it flourished and increased despite the slanders and opposition of its enemies. The closing words of this address are worthy of enduring record: ' Thus, after years of delay on our part, the debt of justice due to Africa's sons has begun to be considered. Guided by experience and cheered by success, we come to bind ourselves afresh to the holy work, and to renew the solemn obligation which the enterprise of negro salvation and instruction imposes on us. Into this long-neglected field of danger, reproach, and toil we again go forth bearing the precious seed of salvation; and to the protection of the God of Missions our cause is confidently and devotedly commended.'

"In 1832 we find the return made of four distinct colored missions from the Georgia Conference, which shows that this Conference had started out with all the zeal of the mother Conference. Indeed, this year, she not only ran abreast, but ahead, reporting four missions to two in the South Carolina Conference. This looks a little strange at first, but is easily accounted for by the transfer of a part of the territory of the South Carolina Conference, including one of its missions, to the Georgia Conference. This was the Little River Mission which, although it was established in Georgia, was nevertheless at first under the control of the South Carolina Conference.

"The other three missions in Georgia at this date were those on Broad River in the Athens District, the one near Macon, and the one on Sugar Creek, in the Milledgeville District. The names of the missionaries serving them were: Robert G. Edwards, Whitman C. Hill, and John Collinsworth—all names honored as pioneers in Georgia Methodism. John Collinsworth was especially noted for the access he had to the hearts of the slaves and the confidence of their masters. He was then a man in the prime of life. He died September 4, 1834, while stationed at Eatonton, Ga.

"The two missions in the South Carolina Conference were the Pon Pon and Combahee Mission, and the one on the Santee River. Rev. George W. Moore was the missionary to the former, with Rev. John R. Coburn his colaborer, while Rev. Christian G. Hill had charge of the latter. The number of members returned on these two missions alone was 1,395. Another cause of the decrease in the number of missions in the South Carolina Conference was that during the year 1831 the negroes served on the Savannah River Mission had been put into the regular work of the circuit. This mission must not be confounded with that of the Savannah Back River Mission established by the Georgia Conference in 1834.

"In 1832 we find the Tennessee Conference following the example of the Georgia and South Carolina Conferences and establishing two missions to the blacks. But though established by this Conference, these missions lay in the bounds of another state—the one in Madison and Limestone Counties, and the other in Franklin and Lawrence Counties, Alabama. The two missionaries sent to serve these missions were Thomas M. King and Gilbert D. Taylor. This makes eight slave missions in operation for the year 1832.

"The reports from these missions, with but slight exception, were encouraging. The good work had spread; the minds and hearts of the planters had been opened to the marked benefit of the system, and in several instances they were beginning to contribute liberally toward the maintenance of the missionaries.

11

"The Rev. George W. Moore, writing from the Pon Pon and Combahee Missions, in South Carolina, in February, 1832, said: 'At no time has there been more fixed attention to the word than at present. If we are to decide on its advantages from the statements of those who are best acquainted with the colored people, the master and overseer, it is their decided conviction that much good has been done.'

"On the Santee Mission, same Conference, where that good and true man, Christian G. Hill, was in charge, matters were also in a highly prosperous condition. During one quarter he received on trial eighty-six adults and had the accession of three large plantations to the mission. He had, too, a class of nearly two hundred children under catechetical instruction.

"In January, 1832, the Georgia Conference, in session at Augusta, passed a resolution to the effect ' that in the opinion of the Conference it was the duty of the missionary to the slaves and the colored people within its bounds to consider them his special charge, to collect them into societies and divide them into classes wherever it is practicable; that he should carefully instruct them in the doctrines of Christianity and bring them under the discipline of the Church, as in the case of all other members.'

"On the missions within the bounds of this Conference everything seemed to be in harmonious working order. Near Macon was at this time one of the most prosperous missions. This mission had been organized by the Rev, Whitman C. Hill. He was succeeded in 1832 by Rev. Jesse Sinclair. This mission embraced a tract of thirty-five miles in length and about twenty in breadth. It lay west of Macon, in the counties of Bibb, Monroe, and Upson. By the summer of 1832 Mr. Sinclair reported 12 regular preaching places, nearly 500 members in full connection, and with nearly 100 on probation. Among many things of interest, he wrote of a quarterly meeting just held in which many of the slaves spoke at love feast 'calmly and rationally on the goodness of God in their awakening and conversion.' Their faces shone with a new light, the tears streamed down their cheeks. Many of the owners of these slaves were present and joined with them in the praise of God, weeping as they wept and rejoicing as they rejoiced.

"During the year 1832 (report made at the beginning of the year of 1833) the South Carolina Conference appropriated $1,519.45 to Missions, and the Georgia Conference $856.25, the greater part of which went undoubtedly to the keeping up of their slave missions. The Rev. Mr. Chreitzberg, the able statistician of the South Carolina Conference, writing in reply to the author's inquiry, says: 'You can safely set down fully two-thirds of the amount from each year's Mission report of the South Carolina Conference as appropriated to slave missions.' We suppose this will hold good of other Conferences having these missions in their bounds. It is certainly not an overestimate, as for several years after the establishment of slave missions the total amounts collected for Missions by the South Carolina Conference were appropriated, with but little reservation, to the keeping up of its missionaries in the slave mission fields.

"What amount the Tennessee Conference contributed to the support of its two missions in Alabama, during 1832, we have been unable to learn. The total colored membership within the bounds of these missions at the close of the year 1832 was something over 2,500, and the three Conferences reporting special missions to the slaves had a colored membership of nearly 26,000.

"Now it must not be supposed that because no special missions to the blacks had at this time been established in the other Conferences they were neglectful of this work. Not so; there was not at this date a single Conference within the Methodist Episcopal Church that had not, in some way or other, made provision for the spiritual enlightenment of the blacks. A large part of this mission work was done by the regular ministry. There was not a circuit of any size that did not have its colored charge, or its colored membership. Thus the Kentucky Conference, which, up to 1838, had established but one mission to the people of color (that in Lexington and vicinity) had a colored membership of 5,854. So, too, of the Holston and Virginia Conferences which, for several years later, did not establish separate and distinct missions for the blacks; the former had a colored membership of 1,820, and the latter 2,951. What was true of these Conferences was also true of the others, to a greater or less extent.

"The year 1833 opened with five missions in the Georgia Conference, ten in the South Carolina, and one in the Tennessee—sixteen in all, a wonderful increase over the previous year. Record is also given of the establishment of a mission partly to the whites and partly to the blacks, by the Baltimore Conference on Mattawoman Creek; but as no further account of it is obtainable from the Minutes, no estimate of it can be given. The two missions under the control of the Tennessee Conference in Alabama were now placed in the work of the circuits, and no separate account of them is available.

"On June 5, 1833, the Rev. A. Hamill, presiding elder of the Savannah District, reported the mission to slaves in Burke County, Georgia, under the management of the Rev. L. C. Peck, in a highly prosperous condition. There were twenty-six appointments in all, with a population of nearly two thousand slaves enjoying the preaching of the gospel. 'The planters,' wrote Mr. Hamill, 'are generaly inclined to favor the introduction of Christianity among their slaves.'

"The Savannah River Mission, under the charge of the Rev. Samuel J. Bryan, had, in addition to a large membership, six schools in which 214 children were regularly catechised and instructed in the knowledge of God. Mr. Bryan mentions several instances of masters and slaves being gathered around one common altar, beseeching mercy from the throne of grace.

"There was another mission near Savannah, that was known as the Ogeechee Mission, which was this year served by the Rev. John M. Remshart. The prospect, as reported by this noble old soldier himself, was 'cheering and full of interest.' At one meeting he received twenty-seven members on trial. At every preaching place he had large congregations, 'eager to hear the word of life.' Some of those who had but lately embraced religion could tell, though in broken language—'a whole and perfect experience.' 'By the help of the Spirit,' continues this consecrated missionary, 'we shall continue to sow the seed, looking to God for the shower.'

"From South Carolina the reports were fully as cheering. But the brave missionaries, of course, did not find it all sunshine and easy sowing.

"About this time a report from the Rev. Thomas D. Turpin, the missionary in charge of the May and New River Mission, speaks of one of the many obstacles in the way of the mission work—doubtless one of the most stubborn against which they had to contend. A number of the negroes on this mission lived on a secluded island. Previous to the coming of the missionary, being deprived of Church privileges, they had organized societies among themselves. These were decidedly of Roman Catholic proclivities. Among other things they had a regular form of doing penance. There were three degrees of punishment, inflicted according to the magnitude of the crime. If the crime was of the first magnitude, the perpetrator was condemned to pick up a quart of benne seed (among the smallest of seeds) which had been thrown on the ground by the priest; if of the second degree, a quart of rice; and if of the third, a quart of corn. Many times the poor culprit condemned to pick up the quart of benne seed could not get through in a night. In that case, he had to return to the task on the following night. They also had high seats and low seats, which were used as a means of punishment or reward. It was a rule among the members of these societies, rigidly enforced, never to divulge the secret of stealing; to do so brought dire punishment upon the informer. Against such superstitions and ignorance as this even the bright light of the gospel and the zeal of its noble bearers made but slow headway.

"One of the most interesting of the negro missions at this time was that of the African charge in Nashville, Tenn., under the guidance of that grand old pioneer, Rev. James Gwin. Writing from that place, under date of August 14, 1833, he says: 'The work of the Lord was greatly increased in this mission among the colored people the last quarter. Our campmeeting for this state closed last Thursday, about a thousand colored people attending. Brother McMahon, our elder, addressed them, and administered the Holy Supper. I have never seen so great a display of divine goodness. During the meeting thirty professed to find peace with God, fifty-nine joined the Church on trial; the work spreading all through the city. At our 3 o'clock meeting in the brick church last Sabbath about one hundred fell round the altar, apparently deeply sensible of their lost state. Several professed to find peace, and seventeen joined the society. We have a membership of seven hundred, nearly all of whom profess to be happy in their Saviour; and what greatly encourages me, there is no opposition from the owners of slaves.'

"During the year 1833 there was expended for the support of these missions an amount which, based upon the two-thirds system estimate, will give more than $5,000 from the South Carolina and Georgia Conferences alone. From the South Carolina Conference, according to the statistics gathered by Rev. William M. Wightman, the appropriation was $3,600. We find record of $2,185 paid out by the Georgia Conference.

"Five years of mission work among the slaves had forcibly demonstrated the feasibility, as well as the true Christian spirit of the experiment. Other Conferences beside the South Carolina, Georgia, and Tennessee were now seriously and prayerfully contemplating participation in the good work. More than one of them, in the resolutions adopted in the yearly session about this time, declared it their intention to *urge* upon slaveholders the necessity of paying more attention to the moral and spiritual condition of their slaves. The preachers, too, were urged to do everything they could to promote this work.

"The success of the plan, especially in the South Carolina and Georgia Conferences, had shown beyond a doubt the susceptibility of the negro to the enlightenment of the gospel. Only half a decade had elapsed since the introduction of these missions and the first coming of that noble pioneer, the plantation missionary; and now, in place of the ignorant, superstitious, and imbruted creature that had first met his gaze and appealed to his pitying heart, he had, in many instances, a mild and rational being, earnest, moral, grateful, and rejoicing in the blessed knowledge of a rich inheritance gained through a close and faithful walk with God.

"At the close of the year 1833 there were in the separate colored missions embraced in the Conferences mentioned upward of 4,000 Church members in full connection, in addition to nearly 2,000 more on probation, 800 children under catechetical instruction, more than 150 regular preaching-places, and a population of from 18,000 to 20,000 blacks reached in some way by the missionary. These figures are not given at random, but have been carefully and patiently culled from various sources, principally from the letters of the missionaries themselves in the *Christian Advocate*. In the Nashville African Mission alone there were at the close of this year 819 members in full connection. One mission in the South Carolina Conference also returned as many as 1,155 members. This was the one on Combahee and Pon Pon, the mission which Rev. George W. Moore called 'the child of Providence.'"

CHAPTER XIII.

Plantation Work Continued to 1844.

THE year 1834 opened auspiciously for slave missions. Many hearts hitherto cold were warmed to the work. Tennessee had added another mission to her list (that on Duck River, in the Nashville District), which was placed under the charge of Rev. Joshua W. Kilpatrick. Mississippi, too, had come bravely to the front by establishing her first slave mission, the one to the colored people in New Orleans. Georgia had nearly doubled her list, showing up nine missions, while South Carolina had ten, an increase of one. Two of the missions in the Georgia Conference were in Florida: one in Gadsden County, served by Rev. C. A. Brown, and the other in the St. Augustine District.

"One of the largest and most prosperous missions at this time in the bounds of the South Carolina Conference was the mission to the blacks near Beaufort. This mission was in charge of Rev. George W. Moore. In writing of his work he said: 'In taking a general view of the negroes in this country, it is very perceptive that a decided change has taken place in their general moral character. On a plantation where there are about two hundred negroes, the overseer told me the other day that he believed that not a pint of ardent spirits was drunk in a month on the plantation.'

"Brother Moore recorded a very interesting incident that occurred on this work. On one of the plantations were two little deaf and dumb negroes. Despite their affliction they were always present during the catechising of the other children. Once, soon after catechising, Mr. Moore noticed that the elder of these two little boys seemed much affected. He was very desirous of knowing the cause. The younger boy, not noticing the tears in the eyes of the elder, took him by the hand and brought him to shake hands with the missionary. But on noticing the tears, he seemed to recall what his brother was crying about. The tears, it seems, were not tears of sorrow for sin, but tears of anger, he having, a few moments before the catechising, grown very angry with a little girl who had done him a supposed injury.

"The younger boy now made signs to the elder to go and fight the little girl. At this juncture the old woman who acted as nurse began to tell them by signs how wrong it was to fight. The younger boy, who was the brighter of the two, seemed to read correctly her every gesture. He now turned to his brother, and pointing upward, as though to heaven, and then downward, as though to hell, blew on his hands, and then wrung them as in pain, as much as to say that if the other did fight God would punish him in fire. 'What struck my mind forcibly,' wrote Mr. Moore, 'was how this little fellow, so young and deprived of any particular assistance from any outward circumstance, had conveyed to his mind this knowledge.'

"From the beginning to the close of 1834 most favorable reports continued to come from all the missions. In April Rev. Thomas C. Benning wrote from the missions to slaves on the islands below Savannah, that, though a new work, he had an interesting one which extended to the slaves of five islands. These islands had a population of 80 whites and over 1,200 blacks. There were 180 colored children in classes.

"A little later the Rev. Samuel J. Bryan wrote from the other mission near Savannah, that on the Savannah and Back Rivers. This mission embraced eighteen plantations and reached about two thousand negroes. On one plantation there were 297 members. The planters, as a general thing, were not only favorable to the mission, but liberal. One of them had already begun to give $100 a year to the mission work. One pleasing sign was the readiness with which the children learned the catechism and hymns. It had been only about twelve months since the opening of the mission, yet they could sing with interest all the songs and verses which they had been taught, as well as answer correctly all the questions on the forty pages of the catechism prepared expressly for them by Dr. Capers. There were several Sunday schools connected with this mission. The laws of South Carolina and Georgia, as of other slaveholding states, threw no obstacle whatever in the way of the instruction of the blacks orally in 'the first principles of natural and revealed religion.'

"From the Little River and Sugar Creek Mission in Georgia Rev. Samuel Harwell sent cheering accounts of an interesting and growing work; two new houses of worship exclusively for the blacks; members 'improving in rational, religious enjoyment,' and other encouraging prospects.

"Rev. E. Leggett, serving the Cape Fear Mission in North Carolina under the auspices of the South Carolina Conference, wrote of having gone to his work under many disadvantages, yet of having the mission at the time he wrote generally prosperous. All through the work there was a deep awakening, many inquiring with tears what they must do to be saved.

"During the same year, Burke County Mission, in the Georgia Conference, served by the Rev. L. C. Peek, had twenty appointments, two regular houses of worship, and three more in use; two of them belonging to the whites of the circuit, and the other to the Presbyterians. Everywhere the mission was looked upon with favor by the slave owners.

"From the Wateree (S. C.) Mission, in May, 1834, the Rev. Frederick Rush wrote: 'A great door is opened here for preaching the gospel. The only dissenting voices are from those who have neither might nor means to oppose us.'

"Rev. Charles A. Brown, stationed on the Gadsden County Mission in Florida, sent about this time a letter to the *Christian Advocate* published in New York, in which he declared: 'This mission meets with the approbation of every gentleman with whom I have conversed. The slave owners speak of it with deep interest. They feel for these immortal beings that are committed to them not with the austerity of a reckless despot, but with the charity of Christian masters.'

"From the Forsyth Mission, Georgia Conference, Rev. John P. Dickinson, after reporting an encouraging work that covered fourteen plantations, closed with these words: 'God is preparing a highway for himself in these ends of the earth.'

"In the summer of the same year Rev. Theophilus Huggins, on May and New River Mission, South Carolina, wrote of preaching in a barn and under a stand in the woods to congregations of negroes that averaged not less than 800 to 1,000 each time.

"From the Pedee Mission, same Conference, Rev. John B. Chappell, after speaking of the encouraging prospects of his mission, the kindness of the planters, and his own determination to do all the good he could for the spiritual welfare of this long-neglected people, drew a pathetic picture of the missionary, notwithstanding the deadly malaria of the river swamps, gathering his charge by night under the spreading oak, 'bareheaded, by torchlight, opening to these poor creatures the word of life and salvation.'

"For the support of her slave missions, including amounts contributed by the planters and others interested in the missions, Georgia gave during 1834 a sum closely approximating in round numbers to $3,000. It may have been something more than this, as some items here and there have doubtless escaped the eye of the compiler. The amount contributed from the South Carolina Conference, as per plan of estimate, was $2,615. Like that from the Georgia Conference, it was doubtless more.

"In the meantime quite a forceful impetus had been given the mission work by a most powerful sermon on the subject, delivered by Rev. James O. Andrew (afterward Bishop Andrew) at the Conference session of 1832, held at Darlington, S. C. Bishop Wightman's eloquent pen thus describes that masterful effort:

> He drew a picture of the irreligious, neglected plantation negro, Claude-like in the depth of its tone and coloring. He pointed out his degradation, rendered but the deeper and darker from the fitful and transient flashings up of desires which felt after God—scintillations of the immortal, blood-bought spirit within him, which ever and again gleamed amidst the darkness of his untutored mind. He pointed out the adaptation of the gospel to the extremest case. Its recovering power and provisions were adequate to the task of saving from sin and hell all men, of all conditions of life, in all stages of civilization. He pointed to the converted negro (the noblest prize of the gospel) the most unanswerable proof of its efficiency. There he was, mingling his morning song with the matin-chorus of the birds, sending up his orisons to God under the light of the evening star, contented with his lot, cheerful in his labors, submissive for conscience sake to plantation discipline,

happy in life, hopeful in death, and from his lowly cabin carried at last by the angels to Abraham's bosom. Who could resist such an appeal, in which argument was fused with fervid eloquence? The speech carried by storm the whole assembly.

"In 1833 there were 8 missions to the slaves in South Carolina with a Church membership of over 3,000, employing 9 preachers, and covering between 75 and 80 plantations. In Georgia there were 6 with a membership of 1,266, and about 45 plantations embraced. The two Conferences together gave over $5,000 in support of these missions, beside the amount the planters contributed. Tennessee had two missions, and Mississippi one. What sums were contributed for their support the writer has been unable to find.

"In 1836 both South Carolina and Georgia increased their list of slave missions. Georgia had now 8 missions; South Carolina, 9; Tennessee, 2; Mississippi, 1; and Alabama had just established her first mission, the Canebrake Mission, in the Greensboro District. Twelve missionaries were employed in South Carolina and nine in Georgia. The mission family in the two states alone had increased to nearly 6,000, while the amount contributed for their support was about $7,000. The new mission established in the South Carolina Conference in 1836, that on Waccamaw Neck, brought to light the interesting story of 'Black Punch,' a name deserving, and will doubtless have, perpetual record in the history of Methodism. It is a name peculiarly and touchingly associated with that of the venerated Asbury.

"We copy the record from the pen of Rev. William M. Wightman:

On one of the bishop's tours of visitation, in 1788, on his way to Charleston, S. C., he was passing through All-Saint's Parish, and found, at a creek on his road, a negro engaged in fishing. While his horse was drinking, the bishop entered into conversation with the fisherman. 'What is your name, my friend?'

'Punch, sir.'

'Do you ever pray?'

'No, sir,' said Punch.

With this he alighted, fastened his horse, took his seat by the side of Punch, and entered into conversation with him on the subject of religion, explaining to him in terms suited to his understanding the main peculiarities of the Christian system. Punch was sufficiently astonished at all this, but listened attentively; and as the good bishop sang the hymn,

> Plunged in a gulf of dark despair,

and closed it with a short but fervent prayer, the poor negro's tears came fast and free. The interview over, the bishop bade him an affectionate farewell and resumed his journey, never expecting to see his face again. After the lapse of twenty years, however, when on one of his latest visits to Charleston, Bishop Asbury was waited on by Punch, who had obtained permission from his master to do so, and had traveled seventy miles on foot for the purpose. How touching must have been their second interview! What a harvest had sprung from the handful of bread-seed cast upon the waters! It appeared that the bishop had no sooner left Punch than, hastening homeward with

> The thoughts that wake,
> To perish never—

stirring within his soul, he began to practice upon the instructions of that memorable conversation. He found the knowledge of salvation by the remission of sins after several days of distress and earnest prayer. The change was too remarkable to escape notice. His fellow-servants began to inquire into the matter. Those were strange things which Punch had to tell them. One and another resorted to his cabin to hear further about these things. The interest spread; many were brought to the knowledge of God. One remarkable result followed. An irreligious overseer had charge of the plantation. He ascertained that some new influence was stirring among the people. Punch was holding prayer meeting at night, and this was not to be allowed. He ordered him to desist. Punch accordingly, with a sorrowful heart, dismissed the company of worshipers. A week or two passed away, when one evening the overseer's voice was heard calling for Punch, while the latter was engaged in prayer. In no small alarm he went out, when lo! the overseer was found kneeling under a tree, calling upon God for mercy, and asking the benefit of Punch's prayers. The upshot was his conversion. He joined the Methodist Church, became an exhorter, and finally a preacher.

"The missionary who was sent to the Waccamaw Mission found, on the plantation where Punch lived, between two and three hundred blacks under the spiritual supervision of the gray-haired patriarch. 'I was much interested,' said he, ' on my visit to the old veteran. Just before I reached his house I met a herdsman and asked him if there was any preacher on the plantation. "O yes, massa; de old bishop lib here." Said I: "Is he a good preacher?" "O yes," was the reply, "he word burn me heart." He showed me the house. I knocked at the door, and heard approaching footsteps and the sound of a cane upon the floor. The door opened, and I saw before me, leaning upon a staff, a hoary-headed black man, with palsied limbs but a smiling face. He looked at me a moment in silence, then raising his eyes to heaven said: "Lord, now lettest thou thy servant depart in peace, for mine eyes have seen thy salvation." He asked me to take a seat, and I found, in the following remarks, the reason of his exclamation. Said he: "I have many children in this place. I have felt for some time past that my end was nigh. I have looked around to see who might take my place when I am gone. I could find none. I felt unwilling to die and leave them so, and have been praying to God to send some one to take care of them. The Lord has sent you, my child. I am ready to go." Tears coursed freely down his time-shriveled but smiling face. This interview gave me much encouragement. He had heard of the application for a missionary, and only wanted to live long enough to see his face. After this I had several interviews with him, from which I learned his early history. I always found him contented and happy. In the lapse of a short time afterward, he was taken ill and lingered a few days. One Sabbath morning he told me that he would die that day. He addressed affecting words to the people who crowded around his dying bed. His theme was: "Lord, now lettest thou thy servant depart in peace." He applied these words to himself, and continued his address to the last moment, and death gently stole his spirit away while saying: "Lord, let thy servant depart in peace, let—let—le—" His mistress sent for me to preach his funeral sermon. The corpse was decently shrouded, and the coffin was carried to the house of worship. I looked upon the face of the cold clay. The departed spirit had left the impress of heaven upon it. Could I be at a loss for a text? I read out of the gospel: "Lord, now lettest thou thy servant depart in peace."'

"This missionary, if the writer mistakes not, was the Rev. Theophilus Huggins, one of the noblest soldiers in the ranks, who early entered it with a zeal and devotion surpassed by none.

"There is something else connected with this Waccamaw Neck Mission that deserves to be put in perpetual record, and that is the active and zealous efforts made by the Rev. James L. Belin to Christianize his slaves. Says Rev. A. M. Chreitzberg in a letter to the writer: 'He began the mission work on Waccamaw Neck as early or earlier than the earliest named.' Investigation of the records show that Mr. Belin began the mission work to the slaves as early as 1819, ten years before the Revs. John Honour and John Massey were sent as regular missionaries. Among the first plantations on which he preached were those of Robert Withers and Maj. Ward. With the assistance of the Rev. Theophilus Huggins, Mr. Belin, in 1836, formed the Waccamaw Neck Mission. Mr. Belin continued to the day of his death to labor strenuously for the salvation of the souls of the negroes. He was killed in 1859 by a fall from his buggy. He bequeathed nearly all his large property to the carrying out of this work of salvation among his slaves. In the same year of Mr. Belin's death Rev. Mr. Chreitzberg dedicated a commodious house of worship erected for the slaves. As much as $40,000 of Mr. Belin's magnificent bequest to his slaves survived the wreck of war, and Mr. Chreitzberg, who is a trustee of the fund, writes that, 'the negroes having gone into other Churches, the mission is now kept up to the poor whites.'

"In 1837 there were 25 distinct slave missions throughout the bounds of the following Conference: South Carolina, 10; Georgia, 6; Mississippi, 4; Alabama, 2; Tennessee, 2; Kentucky, 1; and Arkansas, 1. The numbers in the mission family had now increased to nearly 10,000. This was exclusive of those in the regular circuits. The report of the South Carolina Conference Missionary Society declared nearly all the missions in the bounds of that Conference as highly prosperous and promising beyond the most sanguine expectations. A like cheering report came from Georgia. Before these respective societies numerous communications from the most respectable and influential sources, in high praise of the mission work, were read, and greatly cheered the hearts of the workers. The South Carolina Society declared that, 'notwithstanding the troublous times on which we are fallen, and the agitations that have swept in swelling waves through the public mind and the giant shadows cast by pending events, we bless God and take courage.' The missionaries were recommended to concern themselves alone with the moral and spiritual wants of the negro population and to avoid all political discussions.

"The catechising of the young was found a

most promising means of enlightenment. Rev. Thomas J. Williamson, writing, about this time, from the Burke County Mission, in Georgia, said: 'I have become more interested in teaching the young. Many of them progress astonishingly, all things considered. They appear quite anxious to learn, and some of them inquire after the missionary, and wish the time to come when they may meet him again. I discover that a majority of them possess a strong attachment for me, which is very necessary to render me more useful to them. The present generation will soon be past, and the rising one that we now instruct catechetically will take their place. And we hope and pray that by the blessing of God upon our humble exertions the latter will be higher in the scale of religious knowledge than the former.' Mr. Williamson also adds this significant remark: 'The people who attend my ministry are comfortably and neatly clad; and I can assure you that a congregation of negroes in this section of country presents no mean nor deeply degraded appearance, whatever may be said to the contrary, notwithstanding.'

"Rev. William McQuentock, writing at this same period, also bears testimony to the ease and facility with which the minds of the young negroes grasped the first great truths of Christianity. All the missionaries seemed to recognize fully the importance of carefully instructing the children and also to give them every religious opportunity. Rev. Samuel Leard, one of the most faithful and successful of this noble army of light bearers, relates a most affecting incident that took place in the summer of 1837. He was holding a class meeting, when his attention was attracted by the sound of continued sobbing on the outside of the house. Stepping to the door, he there saw the touching spectacle of many children gathered about it weeping as though their hearts would break. They heard some of that which was going on within, the varied and thrilling experience of those cleansed of their sins, and it had pierced their souls. The heart of the good missionary was moved. He determined to hold special services for their benefit. He did so, and was rewarded. Many were converted and brought rejoicing into the Church.

" Rev. John R. Pickett, from the Black Swamp Mission, South Carolina, also wrote of special efforts made by him among the children, which were crowned with rich results. He also spoke of the families of the owners and overseers keeping up the catechising in his absence.

" This year South Carolina and Georgia alone raised nearly $10,000 for Missions—that is, basing it upon the two-thirds plan. That it was in excess of this is strongly evidenced by the report of the Rev. Thomas C. Benning, Conference Treasurer of the Georgia Conference, giving the amount of appropriations for missions from that Conference as $6,282, and adding these words: '*mostly for missions to people of color.*' Another significant matter is that Mr. Benning says in his report that 'it is less this year than it has ever been before.' These words alone will show that the amounts given in the statistical tables are far below what they ought to be. It must ever be a source of regret that these appropriations for the support of slave missions were not separated. The total amount contributed by the South Carolina Conference for the year 1837 was $7,246.78, $2,156.16 of which was contributed by the planters of the different missions.

"At the anniversary of the Georgia Missionary Society, held at Athens, Ga., in January, 1838, it was resolved that renewed efforts should be put forth in behalf of the colored people of the sea-coast. The peculiarities of their location, secluded from the circuits, called for special efforts to give them the advantages of the gospel. Many of them had never heard preaching from a white man's lips until they heard it from those of the faithful Methodist missionary. The picture presented of their wretched condition, 'intrenched within rice dams and surrounded by the pestilential miasma, an isolated, cast-off race, unvisited by the common preacher,' was truly startling, and surely did call for the most zealous exercise of Christian endeavor. But where the 'common preacher' hesitated to go, there went the Methodist missionary, undismayed by danger, strong in the mighty upholding of his own zeal and faith in a sustaining God.

"At the beginning of 1838 much good was done

the mission cause through a widely circulated sermon delivered by the Rev. George Freeman, of Raleigh, N. C., on 'Duty to the Slaves.' He took for his text Colossians iv. 1: 'Masters, give unto your servants that which is just and equal; knowing that ye also have a Master in heaven.' Never had a more forceful sermon been delivered on a more vital question.

"Many affecting scenes were constantly taking place between the missionary and the people. They seemed the most grateful of creatures, as if they could not do too much for him who had come to lead them out of the darkness. Rev. John N. Davis, writing from the Pocotaligo Mission, South Carolina Conference, related a most touching incident that took place at the close of his first sermon on a plantation just added to the mission. As he closed his sermon, many of the poor creatures thronged about him, while with tears rolling from their eyes they said: 'T'anky, massa; t'anky, missie; t'anky, my good preacher, fur de gospel.' It is needless to add in the missionary's own words, 'it was a moving scene.' Doubtless those tears fell upon his already faithful heart with the dew of consecration.

"Rev. Edwin White, on the Burke County Mission in Georgia, also writes of a similar touching experience in an assembly of weeping negroes, to whom he had just preached, crowding up about him to bless him for the light and comfort he had brought them. In that last day how many such pearls—words of blessing and of gratitude from the lips of the poor slave—will shine in the crown of these noble, Godlike men who counted nothing dear, not even life itself, that they might minister to the spiritual comfort of such as these!

"Many other similar instances could be recorded; indeed, they were constantly occurring. Nor were the children less grateful. Revs. Thomas Ledbetter and William C. Kirkland, after writing many interesting things of their work on the Beaufort Mission, spoke of the great joy with which the children of the various plantations of the islands hailed the period of the missionary's regular visits. How eagerly they ran to open the gate! how they crowded up about him, touching his hands, his clothing with the most affectionate freedom, yet with an unmistakable air of veneration mingled throughout it all. When he went away, there was the same readiness to open gates, but not the same air of cheerful alacrity, while the tear-filled eye and the tremulous lip showed the depth of feeling even in their young hearts, as they looked at him wistfully with the earnest reminder: 'Come back again soon, sir.'

"That the gospel preached by the faithful missionary had power to reach all hearts, the following incident, related by Rev. S. D. Laney, missionary to the Pedee Mission, will show: 'Jim had stolen some of his master's corn, and was absent from the preaching, and on my inquiring after him, one remarked thus: "Ah, massa, he 'fraid you preach at him, dat make him no come to-day." One who is guilty of an offense of this sort is looked upon with general contempt. This is an effect of the gospel being preached to them.'

"At the end of the first decade of slave missions the ground covered, in South Carolina alone, extended from Waccamaw Neck and Pedee River on the east to the Savannah River on the west, and embraced 234 plantations. These plantations were served by 17 missionaries under the general supervision of three superintendents. These missionaries preached at 97 appointments, and had under their regular pastoral charge 6,556 Church members, to whom they furnished the preaching and administered the sacraments and discipline of the Christian Church. And, further, they had under regular catechetical instruction 25,025 negro children.

"Truly these active missionaries had not been as 'dumb driven cattle,' but as 'heroes in the strife.' Imperishable should be the record to their memory.

"The year 1839 opened with 54 special missions to people of color throughout the various Southern Conferences having them in their bounds, with a membership in this mission family alone of between 18,000 and 20,000. This did not include the members in regular charges or the colored members in separate Churches in the cities and larger towns, known as city colored charges, but simply included those served by the regular plantation missionary.

REV. J. A. BEEBE,
Bishop of the Colored M. E. Church.
(See page 380.)

"Some of these 'African charges,' as the city colored Churches were styled, were at several places in excess of the white membership. Very few of them that did not run largely into the hundreds. Thus the Kentucky Conference, that only reported in the bounds of its two regular missions to the slaves 313 members, had in the Louisville colored charge alone 495 members. The largest colored charge of all was that in South Carolina, at Charleston, which numbered 3,742. The next largest was the Sharp Street and Asbury, of Baltimore, 2,600; and the next the Nashville African Mission, well up in the hundreds. Virginia, which up to this time had not reported a single special slave mission, had, in all the larger cities and many of the small towns, flourishing colored charges, noticeably that at Norfolk, which numbered 337—seven more than the white membership of the city. The total colored membership for 1838 throughout the various Conferences having special slave missions—the Georgia, South Carolina, Kentucky, Mississippi, Alabama, and Tennessee—was 58,313, of which 27,630 were in South Carolina and 10,180 in Georgia. This does not include the other Southern Conferences, each of which had a large slave membership scattered through the various circuits and charges. The total colored membership of 1839, lying in the Southern body, was 84,332. In 1839 Texas, too, added her first colored charge—43 members.

"In 1841 Virginia established her first slave

mission (the Prince Edward Colored Mission), which was put in charge of Rev. Matthew N. Dance. From that time on we find his name constantly associated with this work, as also those of Benjamin Devaney, Samuel Phillips, and Lewis Skidmore.

"Kentucky had, in the meantime, thrown her two missions into the regular circuit work, and cared for them there. In the next year after Virginia, 1842, the North Carolina Conference, also, came to the front with her first regular slave mission, the Roanoke Mission, in the Washington District. But up to this time she, too, had been far from idle in the matter of the spiritual care of her slaves. Like the Kentucky, Holston, and other Conferences, she had made faithful provision for them through her circuits and charges. At the time of the establishment of her first regular slave mission, she showed a total colored membership of 9,373. The names of some of the noble veterans who were the earliest in this work from the North Carolina Conference were Bennet T. Blake, William Carter, R. J. Carson, Joseph Goodman, and Thomas J. Cassaday.

"In this year (1842) Arkansas established her second regular slave mission, or what was at that time her only one, as the other had been put into the regular charge. This second mission, which was the first she kept running as a regular mission, was known as the 'Red River Colored Mission.' It is but proper to remark at this point that Arkansas was actively engaged in caring for the Indians, numbers of whom were within her borders. But she too had been faithful in the care of her colored people, showing at that time a total colored membership of 828. The names of A. L. Kavanaugh, Henry Hubbard, and Alexander Avery appear prominent among the first of her slave missionaries.

"South Carolina, Georgia, Mississippi, Tennessee, and Alabama were advancing in the good cause. Plantation after plantation was put into the hands of the missionary. East, South, and West fields stretched white to the harvest. Louder and more prolonged grew the cry for more laborers. The Church responded with promptness and energy. Said one of the most zealous of the Conference Treasurers at that time: 'Though our funds are exhausted and we know not where the next are to come from, still this work *must* go on, these missions to the slaves *must* be kept up, cost what it may.' He but echoed the sentiment of every Christian heart when those words were uttered. Poor Ethiopia struggled in the bonds of pagan darkness—bonds far more terrible than any that bound her bodily. Her wailing cry fell on the ears of a Christian brotherhood, who heard, pitied, and succored.

"In the meantime the work had spread even to the wild frontiers of Texas. Through the kindness of Dr. Homer S. Thrall we are enabled to give a few points touching the early mission work to the slaves in Texas. These would otherwise have been left in obscurity, as the Minutes do not give these missions as colored missions, but simply as missions. This makes the author fear that injustice has been done in other directions and many missions that were colored missions have been left unrecorded. This difficulty we have endeavored to avoid as far as possible by noting the membership given, whether under white or colored column. But often this discouraging line has met the eye: 'No returns given.'

"Says Dr. Thrall: 'The first report of members of the Methodist Church in Texas was in 1839, and there were reported then 43 colored members. We have but brief records of the work of Dr. Martin Ruter, the first superintendent of the mission work in Texas; but in those notices it is stated that he, and indeed all the preachers, devoted Sunday afternoon to the slave population, wherever there were slaves to preach to. There was a universal willingness on the part of the planters to have their negroes preached to and catechised. The first preacher appointed exclusively to the slaves was Jesse Hord to the Brazoria Mission, in 1843. At a later period J. W. Devilbiss, Joseph P. Sneed, Robert Crawford, Francis Wilson, M. Yell, and others equally worthy were employed in the work. At the organization of the Texas Annual Conference, in 1840, there were reported 230 colored members. Ten years later there were 1,847, and in 1860, 7,440, with 20 missions to the colored people, mostly, however, connected with white charges, the same preacher serving both congregations.' "

The remaining notices, required to bring the history of the work up to the year 1844, will be found in the various contributions to this volume made by the missionaries themselves, and in the extracts from a large variety of articles which will not readily conform to the division of the work adopted by the editor. It is our purpose to show, firstly, the interest taken in the salvation of the slaves by the white race of the South, slaveholders and nonslaveholders alike; secondly, we propose to show that the division of the Church in 1844 emphasized and enlarged that interest, but did not create it.

For this purpose we think that the year 1844 forms a definite historical era. Whatever existed prior to that time was not the product of that time, and inasmuch as the sending of the gospel to the African slaves was an enterprise that had grown into proportions nearly or quite equal to the missionary efforts in behalf of the white race, the reader will be able to see how greatly the cause of Christ was placed in peril by the action of the General Conference of 1844.

In order to bring the statistics of the plantation work from 1829 to 1844 distinctly into view, we append a table which gives in regular order from year to year the number of missions to slaves established by the various Conferences, the number of missionaries, the number of Church members among the African slaves, and amounts appropriated by the several Conferences for the support of the work.

STATISTICS FROM 1829 TO 1844.

Year.	Conference.	Missions.	Members.	Missionaries.	Amount Appropri'd.
1829	South Carolina...	2	417	2	....
1830	South Carolina...	3	1,077	3	$ 216 00
1831	South Carolina...	3	1,242	3	727 67
1831	Georgia..........	1	115	1	....
1832	South Carolina...	2	1,395	3	1,519 45
1832	Georgia..........	4	936	4	856 25
1832	Tennessee........	2	190	2	656 35
1833	South Carolina...	9	1,426	11	3,600 00
1833	Georgia..........	5	1,105	5	25,00 00
1833	Tennessee........	1	819	1	465 00
1834	South Carolina...	10	2,913	11	2,615 00
1834	Georgia..........	9	1,385	9	2,818 65
1834	Tennessee........	2	824	2	850 00
1834	Mississippi.......	1	....	1	....
1835	South Carolina...	8	3,134	9	2,821 42
1835	Georgia..........	6	1,266	7	2,445 00
1835	Tennessee........	2	621	3	....
1835	Mississippi.	1	....	1	....
1836	South Carolina.	9	4,417	12	4,194 00
1836	Georgia..........	8	1,357	11	2,749 58
1836	Tennessee........	2	701	2	950 00
1836	Mississippi.......	1	523	1	757 72
1836	Alabama.........	1	139	1	165 00
1837	South Carolina...	10	9,693	12	4,831 20
1837	Georgia..........	6	1,298	7	4,118 00
1837	Tennessee........	2	810	2	....
1837	Mississippi.......	4	459	4	1,440 00
1837	Alabama.........	2	383	2	745 65
1837	Kentucky........	1	....	1	....
1837	Arkansas........	1	....	1	204 50
1838	South Carolina...	12	6,556	13	4,530 36
1838	Georgia..........	6	1,381	6	2,860 22
1838	Tennessee........	5	960	5	1,056 72
1838	Mississippi.......	5	710	5	1,485 40
1838	Alabama.........	2	....	2	911 42
1838	Kentucky........	1	718	1	756 00
1838	Arkansas	1	130	1	....
1839	South Carolina...	18	7,160	24	4,464 80
1839	Georgia..........	16	3,864	19	3,398 74

Plantation Work Continued to 1844.

Statistics from 1829 to 1844 (Continued).

Year.	Conference.	Missions.	Members.	Missionaries.	Amount Appropri'd.
1839	Mississippi	10	3,672	12	$ 3,741 26
1839	Alabama	6	1,671	6	1,800 00
1839	Tennessee	9	2,316	10	2,700 00
1839	Kentucky	2	505	2	600 00
1840	South Carolina	18	7,631	24	3,780 90
1840	Georgia	15	3,972	17	3,100 00
1840	Alabama	9	2,691	9	2,326 00
1840	Mississippi	8	3,908	10	2,400 00
1840	Tennessee	7	3,251	8	2,100 00
1840	Memphis	4	769	4	1,200 00
1841	South Carolina	16	7,557	21	4,950 80
1841	Georgia	12	3,913	14	4,821 06
1841	Alabama	8	2,793	8	2,160 24
1841	Mississippi	10	4,302	12	2,432 00
1841	Tennessee	5	1,120	5	1,213 43
1841	Memphis	5	923	5	1,500 00
1841	Baltimore	2	....	2	600 00
1841	Virginia	1	....	1	300 00
1842	South Carolina	17	7,866	25	5,576 79
1842	Georgia	13	3,787	16	3,978 45
1842	Alabama	8	2,009	9	3,028 25
1842	Mississippi	7	2,466	8	3,028 96
1842	Tennessee	4	1,624	4	1,200 00
1842	Memphis	7	1,567	8	2,037 10
1842	North Carolina	1	....	1	300 00
1842	Arkansas	1	125	1	300 00
1842	Virginia	2	261	2	600 00
1843	South Carolina	16	7,262	23	7,695 22
1843	Georgia	11	3,291	13	4,464 55
1843	Mississippi	9	2,187	10	2,392 50
1843	Memphis	9	2,261	10	1,812 25
1843	Alabama	6	2,131	7	3,364 95
1843	Tennessee	4	696	4	1,512 36
1843	Virginia	3	428	3	900 00
1843	North Carolina	2	153	2	908 50
1843	Arkansas	1	138	1	300 00
1844	South Carolina	16	7,922	21	7,356 20
1844	Georgia	9	3,051	11	3,870 30
1844	Memphis	10	2,655	12	2,134 10
1844	Mississippi	10	3,419	12	1,624 95
1844	Alabama	9	2,146	10	2,864 85
1844	Tennessee	6	1,707	6	1,820 75
1844	Florida	3	530	3	905 90
1844	North Carolina	2	148	2	902 20
1844	Virginia	2	357	2	600 00
1844	Arkansas	1	128	1	300 00

Thus it appears that from the small beginning of the two plantation missions in 1829, with 2 missionaries and 417 members, within fifteen years the work had grown to 68 missions, 71 missionaries, and 21,063 members. The amount appropriated by the South Carolina Conference was so small that no record had been made of it for the year 1829, but in 1844 the Southern Conferences paid $22,379.25 for this work, South Carolina leading the list with $7,356.20.

It has already been stated that the actual amount expended cannot be accurately known because many contributions were given under circumstances that rendered it difficult to ascertain the amounts and the names of the contributors. Presents in kind to the family of the missionary, valuable as the money itself, could not always be rated in that way for obvious reasons, yet they lessened the cash requisitions upon the missionary treasury and gave great aid to the cause. After making as thorough an examination as the case will allow, there can be little doubt that the Southern Conferences contributed fully $200,000 to the special work of sending the gospel to the slaves on large plantations between the years 1829 and 1844.

Of the total amounts reported to the Annual Conferences, $168,458.87, the South Carolina Conference paid $58,879.81: Georgia, $41,980.80; Mississippi, $19,302.79; Alabama, $17,366.36; Tennessee, $14,524.56; Memphis, $8,683.45; Virginia, $2,400; North Carolina, $2,110.70; Arkansas, $1,104.50; Florida, $905.90; Baltimore, $600; and Kentucky, $600.

CHAPTER XIV.

NOTES FROM THE PIONEERS.

NO description of any movement can be better understood than by giving close attention to the words of those who were the leaders in that movement. Many of the pioneers in the plantation mission work have left such records to the Church, and from these we will endeavor to give the reader an insight of this enterprise at its commencement. Tedious details will be avoided, and much of the matter that was instructive and profitable when these accounts were written, must, of necessity, be omitted. Time has rendered many allusions obscure, and incidents that derived their chief interest from local causes have ceased to be attractive to the modern reader. For these reasons we shall abridge from time to time, and sometimes it may be that we shall remodel a communication. The object is to unfold the surroundings, and to give to the mind of the reader a distinct picture of this missionary work.

The first of these " Notes " was written by Rev. G. W. Moore, of the South Carolina Conference. As fair samples of these sketches, we will vouch for the reader's interest in the details of " Life among the Lowly."

Combahee, Pon Pon, Beaufort, and Cooper River Missions.

By Rev. George W. Moore, of the South Carolina Conference.

The Combahee Mission may be considered a child of Providence. It had its rise in the following manner: A Mrs. Bearfield, a pious old lady, a member of the M. E. Church, was employed by Mrs. Charles Baring to look after and attend the sick. Through her an invitation was extended from Mrs. Baring to one of the preachers of the Black Swamp Circuit to visit the plantation and preach to their people. The preacher, however, did not attend, in consequence of Mr. Baring not being at home at the time, he supposing it would not be prudent for him to do so. At his failure to come Mrs. Baring was greatly disappointed.

Being in the neighborhood and hearing of Mrs. Baring's disappointment, I proposed to go, and accordingly did so. I stayed with Sister Bearfield, and went out that night and preached to the blacks in a large room near Mrs. Baring's dwelling. We had quite a good meeting. Sister Bearfield got so happy she shouted. Mrs. Baring had company that evening, among the guests being the Episcopal minister. He, with the family, I was afterward told, stood near the window during a part of the service. Soon after the meeting closed, Mrs. Baring sent a servant with refreshments to me and an invitation to call on her the next morning. I did so, and had quite a pleasing interview with her, in which she expressed her satisfaction at my coming and desire for the continuance of my visits to her people. This was in the year 1828. Brother Samuel W. Capers and myself, being on the Orangeburg Circuit, our appointment reaching down near Mr. Baring's plantation, we embraced that place in the plan of the circuit, and preached there regularly. The next year, I think it was, it was set off for regular mission work, and Rev. John Honour appointed missionary. The year following I was sent to the mission, Brother Honour having died in the work. This year the mission also embraced Mr. John Dawson's plantation in St. John's and was called the St. John's, Pon Pon, and Combahee Mission. There was a church built in the vicinity of Mr. Dawson's place for the blacks, which still exists, and in which I preached to a large congregation of devout worshipers last Sunday. The place is now connected with the Cooper River Mission, and embraces members from several plantations in the neighborhood.

The Pon Pon Mission, when I took charge of it, embraced Col. Morris's place on the Bluff, with several places on the other side of the river belonging to the estate, and Gov. Aiken's place on Jehossee Island. I generally preached in an old cooper shop opposite the Bluff Place, where the negroes from all the other plantations attended. Here we usually held a sunrise prayer meeting and catechised the children from the estate place. I have often been interested in seeing the little fellows running on the rice bank toward the cooper shop, and entering almost out of breath. The first thing they would do would be to clasp my hand and tell me "how-dy," and while upon my knees in prayer they would get as near as possible, some of them leaning against my feet with their heads. The negroes from the Bluff and the estate all worshiped in the cooper shop, and O how often has my heart rejoiced in their joy at the knowledge of the gospel of Christ Jesus!

Col. Morris and others would attend sometimes with their families and with the overseers and their families, and often around the same altar you could see several of those white persons mingling their cries for mercy with those of the blacks, and many together found the pearl of great price.

Among the most prominent of the colored leaders on this work there was January, a very faithful man, who generally held a long reed in his hand, and if he saw any one asleep he would give them a tap on the head to wake them up. In the love feast if any one would speak as he thought a little too long he would cry out: "Short and sweet, my hearty, short and sweet."

These love feasts were precious seasons, and highly prized by the members of the Church. You could see two or three up at one time waiting to speak. On one occasion one of the members, hearing some of the others speak of their trials and difficulties, said: "My bredren, I hab my dif'culties an' trials too, but de Lo'd so good to me I ain't hab time to t'ink ob dem fur de mercies he sends me long wid 'em." Another said: "My bredren, I hab my hard bone fur to chaw, an' my bitter pill fur to swaller, but bredren, I tell you what, 'ligion makes de bone turn to marrow an' de bitter to sweet. 'Ligion's jus' like de spring in de back country, de furder you go de sweeter de water tastes."

Their sweet songs, sung with a fervidness indescribable, added much to the pleasure of the occasion.

We generally preached at the estate place in the morning, and in the afternoon at Jehossee. Here we preached in a room next to the hospital, so that the sick might hear as well as those who were not sick. Gov. Aiken was exceeding kind to us; so was his overseer, Mr. Bagwell. The first letter I received from Gov. Aiken, inclosing his donation of $100, impressed me sensibly. It had the same effect upon Bishop Andrew, who asked me to let him keep it.

The overseers would generally send up to the estate place for us a large boat rowed by six or eight hands. I remember a conversation that took place between Dr. Capers and one of the hands on the boat. The Dr. asked him, among other things, how he liked the overseer, which is the test question among the negroes. In reply he said: "Massa he good man; he nebber promise nuffin he no gib you. If he promise you whippin', you's as sho' to git 'em as if you had 'em on you' back."

I soon found the secret of the good government on this place; it was decision of character. I visited the place at all times during the year, and I never, to my recollection, heard the overseer swear, get in a passion, or whip a negro during all that period, and it was all because the negroes understood that he meant what he said, and a promise was as good as performed.

I have already mentioned that in preaching at Mr. Charles Baring's we occupied a room near to his dwelling. Adjoining this was another of smaller dimensions, where the white persons who attended sat, among whom could generally be seen Mr. and Mrs. Baring, who took a deep interest in the welfare of their people. I have often seen Mrs. Baring, when the negroes were singing, catch the motion of their bodies and do just as they did. On one occasion, when taking my seat at the dinner table, Mr. Baring took my hand, and, while under the influence of much feeling, said, with emphasis: "Sir, this [referring to the service that had just taken place] must do good, it will do good, it *shall* do good." And he pressed my hand very warmly in his. At another time, when about leaving for their summer residence, they asked me to retire with them to a private room and there engage in prayer for the salvation of their people.

On one occasion I preached to a British Admiral, who was an American born citizen, who was on a visit to the family. He sat in the rear of the negroes and was quite attentive during the service.

Mr. Baring was most generous in the support of the mission, and I believe at one time carried it entirely. His good wife was not one whit behind him in zeal. Often when coming from the service I have heard her say to him: "Now, Charles, I hope you will take to heart what Mr. Moore has said." Noble woman, I hope she is in heaven!

The Beaufort Mission was attached to the Combahee and Pon Pon in 1832, and John R. Coburn sent with me to serve the work. The Beaufort Mission had its origin through a religious revival that took place among the Baptists and Episcopalians in Beaufort and vicinity, instigated by Rev. Mr. Daniel Baker, a Presbyterian minister. The stores were closed and business in the town suspended for several days, so great was the interest taken. This revival caused the planters, several of whom made Beaufort their summer residence, to turn their attention to the condition of their slaves. Not being able to get the services of an Episcopal or Baptist minister, they, through the influence of Mr. Pinckney, who at the time had the services of a Methodist minister on his plantation on the Santee, applied to our Conference for help, and Beaufort Island was taken in along with Combahee, Pon Pon, and Wappahoola, the mission having that name at the time.

One pleasing part of the Beaufort work was that the young ladies took quite an active part in the instruction of the colored children, both in Beaufort and on the plantations of their fathers.

Frequently I found them under the shade of the spreading oak, with a group of little negroes around them, instructing them in the catechism. The planters too were active in the work. Some of the wealthiest and most distinguished gentlemen would spend every Sabbath afternoon in imparting religious instruction to the negroes, young and old.

I commenced my labors in Beaufort by preaching to the negroes in the old Tabernacle Church, belonging to the Baptists, and holding prayer meetings, with the assistance of a few Christian gentlemen, in the Episcopal lecture room. We soon enjoyed as great a revival among the colored people as there had been among the whites. I extended my labors to Paris, Cat, St. Helena, Dathan, Coosa, Lady's, Beaufort, and Big Islands, and on the mainland, where we soon enjoyed much prosperity. I left the converts free to join the Church of their choice. At one time, with my full consent, over two hundred of them were added to the Baptist Church.

The mission at that time was similar to a circuit, I went regularly round, week day and Sunday. We preached on Paris Island on Sunday, the negroes from all the plantations attending. We had no church building at that time, but occupied a house on the plantation of our patron, Mr. Robert Means. We would also preach at some of the other places at night. I recollect on one occasion preaching with a negro holding a lightwood torch at my back to throw light on my Bible and hymn book. At first we preached at two or three places on the island on Sunday, as we confined our labors a good deal to plantation preaching. We catechised during the week, and also preached at several places on week days. Robert Means, Esq., Dr. Thomas Fuller, Rev. S. Elliott, Mrs. Habersham, and William Eddings owned the entire island, and we had access to all the plantations.

There were two very remarkable cases of the power of the voice of conscience that occurred on this island. After one of my sermons on Mr. Means's place, a woman got possession of the key of the house where the molasses was kept. She went to steal some to send to a woman on a neighboring island, and when she had put the key in the door, she stood motionless, having no power to open it, and was found in that position by the driver. I was an eyewitness to her agony. She could neither move nor speak. Afterward she seemed very penitent, especially when she knew that I was acquainted with all the circumstances.

The other case was that of a man who attempted to get into the corncrib and carry off a sack of corn. He was discovered and taken down by the driver, having no power of his own, either to go forward or to come back. How long he had been in that position was not known.

From Paris Island we went to Cat Island, owned by Rev. R. Fuller. Here we preached on week nights, the negroes assembling in a vacant house on the place. On one occasion when Brother Coburn preached, the negroes were so much pleased with his preaching that they begged him to remain for the next day and preach again. This he consented to, and at an early hour the place was filled. One fact I have often noticed is that not only on the cotton but also on the rice plantations those negroes who are industrious can accomplish their task during the hoeing season by the middle of the day, and thus have the afternoon to themselves.

Our next appointment was on St. Helena Island at Rev. Mr. Field's, Col. Stapleton's, and Dr. Scott's. From there we went to Dathan, owned by Dr. B. Sams and Mr. L. Sams, his brother. At the different places on Dathan we preached at night and catechised the children during the day. At Dr. Sams's, however, we preached on a week day, the negroes coming out of the fields to assemble at the appointed time in a large cotton house. At the close of the services the smaller negroes would remain to be catechised. At Mr. L. Sams's we preached at night and had some most attentive hearers. Here there was soon erected a very comfortable house of worship.

From Dathan we crossed to Mr. Barnwell's place on Coosa Island and preached at night, and then crossed over to Lady's Island in a canoe, swimming our horses alongside the boat. Here we also preached at another of Mr. Sams's places.

On Beaufort Island, where my family lived, we

preached at Mr. Josiah Smith's plantation, at the Misses Elliott's, and the place now owned by Mr. L. Sams. All these appointments were on Sunday. We also preached at Rev. Mr. Barnwell's, on Laurel Bay, Broad River. Rev. Mr. Barnwell commenced his ministerial career by preaching to his own blacks and holding prayer meetings with them every morning before sunrise. We also had an appointment at a place called Myrtle Bush in an old brick dwelling. Here we had some refreshing times. Old Palidore, the colored leader, was a remarkable man. He never began his prayer without calling God's blessing upon the missionary who had come so tedious a journey to tell them of the Saviour.

While preaching at this place once, in reference to besetting sins, I touched upon a sin then prevalent among them, that of taking cotton out of the house and carrying it to the field and bringing it back at night saying that they had picked it. While speaking a woman fell upon her knees and looked very earnestly at me, as if to question: "*How* did you find that out?"

One of the most flourishing places on the mission was Big Island, owned by Mr. Thomas Cuthbert, who was greatly interested for his people, and among the most liberal patrons of the work. He very soon built a comfortable church, and allowed his people to attend week days as well as Sundays. On preaching days he would not permit any of his people to do anything to interfere with the hour of service. Every time we visited his place he gave up the labor of sixty hands for half the day. On this place I baptized thirty at one time, twenty-nine by immersion and one, the driver, by pouring. Mr. Cuthbert and his little daughter, he being a widower, were generally present at the church. He would always commune with his people.

In going to and fro on my work on the mission, I have ridden horseback, in a gig, and often on a negro's back. Sometimes it would be in a boat pushed through the mud. Often I have had to be pushed some distance through the mud to get to water to baptize the negroes.

Our great enemy was superstition, which prevailed to an alarming extent. Idolatry too entered greatly into negro worship. I remember on one occasion, while preaching, a woman was so much excited she rose and fell at my feet, embracing them in her arms. I had a great effort to contend with this inclination to man-worship. At another place, when leaving, an old woman came after me, begging me on my return to bring my "big book" with me and find out whether she was an old witch or not. I thought she gave me a difficult task to perform, but I determined to please her so far as I could. Accordingly on my return I read to her from the Bible and told her that, according to that, she was not an old witch, and advised her not to play the witch any longer. She left me perfectly satisfied.

I have already stated the commencement of the Cooper River Mission, where I am now laboring. The mission embraces two appointments for preaching on the western side of the Cooper River, one on Back River, which serves the plantations on that river and those on the opposite side. The other appointment is at the church near Wappahoola Creek, a branch of the Cooper River. I catechise during the week and on Sunday in this part of the mission. This place serves the negroes on that creek and several of the plantations on the western branch of the Cooper River. I catechise throughout the mission both during the week and on Sundays. In this part of the mission there are two church buildings, one of them old Cumberland, removed from Charleston. Here we have large and attentive congregations. At Cumberland the planters and their families usually attend, and also commune with the people. On last Sunday there were persons present from seven or eight different denominations, and five of those denominations were represented at the Lord's table. It was a pleasant sight to behold.

On the other part of the mission I have three appointments and two churches. At Bonnoe's Ferry I preach at Dr. Prioleau's, sometimes in a negro house and sometimes under a widespreading oak. I also preach under an old brick shed, where the negroes from several of the plantations on the eastern branch of the Cooper attend. We hope soon to have a church here. Another appointment is at a very comfortable church given to the mission by Mrs. Simons. This church, which is large and commodious, serves the negroes on both the eastern and western prongs of the Cooper River. Mrs. Simons also left a very comfortable house as a parsonage. Another appointment is on the opposite side of the western branch at the plantation of Col. James Gadsden, where we have a large society and a very good church building. In all the Cooper River Mission has five Sabbath appointments and four churches served every other week. At the last Conference I reported 649 members in full connection and 318 catechumens. I would suppose that there were from 2,500 to 3,000 negroes within reach of the appointments. Our average attendance at each place is from 100 to 150.

Since the establishment of these missions there has been a great reformation in the condition of the negroes. Whereas before many were lazy, immoral, untrustworthy; they are now industrious, cheerful, and worthy of confidence. Many of these negroes are left in charge of the plantations during the absence of their masters in the summer. On one occasion an old negro told Brother Coburn that the gospel (meaning the preaching of the missionaries) "had saved more rice for massa than all the locks and keys on the plantation." It has also happily affected their domestic relations, joined many of them lawfully, made them better husbands and wives, and improved their condition in various other respects. I have often been awakened in the morning by the songs and prayers of the negroes, some of whom attended regularly to their family devotions. The negroes generally are fond of class meetings and love feasts, and are very apt to give some expression of approbation when pleased with preaching. On the whole they are a very grateful people.

THE WATEREE AND BLACK MINGO MISSIONS.

By Rev. Frederick Rush, of the South Carolina Conference.

At the beginning of the year 1834, at the Conference held in Charleston, Bishop Emory appointed me to form a mission to the people of color on the Wateree River. I first consulted the planters in the neighborhood of Camden, and obtained their permission by certificates to operate on their plantations. This was the first missionary effort to people of color in that section. Previous to this time, however, the question had been considerably agitated. There was much talk for and against it. The overseers generally were opposed to it, but the planters seemed to take to the idea.

Mr. James C. Doby made his house my home and stood by me at every point of opposition, also Col. W. W. McQuillay and others who were determined to give the mission a fair trial. In a short while I had as much ground as I could occupy, and the planters to a unit soon expressed their opinions earnestly in favor of the work.

Sometime in April, while enlarging my new field, I went to Mr. Stratford's, about twelve miles above Camden, to have an interview with him respecting his plantation. He soon gave me his consent to take it into the work. This was on Thursday or Friday, and the rains beginning to fall, then heavy floods came and detained me there three or four days, during which time I preached three times to the family and servants, also to such of the whites and blacks as came from the neighboring plantations.

During my stay there I conversed with an old negro belonging to Mr. Stratford. He was from Africa, and totally ignorant of spiritual things. He said that in their country they had all heard of the devil, but none had ever heard of the other one of whom I told him, Jesus the Christ. He took my advice and began to call upon the name of the Lord for enlightenment and mercy. He was soon happily converted. The next morning after this happy conversion he went to the field as usual. Soon after he commenced his work, he saw his master coming into the field. Mr. Stratford was then seventy years of age, and up to this time had made no effort to get religion. The old African dropped his hoe and ran at once to meet his master, telling him in his broken way of the Jesus he had found, and entreating him also to seek the blessing which Jesus only could give. Mr. Stratford was melted to tears. He told me afterward that he did not wish to be seen crying by his slaves, but that he could not help it. This was the start of a great work here. Soon after that affecting incident in the field, Mr. Stratford joined our Church, and I baptized him and his daughter and twenty-four of his negroes at one time in his house. Not long afterward he was thoroughly converted after some hours of the most earnest prayer, and like his servant, George, he rejoiced greatly in his new-found happiness in Christ.

I formed a society and preached here for a few weeks under a bush arbor. By the end of the year we began to worship in our new and commodious chapel, which had, in the meantime, been built. I left this place with sixteen white and I believe about forty colored members. I do not remember the exact number on the entire mission, but I know that I left it in a very sound and prosperous condition, and that the planters generally requested its continuance. I was there but one year. Brother W. A. Gamewell was my successor.

The next mission field to which I was appointed was the Black Mingo Mission, during the years 1832–33. This mission had been formed by Brother Abraham Nettles, and I went to it in the second year of its existence. There were thirty plantations served on the mission, with 9 preaching places, 49 white and 586 colored members. That year I catechised about seven hundred children. I remember also that the contributions from the planters more than covered the expenses of the mission. That year I formed a society at Cedar Creek, on the Williamsburg District. It had 35 whites and over 100 colored members. These whites were chiefly among the patrons of the colored mission, and the society was principally for their benefit, but there were the number of colored members I have already stated. By the advice of Brother Derrick, the presiding elder, they were transferred to the Black River Circuit, and it is at this time one among the most important societies of that circuit.

The patrons of the Black Mingo Mission were all warm friends to the work, especially Mr. William Burrows and Mr. J. B. Pressley, who were very active in its starting, and whose zeal was as warm as ever in 1853.

At Mr. G. Cooper's, one of the patrons, I went to see a sick negro who was very old. He told me that he was a member of the church, and had been going to church as faithfully as he could until stricken down with the weight of years and sickness, but that there was one thing that troubled him a great deal. This was about three Gods of whom "mossa" (the missionary) had told him. He was bothered to know which was the head man and to which he should go when asking for anything. I began and tried to explain to him as clearly as I could why the *three* persons in the Godhead were *one*. The Lord graciously helped his infirmities while I was talking, and he soon saw clearly. He was filled with deep joy when he realized God the Father and Christ the Saviour. His cheeks glistened with tears and his countenance beamed with joy. In a few days he died in great triumph. I will add here that his master is a very pious and upright man, and that few men afford their servants more religious privileges than Mr. Cooper. The great darkness and superstition of his race stood in the way of this poor old man; the veil was so thick it was long ere he could see through it clearly. This circumstance, when it became known, did much for the cause of colored missions, by showing the importance of visiting and catechising even the grown negroes on various religious subjects. I left this mission in a prosperous condition, and Brother J. Parker was my successor.

In 1834 I was appointed to the Cheraw Mission. From the moment I took hold of the work I realized that it was not missionary ground, and so, through my advice, the Conference discontinued it, to devote its time and money in more promising fields

Twenty-two Years in the Mission Fields of South Carolina.*

By Rev. Charles Wilson, of the South Carolina Conference.

I received my first appointment to the mission field at the Conference held in Charleston, S. C.,

---

*Abridged from a manuscript found in the collection of Rev. H. A. C. Walker, who proposed at one time to publish a "History of Missions to the Blacks."

in 1834, to the Combahee, Ashepoo, and Pon Pon Mission. I was sent as a colaborer with Dr. Boyd, who had labored there a part of the previous year with Brother Coburn.

This mission was in the midst of the rice fields, then looked upon as "the graveyard of South Carolina." But despite this, I knowingly slept in their midst two or three nights of every week the year round. During such times, in the sickly season of the year, I have known as many as two corpses to be carried to the graveyard within hearing of my room. Whether this exposure of myself was a piece of recklessness on my part or not I do not now pretend to say, but this much I can assert: I never enjoyed better health.

We had at that time but one appointment on Combahee River. This was at the plantation of Mr. Charles Baring. He was a warm and zealous friend of the missionaries. If I am not mistaken, it was at this plantation that the blessed work of missions to the slaves had its beginning. In addition to the negroes on this place, we had those belonging to Capt. N. Heyward, one of the largest slaveholders in the state. He had some eight or ten plantations, all lying together on the Ashepoo. We preached on three plantations: those of Edward Webb, J. G. Godfrey, and Hon. Barnwell Rhett. At the latter place we also had in attendance the negroes from Mr. Thomas Rhett's plantation. On the Pon Pon we preached on one of Mr. Baring's plantations; on Mrs. Morris's, at that time under the direction of Col. Morris; and on Mr. Aiken's, on Jehossee Island. In addition to these we had one or two small places at which we preached occasionally. At the regular appointments we preached every Sabbath from two to three sermons. A portion of each week was devoted to the work of catechising the children and visiting the sick and aged.

We preached in barns, cooper shops, hospitals, and other plantation buildings, which were generally fitted up in comfortable style. So far as we could judge we had the entire confidence of the planters, which they evidenced by their kindness and liberal hospitality. As to the negroes themselves, their artless expressions of gratitude, their rapt attention bestowed upon our sermons touched us deeply and made us all the more resolve to be faithful. In the early part of this year we added another plantation to the mission. This was that of Mr. Mason Smith, one mile above the ferry. A touching incident is connected with the establishment of this mission. Going to keep the appointment, Mr. Smith met me, telling me how glad he was to see me, and how gratified at the prospect of having regular religious service among his blacks. He accompanied me to the house where the meeting was to be held. We found it well filled with a neatly dressed congregation, with countenances giving ample proof of their own joy and gratification in the prospect before them. I read a chapter in the Bible, gave out and sung a hymn, the negroes all joining in. I then prayed and preached a sermon, which I endeavored to make as plain to them as possible.

At the close of the sermon Mr. Smith arose and addressed himself with deep emotion to his people. He said: "Now, my people, you have heard preached to you this day from that blessed book [pointing to my Bible] the very truths I have always been trying to impress upon your mind; and now I feel perfectly willing to commit your religious instruction and spiritual welfare to these men of God. May God be with you!" By this time his feelings got so completely the mastery of him that he burst into tears and rushed from the room, praying God's mercy upon them and upon himself. The emotion displayed by their master had an electrifying effect upon the negroes, and scarcely have I witnessed such a scene as now took place. The result was many converts to the Church. And never have I known a more submissive and orderly plantation in my life as a missionary, nor a Church that gave less trouble in the administration of the discipline. It was touching to see the love and gratitude bestowed upon their minister, and they were always desirous of making him some little gift.

It was the regular custom to catechise the children on this plantation every Monday morning about 11 o'clock. Sometimes the grown people working near the house would also come to take part. When the catechising was over, the little ones would scamper away to the cabins, returning in a few minutes laden with their modest gift of eggs for the minister. Some would have six, some five, some three, and so on. These they would spread out on the ground in front of him. On one occasion these offerings numbered no less than seven dozen.

In the winter of that year, or in the early spring of the year following, we obtained permission to preach on the plantation of Mr. Thomas Lowndes. He was a near neighbor of Mr. Smith, and owned a large number of slaves. Mr. and Mrs. Lowndes both appeared deeply interested in our work, and not only entertained us hospitably during our stay in that section, which was only during the winter and spring; but also made every arrangement for our comfort at their house in their absence. Our congregations here were generally large and our preaching to them productive of much good. A number soon became members, and adorned their professions by a life of consistent piety. Mr. Lowndes was a most liberal patron of the mission, giving regularly one hundred dollars per annum to its support.

At the time that our missionaries first found their way among the larger plantations of lower Carolina, the Episcopalians had a few churches scattered about, principally in the upper borders of the rice-growing section. These were built mostly, if not altogether, for the accommodation of the planters and their families. Consequently they were only preached in during the winter and early part of the spring. As may be supposed, a sermon prepared expressly to the taste of the learned and enlightened could be of little use to the profoundly ignorant. Hence the coming of the Methodist missionaries with their plain and simple story of the cross was like the opening of a new world to the spiritual mind of the negro.

During this year, 1835, Hon. R. B. Rhett put up at his own expense a comfortable church building on his plantation on the Ashepoo. Here we preached regularly to his own negroes and to those of his brother, Mr. Thomas Rhett, never failing to have large and interesting congregations. Through the lavish kindness of Hon. Mr. Rhett I and my family occupied his residence during his stay in Washington. This put me in the center of my work, and enabled me to leave home after 8 o'clock in the morning, reach the most distant place in my charge, catechise the children, visit the sick, and return before 2 in the afternoon. On Sabbath mornings I was also enabled to hold sunrise prayer meetings on the neighboring plantations and to return home in time to set out for my regular day's preaching. This kind hospitality on the part of Mr. Rhett not only rendered my work doubly pleasant and satisfactory, but also of increased profit to those among whom I labored. I could give them far more time and attention and devise many ways for their instruction and entertainment. I now began to spend an hour of each night of the week with those on the place in teaching them the various hymns used by the Church. Having a natural ear for music, they soon made rapid progress. But these delightful meetings were brought to a close by a severe illness that now attacked me, and laid me low with hemorrhage of the lungs. The devotion of these negroes to me at this period was one of the brightest chapters in my missionary life. I cannot speak of it too highly. As soon as they had finished their daily labors they were at my bedside ready to do any act of kindness in their power. Though weak from suffering, I nevertheless endeavored to talk to all who came, and many scenes that I think God must have loved to witness occurred in my sick room. When at last, having recovered, though with my health seriously impaired, I came away, I believe it was as a much better Christian and a more useful minister.

The Hon. Mr. Rhett was, I think, a truly pious man. He seemed deeply interested in the spiritual welfare of the black population of his country, and contributed most liberally every year to the support of the mission.

At the next meeting of the Missionary Board of the Conference, I believe in February, 1836, the mission was divided, and what was known as "The Barings Mission" taken from it and placed in charge of Dr. Boyd. Brother A. W. Walker and myself were given the other part. This division, I think, lasted only one year. During this year Brother Walker and I had fair success both in preaching to the negroes and in extending the bounds of the mission. We added to it the plantations of Mr. James Lowndes, Dr. Fraser, and Mrs. J. L. Gibbes. We found easy access to the confidence of the planters, and I believe to the hearts of the negroes. All the persons whose plantations we served contributed more or less to the support of the mission.

At the next meeting of the Missionary Board, in 1837, the mission was again divided. The part embracing the Pon Pon River was taken from the Combahee and Ashepoo, and from then until now (1856) has been known as the Pon Pon Mission. Dr. Boyd was appointed to this work, while I was continued on the remaining part, assisted by Brother T. S. Daniels. We had on this mission large classes of children, which we were very particular in catechising. Many of our friends were at this time of the opinion that our only hope of thorough evangelization of the race lay in the children; that the grown up portion had become so debased in sins of almost every kind it was almost, if not quite, impossible to change their habits and instill into them principles of morality and virtue; but I did not share this opinion. While I too had strong hope of the children, I yet had as strong faith in the almighty power of Christ's gospel to enter every heart, no matter how debased, and bring it to the salvation of God. I had continual verification of this belief in the number of genuine conversions among those who had grown gray in vices of the lowest order.

I served the Ashepoo and Combahee Mission for five years. It had proved a most interesting field of labor, abundantly worthy of the money that had been appropriated to its cultivation. In 1839 I was sent to the Pon Pon Mission, and in order to be as centrally located as possible took up my abode in the pine lands of Adams' Run. At Wilton I found that my predecessor, Dr. Boyd, had succeeded in getting a very convenient church erected. The mission embraced nine plantations, with four preaching appointments.

This year we had some trouble with the overseer of Mrs. Morris's plantation, who tried to do what he could to oppose the mission work. Mrs. Morris was away at the North at the time; but when she heard of it, she promptly discharged him and urged us to go on with our labors among her blacks.

In 1840 I was returned to the work. During this year several plantations were added: Mr. Faber's, Mr. Wilkin's, and Mr. King's. By the end of the year every plantation from Jacksonboro to Edisto Ferry, a distance of twelve miles, on the east side of the Pon Pon, was open to missionary labor. Being alone, I had no time for rest, but was kept constantly going.

In the spring of 1841 or 1842, Bishop Ives, of the Diocese of North Carolina, paid Mr. and Mrs. Charles Baring a visit at their family residence on Pon Pon. On my first visit to the plantation after this distinguished arrival, Mr. Baring took me in to get an introduction to the bishop. I found him a pleasant companion and an agreeable talker. He spoke approvingly of the mission work of the Methodist Church among the blacks. As he seemed much pleased with the arrangement of Bishop Capers's catechism, I asked him if he wouldn't hear me catechise the little blacks. He at once consented.

In the meantime Mrs. Baring had gone out and collected the little band and had them all washed and brushed up in fine order, and formed in a semicircle around the front door. As soon as I saw their eyes sparkling with animation, I knew I had nothing to fear in their performance, for it would have been sadly mortifying to me for them to have bungled. Mr. and Mrs. Baring, Mrs. Ives, and one or two others sat on the piazza, while the bishop and I stood on the steps. I commenced and carried them through, and the little fellows were really beyond themselves. Their answers were prompt, distinct, and correct.

At the close Mrs. Baring, filled with gratification, cried out to her husband: "Charles! Charles! they must have a treat! Get something for them!" He walked back into the house, which I thought was unnoticed by the bishop, who had begun to make them a little talk. In the midst of it Mr. Baring reappeared with a large bowl of sugar and a spoon in his hand. Such another breaking up of ranks and charge for the bowl as there was then! The bishop was left to wind up his lecture to unlistening ears.

I spent four years on the Pon Pon Mission. At the end of that time, my health being sadly impaired through repeated attacks of fever, I was given an assistant, Brother Nathan Bird. Having now more leisure, I was again pressed with the old desire to add new fields to my work. Through the invitation of Col. Morris, who had his summer home at Edingsville, I now began preaching on Edisto Island. I found the fields white to the harvest, and the planters almost unanimous in their desire to have the work of evangelization pushed among their people. One of them, Mr. J. J. Mikell, had already gone so far as to erect a comfortable chapel on one of his plantations, not knowing whom he might get to serve his people. My first preaching appointment on this island, the second Sunday in October, 1840, was a memorable one to me. Mrs. Townsend, a zealous and pious member of the Baptist Church, and its most active member on the island, invited me, there being no pastor in charge, to preach at her church. At the hour appointed I reached the building in company with Col. Morris, at whose home I was staying, and found a large collection of blacks and a considerable number of the planters. I next had an invitation from Mr. Lee, the Presbyterian minister, to preach in his church. I again had a crowded house and spoke with much freedom. Mr. Lee, who was a faithful and zealous minister, had already done much efficient work among the blacks on the island. The day following I returned home with the deep conviction that here was a promising door for mission work waiting to be opened. The mission was subsequently established, and I was sent to serve it. Six hundred dollars a year for the support of the missionary was readily subscribed by Messrs. J. J. Mikell, William Seabrook, Maj. Murray, and the Messrs. M. A. and S. Seabrook.

I had on the Edisto Mission, to begin with, six preaching places and eleven plantations to serve. One of these was Gov. Aiken's place on Jehossee Island, which for convenience sake was taken from the Pon Pon Mission and attached to the Edisto. Unlike Edisto, which is a cotton-growing island, Jehossee is mostly a rice plantation and owned entirely by Gov. Aiken. It is naturally a part of Edisto, but has been made into a separate island by the opening of a creek by a canal connecting the two rivers.

The mission on Jehossee had from the first been one of the most promising in the bounds of the Conference. I became acquainted with it in 1834, my first year in the mission fields; and from then to the present time, a period of twenty-two years, I have preached regularly on the place, with the exception of 1837 and 38, when it was in charge of Dr. Boyd.

There is quite a commodious chapel on this island, which has been erected by Gov. Aiken as a place of worship for his blacks. At first it stood in a grove of live oaks on the lawn in front of his dwelling; but his plantation enlarging, it was subsequently removed to a more central spot. Here an addition of twenty feet was made to the building, which had become too small to accommodate the crowds. A portico has also been attached to the front. This chapel has a bell, and a regular sexton in attendance. The occasion is rare when it is not filled to the door with the blacks, with the exception of a small space reserved for the whites. In this church alone sixty-two couples of blacks have been united by the sacred ties of Christian marriage. I recollect to have married here at one time five couples.

From the beginning of our labors on Jehossee Island to the commencement of 1844 our course was generally onward and prosperous. But at that time that terror and destroyer of humanity, cholera, made its appearance for the first time on the island. Gov. Aiken, then in Washington, was duly notified when the disease became epidemic, and, like a man true to his responsibilities, hastened away from his family and business in Congress to afford whatever comfort and assistance might be in his power to his suffering and dying people, and for near or quite three weeks, regardless of danger, passed his time in visiting from hospital to hospital both day and night.

The first case occurred while Brother Bass, who was with me, and I were at Conference. But as soon as we returned and heard of the situation of our charge at that place we went among them, desirous of rendering any assistance in our power, though not without serious apprehension of danger. The first hospital I went into had a corpse lying in the front room in preparation for the grave—a young man, whose mother was sitting by his side and in deep sorrow. I offered what comfort I could, prayed with her, and left. In that day's round of visits I saw four corpses. From the disease's first appearance there were two physicians on the place in constant attendance night and day. About three hundred of the negroes were removed to camp, which was composed of temporary buildings in the woods. Dr. Kinloch was called from Charleston. Brother Bass or I was there every day almost, rendering whatever assistance we could by offering the comforts of religion to the sick and dying, and sympathy to afflicted friends over the dead. The disease continued about six weeks, in which time I think over seventy died.

One of my most important fields on the Edisto Island Mission was the plantation of Mr. J. J. Mikell, already referred to. He had a new and commodious chapel which was largely attended. I soon gathered into the Church at this place a number of orderly and highly interesting people. Our efforts among them were greatly facilitated by a well-ordered system of plantation discipline. Though a firm and decided Presbyterian, Mr. Mikell nevertheless gave his hearty and unswerving support to the Methodist mission. Always, when at home, he and his family attended the preaching at the negro chapel. He was an exceedingly liberal man. Unaided he built a mission house at a cost of $300 in the village, besides providing a winter residence for me nearly all the time of my stay.

On the plantation of Mr. Edward Whaley we had another interesting class. He too was a most liberal patron of the mission, giving annually one hundred dollars.

My labors for the first two years on the Edisto Mission were hard, preaching once a fortnight at all my appointments, and catechising the children and visiting the sick and aged during the week. I have on some occasions preached five sermons and rode on horseback forty-five miles all in a day, leaving home at 4 o'clock in the morning and returning at 8 in the evening, sometimes much later. But the Lord mercifully supported me through it all. At the next Conference I was given an assistant in Rev. J. L. Shuford.

In the early part of the year I learned that Mr. Thomas Hutcheson owned a small island on the west side of the Ashepoo, on which he had about two hundred negroes entirely destitute of all religious instruction; and though I had never seen him, nor had he ever heard my name, yet I became anxious to pay his island a visit, and wrote him a letter informing him that I had heard that he owned a large number of negroes remote from all religious privileges, and that I would be happy to visit his island in the character of a Methodist missionary to the blacks, and referred him to Col. Morris,

Gov. Aiken, and other gentlemen with whom he was acquainted for particulars respecting my object, and immediately received an answer saying that he would be happy to see me; and, accordingly, arrangements were made, and on the appointed day, sometime in May, a boat was sent for me. Upon reaching the shore I found a horse and servant waiting to take me up to his dwelling. I found him polite and glad to see me, particularly on the business on which I had come: desirous that his negroes should have the gospel preached to them. I told him that we would preach to them regularly once a fortnight if he would send a boat for us, with which he seemed delighted.

After preaching to a large congregation in a barn, himself and overseer and family in the number, we parted, all gratified with the prospect, but none more so than the negroes, who seemed to look as if a sort of jubilee was beginning to dawn on Hutcheson's Island.

I asked an intelligent-looking old black man how long he had lived on that island and what they had done in that time for religious instruction. He replied that he had been living there for forty years, and that nearly all the people I saw had been born and raised there; that no minister of any denomination had ever been on the island to his knowledge before; that nearly all the people that had been in the meeting-house that day had never heard a white man preach before; and that they had been wholly dependent upon each other for all the religious instruction they had ever gotten. This statement I believed to be altogether true from my knowledge of the surrounding country and the locality of the island. My heart was filled with gratitude and thankfulness to God for the great privilege of being an honored instrument in his hand of carrying the gospel to those who had never heard it before, although they were in my own native land.

After a year's preaching, at the first opportunity given them, one hundred and eleven came forward, a larger number, I am disposed to think, than ever has been on an ordinary occasion received into the Church at one time within the South Carolina Conference. They all, with but few exceptions, proved true to their vows.

But this mission had a sad ending, for Mr. Hutcheson, not long after this, dying with brain fever, the estate fell into the hands of his mother, who was a Roman Catholic. I called to see her, and when she learned that it was her son's wish that the mission should continue, she expressed her willingness to have it so. But in a few days thereafter she had a visit from her priest, which put an end to the work in that part of the field.

In 1847 my assistant was removed to the Beaufort Mission, and Brother R. P. Franks appointed my junior. Other plantations were added. In 1850 Brother Banks labored with me. In the beginning of the succeeding year he was removed and Brother H. A. Bass appointed in his place. And from the beginning to the present time we have held firmly the confidence of all concerned. Our labors have doubtless proved a great blessing to the inhabitants of Edisto Island.

Nine Years of Plantation Mission Work on the Santee Mission and Elsewhere.

By Rev. Samuel Leard, of the South Carolina Conference.

In the year 1836 I began my mission work among the blacks on the Manchester Mission. I had my headquarters for a time at Manchester, which stood about four miles from the Wateree River on the Sumter side. It was the central point of a large population, both white and black. Very few of the whites belonged to the Methodist Church, being for the most part Baptists and Episcopalians. But there was a large colored membership collected, mainly by my predecessor, Rev. Sherwood Owens. We had for our preaching place in Manchester an old frame church building, which had served as a church for many years. There we had a large colored society, and a still larger number of the little negroes under catechetical instruction.

The prominent planters of the neighborhood were generally patrons of the mission. Among these were Mrs. Belsar, Mrs. Moore, Judge Richardson, and many others.

The children were catechised during the week at their plantation homes, and generally made fine progress.

REV. SAMUEL LEARD,
Of the South Carolina Conference.

From this central point our work extended above to Statesburg, and down the river until it finally reached Murray's Ferry, on the Santee River, and some sixty miles above the city of Charleston. Going down the river from Manchester, we soon reached Broughton's, a very public place; and below him Mr. Mat James, Col. Richard Richardson, Mrs. Richardson, Col. Peter Richardson (the father of the present Governor of South Carolina), Dr. Boyd, and Col. David DuBose, all of them wealthy and refined gentlemen. They owned large numbers of slaves, and were sincerely desirous to see them Christianized and improved in their moral character.

The writer could furnish the reader with an entaining and instructive volume were he to enter minutely into their system of plantation government; their care of the young slaves, as well as of the old; the houses built for their comfort; the nurses provided for the sick and helpless (there was on large plantations a sick house or hospital, and a physician employed by the year to minister to the sick and aged); the watchful care of masters and mistresses over not only the health but the moral and spiritual interests of the slaves. Add to this the earnest desire of the planters to have their slaves Christianized, their willingness to pay for missionary labor, their personal attention to the religious meetings, and we have a picture of Christian philanthropy on the one hand, and of appreciative obedience and satisfaction on the other, such as the world has rarely witnessed under similar circumstances.

Near the center of our mission field, and some little distance from the river plantations, was old St. Paul's M. E. Church and camp ground, belonging to the Santee Circuit. Manchester Mission had no direct connection with this church and neighborhood, and yet, upon the principle of natural and religious attraction, the missionary found here such a home and welcome and spiritual enjoyment as no words can describe. Our mission work extended some fifteen or twenty miles below St. Paul's, including many plantations, and at least two Methodist church buildings and congregations of white and colored members of the M. E. Church.

For two years I spent a part of my time in this delightful Methodist community, preaching to white and colored, and catechising large classes of children.

A charming and beautiful portion of my work lay on the southern side of the Santee along the river swamps, in the Parish of St. John's Berkely, Charleston District, and was called the "Santee Mission." It would be difficult to describe that beautiful section of country as it was then, with its refined and elegant citizens, brave men, cultured women, its contented servants, fruitful fields, and comfortable homes. Alas! the terrible ravages of the civil war left it a desolate waste.

The whole country on both sides of the river

was opened to the missionary, and with a thankful and prayful heart he entered it to sow the seed, trusting in the God of the harvest to grant a gracious yield. For four years I served this mission, from 1836 to 1840, and count them now as among the most useful and satisfactory of my whole ministerial life. I was not ashamed of the work. I felt that I had as much my Master's service to perform here as though I toiled in the most promising mission field of China or India. I gave my heart, time, and what talents I possessed to the work, and God abundantly blessed me. In 1839 I had 740 colored members on the mission. In addition to the children, the preaching and catechetical instruction extended to hundreds of adults outside of the Methodist Church, and perhaps to quite as many children.

The planters and overseers, as a general rule (many of whom were godly men), welcomed the missionary to their homes and plantations; and no one had a better opportunity of studying the character and relations of the master to the servant, and of the servant to the master, than he. The preaching of the gospel was not a new thing to the colored people on the Santee. Rev. Sherwood Owens had preceded me, and had gained the confidence of masters and servants in the fullest degree. In general terms the gospel ministry was a great boon to masses of them. It was a great blessing to them to have their attention directed to the higher interests of the soul and the hope of immortality and eternal life. They were not disturbed in mind by nice points of doctrines or ceremonial parts of Christianity, and hence were prepared to listen to the exposition of the experimental and practical parts of religion. They were not concerned with the questions of what shall we eat or drink or the thought of houses to live in or the care of the sick or even of the clothing they should wear. All these were provided for them by their owners, and while they were required to work, it was not excessive labor, and they had no fears of suffering when old age with its infirmities should come upon them. Cruelty of the owners in any shape was the exception and not the rule. I assert, weighing my words carefully, and speaking from what I know and saw, that no class of poor people in the world were better provided for, and none had fewer cares than the slaves on the large plantations in the lower part of South Carolina prior to and during the war. And while I speak for this section there are others, many others, who can truthfully testify these same things for other sections of the country. The time has come for these facts to be clearly established that the true story may go down to our children and to our children's children.

As the years went on I grew more and more devoted to my work. God's blessing seemed constantly to rest upon it. Especially in the neighborhood of St. Paul's, Rehoboth, and St. Mark's Churches did I enjoy the richest measure of success. Large classes of the young of both sexes were taught the entire catechism prepared for their use by the late Bishop Capers. They also committed to memory numerous hymns and select passages of scripture. Having fine voices generally, their singing was unsurpassed in sweetness and power. The older ones would catch up the refrain, and their voices being of unsurpassed depth and power, they would make the fields, churches, and woods ring with the sacred songs of Zion.

On one occasion I remember catechising a class of fifty or sixty youths and children under the large oak, which stood in front of old St. Mark's, on a Sunday, and in the presence of my presiding elder, the late Rev. Hartwell Spain. Happening to glance around at him during the height of the services, my heart was thrilled to see him bathed in tears. His emotions in gazing upon that scene of the humble blacks being taught the way of life and hearing their tuneful voices raised in loud praise to the Maker of all had almost overpowered him. Surely God and the angels took note of that scene.

The spirit of religion soon spread abroad in the whole community, and harmony of feeling between the white and colored people was unsurpassed by anything I have ever seen. I doubt if I ever shall see its like again. The masters and mistresses exercised the greatest kindness and consideration toward their servants, who in turn were faithful, obedient, and devoted.

In 1843 I served a very important mission field not far from Georgetown, S. C., called *North* and *South* Santee Mission. It included the large rice plantations on either side of the two branches of the Santee River and the large delta between them. This was a region of immense wealth, great fertility of soil, and of extensive planting interests. Here thousands of slaves cultivated the fields of rice. I have a lasting impression of the culture and refinement of the planters and their families, of the care they took of their slaves, of the protection furnished to them against imposition and cruelty, and the almost perfect system of plantation regulations. This last included even the negro's church going, and was most particular as to the hospital service and the marital relations of the sexes. I remained but one year on this very inviting but laborious field of mission work, and left it with regret, despite the arduous labors entailed.

The mission fields in the low country of South Carolina were largely self-sustaining, the contributions of the planters covering largely the appropriations made by the Missionary Society. To the planters of Lower Carolina great praise is due for their liberal support of our domestic missions.

Years of various itinerant service, on stations, districts, and circuits succeeded, until, having finished two years on the Black Swamp Circuit, in the Beaufort District, I was sent by the bishop to organize and serve a mission field called the Bluffton Mission, including the mainland and islands in the neighborhood of the May and New Rivers, Calliboga Sound, and Broad River. This interesting field of mission labor was occupied until the battle of Fort Walker, on Hilton Head Island, in 1861. The lovely village of Bluffton was abandoned, and finally the whole coast yielded to the arms of the United States.

In addition to my work on the regular missions I constantly had large numbers of the colored people under my charge in the various cities and towns of South Carolina. In Charleston, in the years 1846 and 1855, when pastor of the Cumberland Church, I had some 1,200 colored people under my pastoral care. There was not a night in the week that we did not have some Church or society meeting in their behalf in the large basement story of the church. On Sundays hundreds of them occupied the large galleries in the body of the church morning, afternoon, and night, for there were three services every Sabbath. Besides, their monthly love feasts and sacraments were duly administered. I never failed to visit them in their own houses during the week or when they were sick or dying. I leave the reader to imagine the amount of labor involved in a pastorate of twelve hundred souls, in addition to the cares and labors bestowed on two hundred white members. As can readily be surmised, it was no child's play.

In closing this article I cannot forbear to remark that from the moment my work began among them in 1836 to the present time—when an old man worn in my Master's service I await the voice that is to call me hence—I have had the negroes' moral and spiritual welfare sincerely at heart. I have known them all my life. I have mingled with them, talked to them, wept over them, prayed with and for them. I have studied every phase of their character from that of the tattooed African fresh from his native land to the aged and dying Christian, telling forth in clear, unbroken English the preciousness of a crucified Saviour. I have rejoiced with them when one of their number reached a plane of sincere usefulness and ability. I have felt for them when tricked by unprincipled politicians to serve their own corrupt ends. I know their needs and their weaknesses, while I, at the same time, bear willing testimony to the faithfulness and integrity of the many who have come directly under my notice, and I pray God, in his own good time, to bring them to that state or condition in life which, in the wise fulfillment of his purpose, he deems the best and fittest for their good.

The Pedee and Upper Santee Mission.*

By Rev. S. D. Laney, of the South Carolina Conference.

In 1838 I was stationed on what was then called the Pedee Mission. This mission was afterward

---

*Abridged from the original manuscripts among the papers of Rev. H. A. C. Walker. The writing bears the date of May 10, 1856.

merged into the Liberty Chapel Mission, near Mars Bluff.

The year I labored on this work it extended from Mars Bluff near to Society Hall on the Great Pedee. But the most important, or at least the most interesting, portion was that which lay on Lynch's Creek in Darlington District, and covered the plantation of Moses Sanders, Esq., who then resided in Darlington village. He was one of the mission's strongest supporters, but unfortunately died at the close of the year. This was doubtless the cause of the mission being discontinued for a time, though Mr. Sanders left a liberal provision for it in his will.

Captain Gibson was also a warm patron of the mission, as was Maj. Cannon, both worthy members of the M. E. Church, South.

In the early part of the year I made a visit to John McLenehen, Esq., who cordially invited me to take his plantation into my work, which I did. Mr. McLenehen was a highly respected member of the Presbyterian Church, as was also his accomplished lady, but both were warm supporters of the mission, and were constantly contributing to the comfort of the missionary. At this appointment I formed a good society and had a most interesting class of catechumens among the children. Gen. Williams, of Society Hill, and the Hon. Mr. Erwin, of Darlington, and others whose names I cannot now recall, were also patrons of the mission.

At almost every appointment I had a class of

catechumens. These afforded me the rarest delight in the catechising. One class I recall with special pleasure. This was at Springville, the residence of Maj. Cannon. On one occasion I invited the Rev. Ira L. Potter, then in charge of the Darlington District, to go out to this appointment and witness the exercises. He listened with the greatest concern, and was greatly affected after hearing the children answer the questions with such intelligence and promptness, as well as sing the doxology and stanzas of various other hymns without a jar. There was in this class one little fellow of about ten or twelve years of age that I specially recall for his quick ways and readiness of thought.

Great respect was given the missionary on this mission. Especially did the blacks look up to him with great trust and veneration. Our strongest foe was superstition, which is always the bane of the ignorant. Especially did I find it to predominate in this race. But always I found the blessed gospel of Christ with the power, if rightly comprehended, to dispel this state of feeling from the mind. In a good many instances I saw fruit through the course of this year.

Whether, upon the whole, this was a mission proper, is very questionable. Very nearly all the appointments were accessible to the preachers of the circuit. The mission money was paid into their hands and reported to the credit of the circuit, while I think a majority of its patrons were members of the circuit charge.

There was at this time in the vicinity of Mars Bluff a very corrupt state of society. I was frequently interrupted in my services with the blacks. On one occasion a great blustering man threatened to whip me for reproving his wife for boisterous talking in the congregation. I had thought at the time that it was one of the negroes. But I met him coolly, and so, after swearing around the house for awhile, he left. I really felt during the progress of the year 1838 that the neighborhood of Mars Bluff was a modern Sodom. But thank heaven! they were not all depraved. There were some very worthy citizens, and some who were pious. Other difficulties attended my work during my connection with this mission, but there were none so formidable as at Mars Bluff. But even there I had many seasons of refreshing in the colored congregation, and left them at the end of the year in a healthy condition. The next year they were transferred to the Darlington Circuit.

It was at the close of this year that an incident transpired that showed to what an extent the influence of the missionary extended. It happened while I was on my way to the up country in company with Rev. Ira L. Potter. As we passed along through a portion of the Wateree Mission, then served by Brother Whatcoat A. Gamewell, we discovered on a river plantation a large group of little negroes performing some light work by the roadside. The thought struck me that they were

Brother Gamewell's little negroes. As we came near to them I observed to Brother Potter that I would test the matter and exhibit to him a season of interest. When we came within speaking distance I began the catechising: " Who made you ? " I asked. "God!" immediately shouted many voices. As the question was answered they dropped their work to a man and eagerly rushed after us; and for nearly a half mile they trotted along after us, answering questions until I could proceed no further from memory. I mention this instance to show what interest even the children took in this work of grace, and how well they were trained by the worthy missionary.

During the Conference year of 1840 I served the Upper Santee Mission, which lay on the south side of the Santee River in the bounds of the Charleston District, but in the order of the Conference in the Columbia District. Brother H. Spain was the presiding elder, but from some providential causes made no visit to it during the year. I was left wholly to myself, the Lord being with me. It was a year of great affliction to me, physical and mental. My mind was gloomy the greater part of the year. Much sickness prevailed, and many deaths occurred both among the whites and blacks. I visited and prayed with the sick and dying until I was compelled to abandon my post, driven away by the poisonous malaria. But I think the Lord helped me to sow some seed eternity will show. I preached and catechised at four different places each Sabbath. Maj. Porcher was one of the warm supporters of the mission.

Another important appointment embraced the people belonging to the "Santee Canal Company," called "Big Camp." The entire work lay up and down the river between Pineville and Vane's Ferry, embracing the settlements of Mrs. Marion, Mrs. Gaillard, James Gaillard, Peter Gaillard, T. W. Porcher, and others. I have never before or since encountered beings in human shape so far removed from civilization and Christianity as the blacks on this mission, and yet I found their owners intelligent and refined. It was with the utmost difficulty that I could understand the language of these negroes. I noticed one peculiarity of expression which I never found among others. They invariably used the masculine gender. If it was a female, it made no difference: she was called "he." There were but two classes of the white population here—namely, the owners and the overseers—consequently the negroes did not mingle with a third class of whites as at Mars Bluff, and this may account, in a great measure, for their being under the influence of manners entirely their own. But they labored less and were better provided for here than at any other place under my observation. It was on this work that I became acquainted with that truly pious man of God, Rev. Joseph Warnock, who himself became a missionary, and died not long since in the city of Savannah, Ga.

This mission was discontinued at the close of

the year, and I think the ground is now mostly occupied by the Protestant Episcopal Church, as I noticed in Bishop Daves's late report that there were several of my old places embraced.

My Year on the Beaufort Mission.

By Rev. A. M. Chreitzoerg, of the South Carolina Conference.

In the year 1843, which was the fifth of my itinerancy, I was sent to preach the gospel to the slaves on the Beaufort Mission. I was only the junior on the work, that noble old veteran in the cause, Rev. Thomas E. Ledbetter, being the senior. I felt honored in having been assigned to this important field of labor thus early in my ministry, as I knew our Conference was careful always as to whom they intrusted with a work so delicate in many ways.

Both Brother Ledbetter and myself had our families with us, he in his own house at Beaufort and I in a hired one at the same place.

Our work lay in and around Beaufort, principally around it, among the plantations situated upon Lady's Island, Paris Island, Dawfuskie, and others not necessary to mention. These were reached from the mainland by boats which the planters kindly placed at our service. We could cross and recross at any time we pleased.

The plantations served belonged to some of the most prominent families in the state: the Smiths,

Barnwells, Cuthberts, Elliotts, etc. With but one or two exceptions the planters were all sincerely in sympathy with the work of evangelization among their slaves. They threw no hinderance in our way, but put forth every effort to interest the negroes in the religious services. In many instances they and their families were members of other Churches, yet frequently attended our appointments.

During the week myself and colleague visited the different plantations, catechising the children. In some instances there were as many as two or three hundred of these children, all kept together under the care of an elderly female, and orders were given to have them all assembled whenever the preacher came on his catechising rounds. In no instance that I can recall were these children kept away at work or for other purposes during the occasions of the missionary's visit; but, on the other hand, were always assembled, generally smiling and clean for their instruction.

On Sundays we would preach twice, thrice, and even four times a day, to old and young alike. It was no holiday time, this work of a plantation missionary, but one that required the utmost concentration of effort, the most unflagging spirit of zeal, and, in some instances, a self-sacrifice that was heroic. Especially was this true of those whose labors lay among the slaves of the rice plantations. Here their lives were constantly in jeopardy from the deadly miasmatic exhalations of the rice fields; but thanks to the watchful care of a beneficent Providence, and to the retreats afforded by the pine lands, but few of them died. As to the slaves themselves they seemed to thrive better in these localities, owing to their similarity in temperature and topographical features to their own country.

But despite these drawbacks and the many hardships and discouragements with which I had often to meet, my year on the mission was pleasant and of much satisfaction to me. There were many charming families. In the home of one of these especially were many happy hours passed, delightful to look back upon even at this distant day. This was the family of Capt. John Joiner Smith, himself one of nature's truest noblemen. His plantation was known as "Old Fort," and was situated on a bend of the river about five miles distant from Beaufort, and in plain view of the city. The place was so called from the remains of a structure, composed of shells and lime, supposed to have been built by the Spaniards.

Capt. Smith and his wife were Episcopalians, but were both earnestly devoted to the Methodist mission, giving liberally of their substance to its support. They took a personal interest in each slave's spiritual condition, constantly inquiring thereinto with the devotedness of the missionary himself.

At this plantation there was a most comfortable church, which its black members took great delight and pride in adorning for their missionary's coming, with such simple material as the forest gave them. Around the upright posts of the neat pine pulpit their zealous hands would twine the beautiful drapery of the long gray moss, while graceful festoons of the same moss would hang in front with cords and tassels attached, the latter formed by the bur of the pine. In the rear swept the waters of the river, while in a grove that surrounded the building was the burial ground of the negroes, kept ever clean and neat. Here year after year, ever since the coming of that noble old pioneer, George W. Moore, the founder of the mission in 1833, the slave had been taught of Jesus and the resurrection; had been pointed to the Lamb of God who taketh away the sins of the world.

The service would begin with the rising of the missionary in the pulpit, followed by the simultaneous rising of the entire congregation, who would repeat after him line by line the Apostles' Creed. Then came explanatory questions, which were readily answered. The Commandments would next be repeated, and then the reading of a portion of Scripture, which was always carefully explained. After that a hymn was sung, a prayer offered, and the sermon began, followed all the way through by the closest attention and constantly responded to by a nod of the head, a gentle clapping together of the hands, or a deep "Amen!" according as their religious fervor moved them.

I found them a grateful and faithful people, much

devoted to their old spiritual instructors, and constantly inquiring after them. Especially had Brother Moore won their deepest affection. I shall never forget a touching incident that occurred illustrative of this. In one of the charges was Fortune, a fine specimen of his race: honest, intelligent, and one of the most consistent members of his Church. I could scarcely believe that he had once been one of the worst negroes on the plantation, and, on questioning him as to his conversion, was deeply moved by the expression of his face and the tone of his voice as he replied: "Yes, sir; all that you have heard is true. I was what they have told you, even worse than that. I never can forget how Mr. Moore, when I was a wicked sinner, walked his horse six or seven miles to talk to me all the way about my soul. I would walk this day twenty miles to hear him preach once more!" That walking six or seven miles with the earnestly devoted missionary, who showed that he set a precious price upon this soul, a negro's soul though it was, moved Fortune as nothing in his stormy life had ever done before, and resulted in his conversion. Through just such soul-burning devotion as this, illustrated again and again in the life of the plantation missionary, has many a darkened and benighted soul been brought into the light and liberty of the gospel.

Another duty of the missionary, in addition to catechising the children and preaching to the adults, was to visit the sick and aged at their cabins.

In this way he reached a surer and firmer spot in the negro heart than in almost any other; for by these visits he made it plain to the occupant of the humble cabin that he was not ashamed to enter it, or to grasp him by his rough and toil-worn hand as a friend and brother; or, kneeling upon the floor beside the rude bed, to offer fervent petition to God in his behalf. In very few instances did it fail to take the simple, rugged heart and bind it firmly to the cross.

It was on one of these visits that I first became acquainted with old Friday. He was a genuine African, not so long from his native wilds and greegree worship that the shadows of them did not still hover about him. But Friday had that in his heart now that shed light upon all the dark places. He was so happy in his religion, so intensely grateful to the man who had first brought him to the light—our dear and departed Brother Coburn—that he came near to drifting back toward the dangerous shoals of his old idol worship by setting up unto himself an idol in the flesh. At one time, if Brother Coburn's name was even mentioned in his presence, new life seemed to possess him. He would roll his sightless eyes around and exclaim: "Way he dey? [Where is he?] Way he dey? Let me see um!"

Friday was fully eighty years old at the time I met him, but his mind was still vivid with memories of his native land. In the clear, peaceful light of the gospel that had come upon him, he was a living illustration of the power of the word of Jesus Christ to tame and make as new creatures his savage race. All Friday's remembrances of having had any form of religion in his native land was that of prostrating himself when the sun or moon arose, and in crying: "Allah Il Allah!" One conversation I had with him deserves to be recorded, as showing the truly benighted condition of these poor creatures when first brought from their native wilds. On entering his cabin I said to him: "Well, Friday, how'dye?"

"T'anke, my mausa, I dey bless de Jesus. Mausa, I jis wake up; I been da dream. I see one all white. He say: 'Friday, you b'long to me.' I say: 'Lord, what you sabe me for, po' sinner?' He say: 'Neber mine, I sabe you.' He say: 'Friday, you lub me?' I say: 'Yes, my Lord.' He say: 'Berry well den, bime by I come tek you home.' O my mausa," turning his sightless eyes full upon me, from which the tears coursed down his dusky cheeks, and extending his arm upward, "I want to go home! I *weary*, I *weary* to get home!"

I said to him: "But you must patiently wait the Lord's time, Friday."

"Trute, my mausa, trute! De Lord no reddy yet. I 'tay here lillie bit longer."

I asked him if they knew anything about God in his country.

"Dey no t'ink 'pon um; dey t'ink dey mek demself."

"How long were you in this country before you heard about Jesus, Friday?"

"Long, long enough, my mausa!"

"Who first talked to you about him?"

A smile of joy inexpressible radiated his withered old face as he cried: "Aha, Mass Coburn! Mass Coburn!" repeating over and over again the name of the missionary, as though but to call its syllables was a delight that thrilled his soul.

Friday rarely attended preaching, his age and infirmities confining him closely to the house. When he did, it was an occasion that made its impression upon all. How vividly I recall one of these occasions! I had already begun the services when, happening to glance up, I saw the old man come tottering in, leaning upon the arm of his son. On entering the church he paused for a moment, clasped his old and trembling hands together and looked upward with a countenance beaming with devout thanksgiving. Never have I seen a look upon a human face that so thrilled me with the intense fervor of its devotion. So grateful was he to be once more within the house of God that his withered old face shone as though the light streaming from the very foot of Calvary gleamed upon it.

At the close of the service I lingered to talk with him. How his grateful expressions toward the missionaries and their work among his people cheered my heart, giving it a fresh impetus in its labors! I could not refrain from asking him if he was sorry he had been brought to this country. You should have seen his countenance as he replied: "Ough, mausa, buckra country too much better dan nigger country! Too much better! too much better! Nigger country you can't go from here to nex' place by yerse'f; nigger meet you in de path; he got knife, he kille you. All you got do in dis country is worrack [work]. Friday got good mausa, good missus; he ole. Friday do not'ing, mausa tek care o' him; anyt'ing Friday want he get um. Berry well den, I jis de wait till de good Massa way up top senna for me."

It was not uncommon often to be sent for to go to see dying negroes. I thank my Master that I never once turned a deaf ear to any of these calls. Once I performed the burial rite over one of these humble slaves at night. The memory lingers vividly to this day.

I left home about sunset, on a calm and pleasant evening, and took my way along the high bluff of the river. The distance was four or five miles, so that it was dark ere I arrived at the plantation. Just before the dead man's door was the corpse, already in its narrow house. Beside it sat the widow, and to her I addressed myself, bidding her trust in God, "the Husband of the widow and the Father of the fatherless." His fellow-servants were seated around, the deep-drawn sigh showing their sorrow for the departed, their sympathy with the bereaved. I addressed them on the uncertainty of life, the necessity of making preparation for death—in a word, I preached Jesus and the resurrection, and by the glimmering of the lightwood fire was the burial service read, and the body committed to the dust.

It was after 9 o'clock as I took my way homeward, and passed through the dark avenue of oaks, trusting to the instinct of my horse to find the way, illumined momentarily by the fitful flash of the firefly. It was a time for serious thought, for a communion with the heart and with God. I asked myself if I had tried in every way to fulfill my duty since I had come to these perishing souls to teach them the way, the truth, and the life? Sweet indeed was the whisper that came in answer to that question. Forgotten now were all the pains and toils of the way. The true missionary glow was burning within. A peace unutterable filled my soul as to myself I murmured the lines:

> Labor is rest and pain is sweet,
> If thou, my God, art there.

I felt that God had indeed been with me; that he had blessed my labors, and I felt the same sweet assurance many and many times afterward on the other mission to which I was sent in 1855: Black River and Pedee, from which I was removed to the upper country of Carolina owing to the debilitating attacks of fever engendered by the rice fields. Here, after several months in the purer air of the Piedmont country, I was fully recovered.

The Congaree Mission, with Other Points and Items.*

By Rev. William Martin, of the South Carolina Conference.

At the Conference that met in Fayetteville, N. C., in December, 1845, Bishop Andrew presiding, I was appointed "a missionary to the plantations of the Congaree River."

To this appointment my heart said "Amen!" God had the past year, in Wilmington, given me great success in my ministrations to my colored charge, and I felt he would again.

Yes, my heart was enlisted in this work of giving the gospel to our servants at the South, and I began with health renewed, and, thank God, I gave to this work six years of the prime of my life and ministry. It was no sinecure. I knew it was hard work and poor pay—in fact, so poor that all our own resources and the income of a school my wife opened were found necessary for our support. But the work paid in many ways besides money: it was a great work, a momentous work, a special one for the South. If we did not do it, no one would or could. No one should think himself too good for it. I for one did not.

This year my mission lay along the Congaree River, reaching down the river from Columbia about twenty miles, and extending to the sand hills on either side. We had on the mission one

---

* It is but just to the memory of Mr. Martin to state that this article is compiled from two or three chapters of reminiscences written by him at different periods for the press.

REV. WILLIAM MARTIN, D.D.,
Of the South Carolina Conference.

regular church building, and one used both as a church and a schoolhouse. At the other appointments we occupied large barns or gin houses, and sometimes in the summer months for preaching and catechising we sought the shade of an umbrageous oak or gum tree. I usually preached at three plantations, generally some miles apart, on every Sunday, catechising after the regular preaching service. I also during the week catechised the children and visited the sick in their humble cabins, where in sickness and death I frequently witnessed evidences of faith and hope that greatly confirmed my confidence in the power of our blessed Christianity to comfort and sustain its believers.

This mission had been previously served by Brother Samuel Townsend, its first missionary, who, at the Conference of 1844, reported 300 Church members and 262 children catechised. In 1845, when I came to the charge, there had been a small increase both in members and in catechumens. There were eight regular appointments in all, and two or three plantations where I preached occasionally, thus reaching a population of from 1,500 to 2,000 souls.

One of my principal appointments was at Mill Creek Church, one of the oldest in the state, and where many stirring scenes in early South Carolina Methodism had been witnessed. It was formerly what was known as a free church, one not supplied regularly, and had been taken into the mission by my predecessor, Brother Townsend. It was now one of my regular appointments, at which I preached one Sabbath in every three. Both white and black worshiped at Mill Creek Church. At one common altar master and slave took the sacrament; and what was very noticeable, there was no irreverent hurrying away at its close, as is often the case.

But with the morning's preaching, singing, catechising, and administering the sacrament, the missionary's day of labor was but half over, for there were the afternoon services, with other ministerial duties intervening. Often I have traveled a dozen miles through the snow or sunshine, whichever the case might be, preached from two to three sermons, held a love feast or class meeting, catechised the children, administered the communion or the rite of baptism, and married a couple, all in one day.

Intimately associated with the religious interests of the servants was the missionary's influence over the masters. So I endeavored, by the grace of my Master, to be all things to all men, to the learned and the unlearned, to the bond and the free. As I prayed for the soul of the slave, so did I pray for the soul of the planter; and two of the wealthiest and most influential of these (with their families) Maj. Lykes and Gen. Hopkins, joined our missionary Church at Mill Creek.

One of the most prominent patrons of our mission was Thomas Heath, Esq. He had a place of worship for his slaves on his plantation, and in every way contributed to their spiritual welfare. Another patron was Col. Wade Hampton. His preaching place was adjacent to the negro quarters. In every way the situation was novel and pleasing. An avenue of large water oaks led from the quarters to the place of worship, forming an impervious shade to the fiercest noonday sun. It was but one of the many appliances for the comfort of the blacks of this large and admirably conducted plantation. The room stood directly over the foaming waters of the creek, that in front spread out into a pond, and in the rear went piping off into a dancing cascade. It was neatly and comfortably fitted up with pulpit and seats.

At this mission, as at the others, there were many living, *speaking* examples of what the gospel could do, and had done, for this race. Usually before the sermon, there was held a class meeting. How rich was the Christian experience of many of these old slaves! How gratefully they testified to their blessings! How fervently they thanked God for the comforts he had given them, for their kind master and gentle mistress; but above all for the blessed gospel that had been brought to their very cabin doors!

One of these ripe Christians was old Daniel, whose hope seemed ever near fruition. Like his namesake, he was a man of faith and prayer; his example ever a practical comment on the good the missions had done among his people on that plantation at least.

After the class meeting the sermon was preached. Then came the catechising of the children. This was done occasionally on the Sabbath, that others beside those in the regular week day classes might receive the benefit of this mode of instruction.

On one occasion as I had finished catechising, and each member of the class had, as usual, come forward to shake hands with me, a venerable old negro handed me a letter which he requested me to read to the congregation. The proprietor of the plantation had sent a part of his force a few years before to colonize a plantation in Mississippi. This was a letter from one of the people out there, telling of their comforts and privileges in that distant country, but especially giving vent, in strong terms, to their gratitude that there they had been followed by the ministry of the gospel. There too they had a missionary to administer to them the word of life, and many had been awakened and converted. This was what was known as the Lake Washington Mission, and which afterward became one of the most flourishing in that section of country.

Six years in all I spent on the Congaree Mission, when I left it to take other work, and Brother Nicholas Talley was appointed to succeed me, which he did, following up the work most faithfully until it was broken up by the war.

Besides this work on the Congaree Mission, I

had other work among the negroes in the cities. I preached to large congregations of them in Wilmington, Charleston, Columbia, and other Carolina cities. The galleries were always given up to them, and long before the regular missions to them began, in 1828, they were considered a part and parcel of the Church.

It cannot be refuted that from the earliest appearance of Methodism in the South the negro has shared largely in the labors and care of her ministry. The Minutes make the first mention of members in Charleston in 1786, 35 white and 23 colored; and when I was stationed in Charleston, with Revs. William M. Kennedy and George F. Pierce, in 1834, we had under our pastoral care 3,249 colored members. All the Methodist churches, as previously estimated, were built with reference to the accommodation of the colored people. They sat under the same roof and enjoyed the same preaching with the white people; they communed at the same altars; they were served by the same hands, and drank in remembrance of the crucified One from the same cup. They shared in the same class meetings and love feasts; they were married and baptized by the same ministers, and thousands upon thousands of them were brought to a saving knowledge of the truth, and were made happy partakers of the gospel hope of salvation.

When I was admitted into the South Carolina Conference (in February, 1828), there were in the limits of the Conference, which then included a large portion of North Carolina, all of South Carolina, Georgia, Florida, and a part of Alabama, 18,460 colored members. This year (1828), as is well known, was the year in which began the systematic operations among the slaves on the plantations. The Minutes show how well and rapidly the work spread, how faithfully and zealously those who had it in charge labored.

At the end of the Conference year 1845, at which time I was sent to the work, Georgia and Florida having been organized into a separate Conference, there was in the South Carolina Conference 25 ministers devoted to the colored missions alone, supported by collections taken up within the Conference bounds, and the colored membership had increased to 41,074. In 1860 we had in the South Carolina Conference alone a colored membership of 49,774. This year there were 30 ministers employed in this great work, and the South Carolina Conference raised for domestic colored missions $24,463.54. For several years previous to the war the South Carolina Conference raised and expended annually for the religious advancement of the negroes sums varying from $20,000 to $32,000, and employed from 25 to 35 of her ministers in preaching to them the glorious gospel of the blessed God.

I was frequently sent for to marry or to bury negroes who had at different times been under my charge. As to the latter sad rite, I had for years standing engagements with many of them, noticeably among these Ned Arthur and Sancho Cooper, of Columbia. I happened to be in Charleston when Ned Arthur died, in 1869. He had been a member of the Methodist Church for more than fifty years, and a preacher and leader among his people for over forty years, honored and respected by all who knew him—a faithful servant and a sincere Christian. He had long since engaged me to preach his funeral, and when dying charged his family to send for me and keep his body until I came. They telegraphed for me, and I left Charleston at 9 P.M., came home, buried the venerable man, and hastened back to Charleston the next night to keep my engagements in that city. I remember a little instance that happened in connection with this burial. On my return I met on the train a Northern gentleman of considerable influence, who expressed great surprise when he learned of the errand from which I was returning. He confessed to much astonishment at a feeling of this kind existing between a white man and a negro at the South.

Sancho Cooper was a pure-blooded African. He was for many years the faithful servant of the celebrated Thomas Cooper, LL.D., second President of the South Carolina College. Sancho had a standing engagement with me for more than twenty-five years to "preach his funeral." At the time of his death he was ninety-five years old, had been a blameless member of the Methodist Church about seventy years, and a class leader for more than sixty years, and throughout had the confidence of all, black and white. For some years previous to his death he was confined to his comfortable cabin, his old master, Dr. Cooper, having left in his will a sufficient living for him in his old age. He, however, still kept his class and prayer meetings, his members coming to him at his own house.

I have been moved to this digression from the regular course of my narrative, and that I might give a consecutive view of my personal observation and experience of the efforts Southern Methodism has been making for the past fifty-four years for the enlightenment, elevation, and salvation of "the brother in black." There appears to have been recently a great awakening in some quarters, both North and South, of interest in behalf of the colored people in our midst. I am glad to see this, but let us not, in our zeal for his future good, forget what our fathers did for him under the most trying circumstances of the past; how for him they toiled and suffered and some of them died; how, when every other white man fled from those miasmatic regions, the humble missionary held on his weary way, teaching the living how to live, and the dying how to die, while trusting in the merits of the blood of the Lamb shed for the redemption of the whole human race.

SEA ISLAND SLAVE MISSION WORK.

By Rev. M. L. Banks, of the South Carolina Conference.

My first experience as a missionary to the slaves was on the Edisto, Jehossee, and Fenwick Mission. It was in 1849. Rev. Charles Wilson was my senior and, as I remember, the founder of the mission. He was the negro's friend. He sacrificed much to show him the way of life, and he succeeded. About twenty years of his ministerial life was spent on this mission. It must have been a severe trial to himself and family to be isolated from congenial companionship during these long years. What but devotion to the negro's spiritual welfare could have reconciled him to this? He was there for near two decades, and likely would have ended his life there but for the war and its results. In those days we had a number of preachers who could adapt themselves to the comprehension of the negro in preaching. Of these Charles Wilson was in the lead. But he never talked nonsense. He never let himself down to the negro's way of talking, but strove to lift him up to his own. I once asked Brother Wilson to give me some lessons in the art of preaching to the negroes. His reply was characteristic. "In preaching to negroes," said he, "I always preach the best I can." He thought that any sort of talk was not good enough for them.

Our work that year covered three islands. Fenwick was difficult of access, with a wide river or sound lying between it and Edisto. Crossing over and back in a small boat was not without its perils. On Fenwick we were furnished with a pony to ride to our appointments. This sturdy little fellow was so used to mosquitoes that he showed little signs of discomfort, though his neck was covered with them as a network.

Jehossee was separated from Edisto by a small creek spanned by a bridge. That, to me, was the most interesting part of the work. Ex-Governor Aiken lived there, and was sole owner of the island. He owned hundreds of negroes, and few slaves ever had a kinder master. His negro quarters looked like a little village, and much whiter and cleaner than many villages I have seen. The large building he had erected for his people to worship in was generally crowded at the hour of preaching. The worshipers appeared in decent apparel, and not a few were dressed like ladies and gentlemen. What a privilege it was to hear them sing! I have sat in the pulpit and listened until I would weep for joy.

Mr. Mikel, another planter, also had a nice church erected for his negroes in a pretty spot. He and his family were in the habit of worshiping with them. They would kneel at the chancel where their slaves did, and receive the holy communion at the hands of the same minister.

The Savannah River Mission lay in sight of the city of Savannah, Ga. Rev. Reddick Bunch and I, both young men, received an appointment to this work in 1851. Bunch was a young minister of good mind, of fine social qualities, and deeply interested in his work. We boarded together with "Uncle Tom Hardee," as he was familiarly called, and I promised myself much pleasure in associating with him. But alas! he died at the beginning of our first year's work. We carried his body to Purysburg, some distance up the river, and laid it away until the resurrection morn. The work was quite enough for two men, but after Brother Bunch's death I had it all to do. In serving the mission I had to travel in the saddle on rice field banks. These banks were ofttimes so soft that even a small horse with a light rider was in danger of going down to stay. What must it have been for a large man like Brother Charles Betts, for instance, who was my presiding elder? He tried it once or twice, however, and got through manfully, but always afterward preferred a route of firmer footing.

Judge Huger, a distinguished jurist, was a prominent patron of the Savannah River Mission. He was deeply interested in the work of the missionary among his people. He talked to me fully of his own spiritual well-being. I trust that, ere he was laid away in the narrow house appointed for all living, he found firm footing upon the "Rock of Ages."

In 1854 I was sent to the Waccamaw Mission with Rev. William Carson as my colaborer. An intimate friendship sprung up between us which has lasted to the present. Having a family, he occupied a part of the parsonage, and Rev. J. L. Belin, a superannuate, with whom I boarded, the other part. The mission extended from a little above the parsonage down the Waccamaw on the right and the seacoast on the left to a point opposite Georgetown across Winyaw Bay. Rev. J. A. Minick spent many years on this mission, and in 1855 went to his reward. His works praise him. To the faithful work he did the mission owed much of its prosperity. His remains and those of Brother Belin lie in sight of the parsonage.

Of the planters who patronized the mission I have very kind remembrances, of one in particular, a Mr. Alston. Whenever the missionary wanted to visit Georgetown, his boat and oarsmen were at his service. They could come and go when they pleased. The distance across the beautiful Winyaw Bay to town was, I think, three miles. Joe Hemingway, one of the overseers, had a Methodist family, and was a Methodist himself. I always felt at home in his family, where I knew a hospitable welcome awaited me.

Combahee was my last mission, but by no means the least. It was first-class, but I dreaded it. My predecessor had had trouble. Could I hope to still the troubled waters and bring about a reign of peace? I was leaving one of the best circuits in the Conference, and I wondered why I was changed. When I found out the reason, I could not but feel the compliment. The planters had been careless on this mission. They had provided no proper dwelling house for the missionary and his family. I found them in a muttering mood over the constant change in preachers. When I spoke to them of the poor accommodations, they seemed for the first time to realize their neglect in that direction, and to be ashamed of it. A comfortable home for the missionary was soon secured, and there was no change of preachers for five years. Indeed I stayed on the work as long as the Yankee gunboats would allow me to stay.

I must here speak of the overseers on this work. They and their families were, in the aggregate, respectable members of society, and connected with the Methodist Church. They lived in comfort, and their tables were spread with tempting viands. The missionary felt at home among them. I had a very warm attachment for many of them, and parted from them with a pang of regret.

Abram Thomas stood at the head of his class as an overseer. He was independent, having a fine plantation of his own in Southwestern Georgia. His salary was $3,000 a year, and besides this his table was furnished, free of charge, with everything the plantation afforded. It took a consideration of this sort to induce him to leave his comfortable home in Georgia. I esteemed Stephen Boineau as a Christian gentleman. He was courteous, refined, intelligent, and pious. His wife was his equal in every respect. The children were orderly and obedient. A better-regulated household I have seldom, if ever, visited. Sib

Jones, Boineau's brother-in-law, was the wag of Combahee. He was pleasant, playful, and witty. If the missionary was ever troubled with the blues, let him visit Sib and they were sure to vanish.

Of the Combahee planters I have very pleasant recollections. They valued the missionary not only as the pastor of their slaves, but as a companion of themselves and families. They welcomed him to their houses, and were not afraid of their families coming in contact with him. It was not so everywhere. They lived in princely style. The dishes on their tables were of the best quality and in great variety. I declined nothing but the wines and liquors, and it was a trial to do that. To hold to my temperance principles under a perfect battery of both masculine and feminine hospitality was not the easiest thing in the world to do.

Charles Lowndes, James B. Heyward, and Daniel Blake had very neat chapels on their plantations, where not only their negroes but themselves and their families worshiped. Charles Lowndes lived the lowest down on the mission. His house was the home of the missionary whenever he chose to make it so. He was a noble, upright, conscientious man, extremely courteous to those in an inferior situation. James B. Heyward lived near the center of the mission. His was an attractive home. He had a large estate, but was a plain man, simple in manner, courteous in deportment, fine-looking, and of dignified bearing. He gave liberally to the support of the mission.

Daniel Blake's plantation lay in the extreme upper end of our mission. He, as I remember, was an Englishman by birth. He was a noble specimen of humanity. He despised affectation and looked with perfect contempt upon all snobbery. There was no man more in sympathy with the work of the South Carolina Conference among the rice fields and cotton plantations of the country than he. Though a member of the Episcopal Church, I think he was about half Methodist. At the handsome church building in sight of his residence, where I preached to the negroes of his place, he was a regular attendant and a close listener. When he had company on preaching day at the church, he proposed to the company that they all go out to the preaching, and they did it. He once said to me that he wanted the missionary on Combahee not only to preach to his people, but to visit his family. He lived up to that sentiment. His house was the missionary's home.

Mr. Blake was a most humane master, and his negroes were devoted to him. I think they would have fought for him to the death had the occasion for it arisen. I remember preaching to his people on the atonement and used an illustration which they interpreted to mean that their master had sold them to a neighbor. The excitement was tremendous. They ran to him from all parts of the quarter to know if such was the case. He explained, and they were content. There was, in their eye, no other master like the one they had.

I think there was not a great deal of clear money made on Mr. Blake's plantation. He fed and clothed his negroes too well and worked them too moderately to admit of that. Among the devout masters who will be saved in heaven with their pious slaves I feel safe in counting Daniel Blake, the missionaries' friend and the negroes' benefactor.

We had no protracted meetings on negro missions. Our preaching was confined chiefly to the Sabbath. Revivals, as conducted among the whites, were not practicable. At the stated appointment, however, we had, now and then, seasons of refreshing. Penitential tears and tears of joy would at times fall like raindrops. A great drawback to the preaching of the missionary was dullness of comprehension on the part of his hearers. Such was to be expected in view of the extreme ignorance prevailing. Intelligence was mainly confined to house servants. But thank God, the experience and practice of religion was not confined to the intelligent. "The wayfaring man, though a fool" may know enough of the way of life to walk therein. It would not be putting it too strong to say that thousands of unlettered negroes on our missions were led into the light of God's countenance by the faithful preaching of their pastors.

I touch now upon the rice field negro's type of piety. Rev. Mr. W—— is credited with the remark that the negro of that time was sadly deficient in the three cardinal virtues of veracity, chastity, and honesty. In these particulars, however, there was marked improvement under the power of the gospel as preached by the Methodist missionary. The marriage relation generally had come to be held sacred, and but few cases of lying and stealing came to the knowledge of the missionary. Still, in our estimate of the religion of our parishioners, there was need of the exercise of considerable charity. Of course their standard of Christian morality could not be expected to measure up to that of their more enlightened white neighbors. Where little is given, little is required. In judging the debased and ignorant, the principle is not always adhered to as it should be. As the negro race advances in knowledge, both mental and spiritual, we must begin, of course, to measure them by a stricter standard. As they grow in intelligence and in the earnest desire for moral and spiritual elevation, so will the efficacy of the gospel to touch and meet every need of their case increase with corresponding force. We must measure one's piety by his knowledge of God's truth. If we do this for the negro, he will compare favorably with any other class or race of equal knowledge of the Bible. For him Christianity has done much. It found him ignorant, debased, scarcely above the brute order in mental and spiritual understanding. It left him as a new creature in Christ Jesus. What may it not yet do for him?

Memorials of the Pioneers.

Rev. Daniel G. McDaniel was born in Georgetown, S. C., on February 15, 1791; was converted at the Light Street Church, Baltimore, Md., when a youth of nineteen, and entered the ministry in the South Carolina Conference in 1821. He served various circuits and missions from that year on to 1854, in which year he died while serving the Wateree Mission for his seventh year. He was a true man, upright, conscientious, and devoted to duty and to the doctrines of his Church. No man in South Carolina or elsewhere did more for the evangelization of the colored race than he. One of the finest tributes to his memory is the monument erected almost solely by the contributions of the negroes, to whom he had been as an apostle of light.

Mr. McDaniel was one of four Methodist preachers who married the four daughters of Michael Schenck, of Lincolnton, N. C. Judge David Schenck, of Greensboro, N. C., is the grandson of Michael Schenck. In recording some of his early recollections of his kinsman, Judge Schenck says:

> I frequently accompanied Mr. McDaniel on his "rounds" to the plantations on the stated days for catechising the children.
>
> The little negroes were drawn up in line, and I was very much astonished at the ease and rapidity with which they answered the simple questions of the catechism. They knew all the essential truths of salvation, and seemed to appreciate them. A prayer, a word of exhortation and kindness ended the visit, and the dear old gentleman never turned to leave without being followed by the "God bless you" from the old "mauma," who had

the children in charge. If any were sick, they were visited and comforted, and the aged received a word of sympathy and encouragement.

The Sabbath services were so novel and interesting that I was greatly impressed with them. The singing was so full of "the Spirit" that the singers often reached a sort of rhapsody or joyful exhilaration that gave peculiar interest to the tune and the hymn. The prayers, rude in language and boisterous in tone, were still full of faith and earnest supplication.

The idiom and vocabulary and provincialisms of this class of people in that region were so peculiar that it was quite difficult at times to understand the language or to comprehend its meaning. At times it was laughable, and at others it impressed the hearer with its force and vigor and directness. The politeness of the negro to a gentleman never failed to elicit respect and a kindly feeling for them.

Mr. McDaniel continued on the Wateree Mission until his death, and was buried at Camden, where a monument was erected over his grave, the result of small contributions by the slaves, supplemented by their masters. He died like a patriarch and was "gathered to his fathers," lamented, respected, and loved by all who knew him.

Mr. McDaniel was a soldier in 1812 in the second war with Great Britain, and was in the battle for the defense of Baltimore. I remember to have heard him relate the anecdote that while the troops were drawn up in line awaiting the attack a tall soldier who stood immediately behind him said humorously, "Dan, you get behind here, and I will stand in front so the balls can't hit you," and stepped forward and made the change, laughing at "Dan's" little stature and remarking how safe he was now. And Mr. McDaniel said that at that moment a bullet struck his comrade dead in his tracks, and he himself was spared. Mr. McDaniel's widow drew a pension from the United States Government as long as she lived.

In the nature of the case, many of the memorials of missionary work, written by the friends of the missionaries, must go over the same ground and employ almost the same language. In endeavoring to avoid this defect we have grouped together such incidents as commend themselves to our notice, giving here and there only a complete article from the pen of a sympathizing friend. One of these articles is entitled: "Recollections of a Plantation Missionary's Daughter," by Miss Isabel D. Martin, of Columbia, S. C.:

Memory carries me back to the time when, early in the morning, through heat and cold, sunshine and rain, I used to see a plantation missionary set out in his buggy and go to preach the gospel to the slaves on the surrounding plantations; and my joy would be full as I would be invited to take my seat in the buggy and go with the missionary on his rounds.

Sometimes we would cross the Congaree with its tumbling shoals, its yellow water, and its never-ceasing voice as it goes murmuring to the sea. Again our way would take us through dense pine forests, where the solemn old long-leaved pines waved their stately limbs, or we would drive through long avenues of oaks draped with long, drooping gray moss. Then sometimes, pleasantest of all, we would drive right through Mill Creek, and while we stopped to let our good old horse get his draught, I would count the shining pebbles at the bottom of the wine-colored stream, or, childlike, clap my little hands at the minnows as they went flitting by.

When we reached the plantation gate, the cry would be heard on all sides, "Preacher's comin'! preacher's comin'!" and from every side we could see the little negroes gathering. At least twenty of the grinning, ebony-faced little creatures would spring forward to open the gate for us and to escort the preacher's buggy up to the "catechising place." Others of the larger children would hurry to deposit the little brothers and sisters they were nursing with the old "maumas" at the hospital; while others, again, impressed with a sense of the decorum of the occasion, would go through the ceremony of hand and face washing ere presenting themselves before the preacher.

At last silence and perfect order reigned. A line would be drawn under the shade of some spreading old oak and the catechising begin. The class was rarely under fifty in number, ranging in age from the toddling wee thing of three and four to boys and girls of fourteen and fifteen, clad generally in the most *airy* of garments. I cannot now recall one instance of bad conduct, nor do I remember once having seen one of the class deprived of the handshake from the preacher, an honor most highly prized by them all, and never denied except in cases of extreme naughtiness.

The preacher would then carry them through Capers's Catechism, the Creed, and Commandments, give them a little—very little—talk, then sing a simple hymn, and afterward, with bared head, kneel upon the ground, and, with all these slave children clustering around him, together they would repeat: "Our Father who art in heaven."

Since that time I have seen God worshiped in many ways. I have knelt with the multitude in the grandeur of a great cathedral, where the "dim religious light" came softly stealing through the pictured glass and the rich-toned organ melted the heart to thoughts of prayer. I have listened to the gospel in the midst of a crowd of gray-uniformed men, whose next orders might be a summons to death. I have heard the words of truth proclaimed on the top of a lofty mountain, where we seemed "to see God in every cloud, and hear him in the wind." I have mingled with the throng around the holy altar in the midst of a wide-spreading forest, where every breeze that swept by seemed to say: "The groves were God's first temples!" I have sat in the rustic church amid the humble country worshipers, sunburned with toil and hardened with care, when I have said to myself: "God is here worshiped in spirit and in truth." Yet now as I look back, it seems to me I have never been in circumstances so pleasing to God and his holy angels, or seen worship so welcome to them as when I saw that man of God teaching the little negro slaves to say: "Our Father."

The catechism lesson being over, the preacher would inquire for the sick. If any were very sick or too old to leave their cabins, he would be taken to them to minister of spiritual things; and sometimes, though, little child as I was, I knew it not, I was very near the gate of heaven. Often I have seen the missionary's face radiant with the light of the throne as he came from these ministrations beside the bed of the dying Christian slave.

As we were leaving a pleasing scene would occur, pleasing to me at least, for then the old "maumas" would come from their cabins with two or three eggs apiece, or the children with old birds' nests, sassafras roots, blackberries, and other simple treasures, to show their love of the missionary by these humble offerings to his little daughter. These scenes would recur at one plantation and another until the whole of a long summer morning would be exhausted, and so would pass the week away.

When Sunday morning would come, the grown negroes, who were at work in the fields during the week days, would assemble for preaching in neat, clean garments. Sometimes this would be in an upper room over the ginhouse, nicely arranged with pulpit and benches, or again in a pleasant little church built by the liberal and pious slave owners. Long before we reached the plantation gates we could hear the untutored voices of the assembled worshipers in songs of praise. Then would follow the simple service of the Methodist ritual and a sermon gloriously beautiful in its gospel simplicity, followed by the repeating of the Commandments and Creed by the whole congregation, occasionally by the administration of the holy communion, and very often a marriage and baptism.

One calm spring morning, beautiful and clear, the missionary and his little daughter, after leaving the preaching place and driving a few miles, stopped at the residence of a planter, whose name is now a household word, a part of our glorious chapter in the world's history—Wade Hampton.

The estate was called "Millwood," and who that has once partaken of its princely hospitality can ever forget it?

After dinner we found the daughters and two little granddaughters of the planter ready to accompany us to the plantation. After the sermon was over the marriage ceremony of two of the house servants was performed, and then the solemn voice of the minister said, "Let those to be baptized be brought forward," when a throng came forth, and in front of the pulpit stood in a semicircle, the parents bringing twenty-two little black babies to receive the holy rite. Each of these babies was dressed in a pretty white dress, and the sleeves looped up with white ribbons. Both ribbons and dresses had been given and the dresses made by the hands of the youngest daughter of the planter. The noble Christian girl has long since gone to her reward, and I have often thought of the joyful meetings there must have been when, in the high courts of heaven, she met some ransomed soul that had gone to glory from her father's plantation.

When I hear the imputation cast—which is, alas! too often the case—that our fathers and grandfathers were sinners above all others, because they owned and cared for their slaves, which were theirs through no fault of their own; when again I hear it asserted that on the Southern plantation nothing was heard but the sound of the lash and the groan of the oppressed, I cannot but think on some of these things which I have herein narrated, which I have seen with my own eyes and know to be true —things to which others can bear witness, which are but an infinitesimal part of that grand work that had its origin and its carrying out in hearts as noble and as humane as ever received the Deity's impress. And when I think how one Church alone —for others there were engaged in this work—the Methodist Episcopal Church, South, gave of her time, her talent, her treasure *the best* that she had, to teach these slaves the way to the one great and universal Father, how I pray God to hasten the day when she shall receive the full measure of her due!

How I wish I could take every reader of this article to a church that has been erected to take the place of one burned down by the soldiers of the United States army on the 17th of February, 1865; for near by I could show them a monumental shaft, plain and uncostly, without ornamental design or sculptured device of any description. And yet that shaft is a more glorious monument than Greek or Roman fancy ever pictured, for it bears this simple inscription:

To the memory
of
WILLIAM CAPERS, D.D.,
One of the Bishops of the M. E. Church,
South,
The Founder of Missions to the Slaves.

We have given a large space to the movement in the South Carolina and Georgia Conferences, not because these Conferences stood alone in the progress of this great work, but because the record of the work in these old Conferences was fairly typical of the labors of missionaries in other states of the South. The peculiar conditions that distinguished African slavery in South Carolina did not exist to the same extent in any of the Southern states. There were not as many large plantations occupied by slaves alone, or by the owners and the slaves, without any environments of social order in white communities.

But there were a few extensive plantations, and the number was gradually increasing in Alabama, Mississippi, and Louisiana, in which the absence of a gospel service was a want felt, acknowledged, and ultimately supplied by the generosity of the planters on the one hand and the heroism of the missionaries on the other.

The Rev. Edwin G. Cook contributes a brief account of the work in Vicksburg, Miss.:

> I here give my recollections of religious services among the colored people in our community (Vicksburg, Miss.), where I lived for many years before the war:
>
> I of course refer to such work as was under the auspices of the Southern Methodist Church. About 1850 the Methodists entered into the new church which they now occupy. The old church was a good brick building, fronting the courthouse, and could have been sold for a considerable sum, but the trustees decided to hold it for the use of the slaves of the city—that is, for the preaching and other services by ministers who might be sent to the Vicksburg Colored Mission.
>
> The minutes before and after 1850 will show the Vicksburg Colored Mission to have been supplied by the presiding elder. It was always understood that this supply was to be Edwin G. Cook, a local elder, the writer of these recollections. In this

old church I conducted all the services directed in the Discipline, including Sunday schools, by oral instruction. Many of the scholars, however, could read the catechism and Bible. I had an official Board of Stewards; and, slaves though they were, the finances were properly managed and the house kept clean and in repair.

The teaching and preaching were intended to be scriptural in doctrine, legal as to practical life, and great caution was enjoined as to profession of real or supposed spiritual attainments. The slave holders generally attended these meetings, as requested by law, to give authority to the services among slaves in the absence of an ordained white preacher. The colored men of this charge, and from elsewhere, would sometimes preach and often exhort and pray most effectively. One colored man I recall was a natural orator. When it was known that he was going to preach, a great number of white hearers would congregate at the church. His name was Henry Adams. He was a large, black, rather coarse-looking, but a good man, sincerely devoted to the work of evangelizing his race, and his work was owned and blessed of God.

One item that I here recall deserves mention. William C. Smedes, one of the most popular lawyers of that time in Vicksburg, an Episcopalian, now deceased, purchased more than fifty slaves from South Carolina and placed them on his plantation below Vicksburg. Mr. Smedes stated to the writer that these slaves applied to him for a Methodist preacher to be sent to them, as many were of that Church, and all had been accustomed to hearing preaching from Methodist preachers in the state whence they had come. Mr. Smedes, having their welfare sincerely at heart, at once made application to Conference for a minister to be sent to these blacks, assuring out of his own pocket the amount usual in compensation for such services. Mr. Smedes's noble example was not the only case among the planters in the vicinity of Vicksburg.

At a dining in New York, when the neglect of religious services to the slaves was charged upon the people of the South, I stated that I knew one slave owner who had a plantation of nearly a hundred slaves left to him on the death of his father, and another besides, on both of which he had preaching regularly by an itinerant Methodist preacher; and that the owner of them not only often closed the services to his slaves, but that he himself was in charge of a colored mission in that city. One of the guests, Rev. P. P. Sanford, spoke up and said he supposed this item was given from report. I replied: "It is given from no report, but from actual knowledge. I am the man in question." They were astonished, and seemed reluctant to believe, if in truth they ever did believe.

I can give but a few scattered items to add to this wonderful history of missions to the slaves. Chapter after chapter could be written, each more wonderful than the other. It is a record of which our Church ought to be proud, that she ought never to let willingly die; too much of it now lies in obscurity. Dr. C. K. Marshall, J. B. Walker, C. F. Evans, of New Orleans, and many of the old preachers of the Mississippi Conference could add much to this information.

I have not lived in Vicksburg since the war. When I visit there, I often meet the colored members of the Church which I served for nearly ten years. It is a great pleasure to me, and they express and show an equal pleasure. My old body servant, who was a preacher when a slave, is now a preacher in charge of a Church of the A. M. E. I visited him lately, and we parted with prayer and the Christian hope:

"Till we meet again."

In order to show the likeness between the workmen engaged in these missions to the slaves in the widely separated communities of South Carolina, Mississippi, and Louisiana, we copy in full a paper from the hand of Rev. H. J. Harris, of Mississippi:

MISSIONS TO THE SLAVES IN MISSISSIPPI.

By Rev. H. J. Harris, Hattiesburg, Miss.

There were no more extensive missionary operations in any Conference than in the Mississippi. At the first our people were somewhat skeptical as to whether it was compatible with the relation of master and slave. The mistaken idea was maintained, among the irreligious especially, that the gospel to the negroes was but another name for abolition interference, and that it would generate insubordination and insurrection. But the test made upon the rice plantations in South Carolina, under the leadership of the lamented Capers and his colaborers, demonstrated the power of the gospel to save the negro in our own land as well as in Africa; and when such men as Wade Hampton and the Pinckneys indorsed it, the cotton planters of Mississippi soon fell into line and became the most enthusiastic patrons of the enterprise.

The Methodist Church was in every place the pioneer in the missionary work among the negroes, and has done more for their evangelization than any other branch of the Church in America, and especially in the South. As far back as 1839, when I was admitted on trial in the Mississippi Conference, and anterior to that date, many of our people who were slave holders recognized the obligation to give their slaves the benefit of religious instruction, but it was imparted under certain limitations and restrictions. When the circuit preacher came on his regular rounds and had "family prayer" with the whites, the negroes were summoned to take part in the worship, and the word of exhortation was also given them. Gradually the sentiment grew until arrangements were made for special services to be had at the "quarters" for the benefit of the negroes. Master, mistress, and their family regularly attended and took part in these services.

As the work progressed—and it was found that the gospel, where rightly administered, made better servants as well as masters—the demand became general for the services of the circuit preacher. About 1846, under the leadership of some of our largest slave holders, the work of regular plantation missions was inaugurated.

Chief among those who first favored this movement was that great and good man, Judge Edward McGehee, of Wilkinson County, Miss. To his worthy name all praise is due as the patron of everything that was good. Under his roof Francis Asbury had lodged, and many other ministers of God found a hospitable home. He owned perhaps a thousand slaves, and had ten large cotton plantations, with an average of one hundred slaves on each. He made it a point that they should be comfortably clothed and fed, have comfortable quarters, and receive ever the kindest attention. Added to this, he provided amply for their religious instruction: had missionaries sent specially to his plantations, with *carte blanche*, to preach, teach, catechise, and in every way instruct the negroes in the way to heaven.

About the same time that prince of merchants in the palmy days of New Orleans, and prominent Methodist, H. R. W. Hill, who had settled several large plantations in the delta region of Mississippi, became enlisted in this good work, and the minutes of the Conference show for years, up to the time of the civil war, that he and others of our large slave holders in that region were careful to provide missionaries to their negroes. Wade Hampton, of South Carolina, became a large cotton planter in that region, and brought with him the ideas obtained from the noble work in his own state, and at once applied to the Conference for a missionary for his plantations. Prominent in the list of appointments for that period appear "Hampton's Plantations," "Hill's Plantations," "Deer Creek Mission," "Sunflower Mission," "Clover Hill," and scores of others where the congregations were made exclusively of plantation slaves. Nor would these planters have illiterate or inexperienced men, but always demanded experienced and competent men, such as they would have preach to their own families.

This writer had the honor of being among the first of those appointed from our Conference to this special work. My field was a new and delicate one to fill. It lay along the Bayou Pierre, a tributary of the Mississippi, running through Claiborne County from east to west, and entering the great river just below Grand Gulf. From its source to its terminus the stream was lined by a most fertile valley on either side, and was one continuous cotton plantation. There were thousands of slaves working these plantations. Their owners were, to some extent, connected with the various religious denominations. The majority, however, were not of any Church at all.

It was my privilege to serve this mission as the first missionary to the negroes in that quarter, and I recur to it as the most complimentary appointment that had been given me up to that time. It had been given me in response to a letter numerously signed, addressed to my presiding elder, Rev. B. M. Drake, the loved and lamented, asking for an able and prudent man.

I had full liberty to arrange my own plans as to the preaching and catechising. These I endeavored to map out according to my best judgment. We were permitted to occupy neighborhood churches, where the slaves from several plantations came together on the Sabbath, while during the week we served them on the plantations. Among others we occupied an Episcopal church, which demonstrated the general interest taken in the work.

In visiting pastorally the sick in the cabins, I witnessed scenes that would gladden the heart of an angel. Not unfrequently when I reached a plantation among the first matters claiming my attention was that some poor slave who was sick desired to see the missionary. Then, accompanied by some member of the master's household, bearing delicacies from master's table—luxuries suited to the palate of a king rather than a slave—we would repair to the sick room of the aged "mauma," at the "quarters," or maybe some poor fainting sick one of younger years. There we would kneel and pray together and sing sweet songs. Often have I seen and heard a young mistress read the precious word of God, then kneel and pray at the sick bed of the aged servant who had nursed her when an infant, and with her own delicate hand wipe the cold sweat from the dying brow.

I have witnessed, too, many a season of refreshing in which master, mistress, and slave alike participated, and seen them all rejoice together. If permitted to gain heaven through grace, I expect to meet many a poor slave to whom I preached the blessed gospel, which is the " power of God unto salvation " to all them that believe.

The following paper relates to a period subsequent to the division of the Church in 1844, but it exhibits the same spirit that actuated the pioneers of 1829:

LABORS IN THE SLAVE MISSION FIELDS OF MISSISSIPPI FROM 1858 TO 1861.

By Rev. J. F. W. Toland, Jonesboro, Tex.

I was admitted on trial into the Alabama Conference of 1858, and was appointed to the mission to the blacks in Lowndes County, Miss., for my first year. Having thus before me a large territory in which to work, I was compelled to preach three times on two Sabbaths of the month, never less than two, and sometimes four. On one occasion, owing to a sick family, I traveled thirty miles and preached three times in one day.

The instructions of the Conference to the missionary to the colored people was to catechise the children at every appointment, as well as to preach to the adults. These instructions were always faithfully carried out.

Many of the negroes on these plantations were of Baptist persuasion themselves, but their owners were either Methodists or of no Church affiliation. But there was no sectarian feeling shown in having the gospel preached to their slaves. Many who belonged to no Church themselves were foremost in their efforts to help the missionary in his work. Prominent among these families was that of the Hairstons. Frequently I preached in the elder Hairston's dwelling house. All the members of the family and many of the neighbors would assemble in one room, while the servants filled the hall, the adjacent room and the gallery. In summer my pulpit was arranged in the porch of the house, the servants all being seated in the yard and the whites in the rooms and hall.

Other planters (Gen. Cocke, of Virginia, and Col. Billups, of Columbus, Miss., among them), having large negro quarters, built a church convenient for the servants of the three plantations. The attendance of each one able to do so was required at this church for each service, though be it said, greatly to the credit of the negroes, this compulsion was hardly ever necessary. They came gladly and in the most teachable spirit. At the church the missionary held his protracted meetings, sometimes to the whites and colored together. One incident connected with an occasion of this kind I must mention. Brother George Shæffer, a name closely connected with the mission work to the negroes of this section, would often come to help in these meetings. Though the services might be to the whites, still a space was always reserved for the negroes, and they were included in the invitations. Old Brother Shæffer was a great favorite with Col. Billups, and he regularly had him once a year to conduct these meetings. It was a sight to see him get happy and go around shaking hands with white and black alike. O he was a grand old man, and the fruit he planted abides to this day. The negroes came to the altar on the same invitation as that to the whites, and the preachers were just as earnest praying for and talking with them. And when communicants were invited to commemorate the death and sufferings of our Lord and Saviour, the old Colonel and his good wife would go up and kneel round the same table with as many of their servants as could be served. It was a picture to be remembered.

The missionary found quite a difference between the intelligence and religious *status* of the negroes on the various plantations. I found these conditions, in the greater part, dependent upon the associations they had had with the whites, as well as the class of whites with whom they mingled. If these associations were of the best, then they had left their imprint on the negro for the best in every way: manners, speech, morals, and everything.

On many of the plantations colored preachers of credit were found. Some of these were really talented as speakers. They gave valuable assistance to the missionary when holding protracted meetings. On one occasion Billy, an intelligent mulatto, a fine speaker—indeed, a natural orator—came to me during the exercises with the mourners and asked me to find for him the hymn which contained the couplet

> Turn, sinners, turn, why, why will you die?
> Why grieve your God and die?

I found it for him, he could read, and he rose to tell his experience. He said that while he was a thoughtless sinner the words, "Why grieve your God and die?" had arrested his attention. He went on, with deep feeling and pathos, to relate his struggles and final conquest. It melted the hearts of all present.

Old Uncle Emanuel was another of these preachers. He was a man of sound piety and of good practical sense. Emanuel was a Baptist, as were all the negroes on Sister Winston's farm; but he loved the Methodists, and he always concluded his exhortations to his people by urging them to pay attention to and profit by the teachings of the missionary. When negroes on the farms of Baptist owners were converted, they usually received baptism at the hands of the Methodist missionary, and were left to pursue their own inclination as regarded Church membership. If they preferred the Baptist Church, they were considered as Baptists, though included in the mission. I am satisfied that there were as many Baptists as Methodists in my charge.

At the next Annual Conference I was returned to the same work. My return was asked for by the planters, for they said that I seemed to understand the negro's nature; besides, the mission was doing a great good among their people.

I must here note one peculiarity of the negro that I was not long in discovering. The first year, when they saw the preacher coming, they would say, "Yonder comes *the* preacher;" the second year, "*our* preacher;" and the third, "*my* preacher." The longer the missionary remained the nearer he got to the heart of the negro. The planters seemed to realize this, and often asked for the same man back again.

At the next Conference the whole territory lying between the Mobile and Ohio railroad and the Tombigbee River on the west and east, Columbus on the north, and the line between Noxubee and Lowndes Counties on the south was thrown into one mission field to the blacks. Brother George Shæffer, who had long been in charge of the colored mission church in Columbus, was appointed superintendent, and Brother James Hood and myself as the regular missionaries. Brother Shæffer was required to visit these missions as often as he thought it necessary. While on these visits, if on my part of the mission, I must fill his pulpit in the city; if on Brother Hood's part, then he had, in turn, to take Brother Shæffer's place in the city.

During this year we had times of great power among the blacks. The wave of revival spread from the country to the city, and from the city back to the country again. I must here say a few words in regard to this colored Church in Columbus, Miss. It was a Church of very large membership, made so by the indefatigable labors of Brother Shæffer, who had served it for a number of years. There were several prominent negro preachers in the Church, possessing exceptional talent, especially in exhortation and song. O if I could once again hear such singing as I used to hear from those negroes! Thirty years and more have passed since then, but I have never heard any to equal it from that time to the present.

My fourth appointment was to a circuit, and my fifth also to a circuit, the latter the Pickens Circuit, in Pickens County, Ala. On this work there were three churches in a rich portion of the county, each attended by a large concourse of negroes. O the times that Dr. Perry, of Vienna, and myself used to have among those negroes! The recollections come back to-day with a force and power that send my heart into a glow.

The negroes would begin assembling in the morning, and by the time services for the whites, at 11 o'clock, were ended, the yard would be filled with the negroes. The service to the whites concluded, they would soon crowd in until the house was packed. Sometimes the throng was so great that many of them could find no space in the house. They began singing, and by the time Brother Perry and I had finished our refreshments the waves of their melody would be sounding out like the beat of the surf upon the shore. Even after the services were over and we had dismissed them, they would linger about the groves until nightfall, singing and praying and shouting.

Dr. Perry has passed to his reward. He died in Gatesville, Tex., but the seed of his sowing is bearing its precious fruit to this day. So many of the old missionaries have passed away that but few remain to tell the story, as thrilling as any there is in Methodism. O that it had been written years ago! There must, of necessity, be much lost, many, too many threads missing from the strand. But the Master has gathered all the broken ends to himself, and in that last day he, and he alone, will show them complete.

In concluding this chapter we avail ourselves of the following "Items of Slave Mission Work in Mississippi," by Bishop C. B. Galloway. A worthy son of a noble state, he enables us to give a record of the principles which governed the slave holders of Mississippi more than sixty years ago.

"It is a significant fact," says the bishop, "that Mississippi retired to private life her ablest and most distinguished statesman because of his supposed opposition to the religious instruction of the negroes. The early history of the state contains no name equal in broad statesmanship and legal learning to George Poindexter. As largely the author of her first Constitution, the codifier of her laws, Governor of the State, and United States Senator, he was peerless at home and the peer of Clay, Calhoun, and Webster in the upper house of Congress. But in 1822 he was defeated for Congress because of a provision he had inserted in the Code of 1820-21 supposed to be unfavorable to the religious training of slaves. Of this defeat Claiborne, in his 'History of Mississippi,' thus writes:

> These provisions were intended as matters of police and as safeguards against insurrection, but a majority of our citizens regarded them as substantially excluding the colored people from religious privileges, and they expressed their disapprobation by casting their votes against their favorite and ablest statesman. He who had heretofore carried every election by large majorities, and had trampled down innumerable slanders was defeated by *a sentiment of religious duty and compassion for the blacks.* . . . With no extraneous influences acting upon them, the citizens of Mississippi, feeling that all mankind are equal in the sight of God, and that all are equally entitled to hear his word, indignantly rejected the law proposed by Mr. Poindexter, and consigned him to private life. . . . The obnoxious provisions proposed by Mr. Poindexter had been rejected by the Legislature in 1822. *The colored people had the same religious privileges as the whites.* They had their colored ministers. They often knelt in prayer in the family circle, in the parlors of their masters. And the very *system of plantation*

preaching which it was charged Mr. Poindexter desired to prevent was in full operation.

"I know of no more significant event in the whole history of the South which more clearly indicates the true spirit of the people toward the moral and spiritual well-being of the negro. A great statesman, almost omnipotent in political influence, was hurled from place and power because he was regarded as unsound on that great issue: 'plantation preaching.'

"As illustration of the system adopted by all the Churches to reach the great mass of the negroes on the plantations, I reproduce a letter written by Rev. B. W. Williams, a Presbyterian minister and addressed to Gen. John A. Quitman, one of the most distinguished citizens of Mississippi.

PINE RIDGE, MISS., September 4, 1831.

To Gen. John A. Quitman.

Honored and Dear Sir: I doubt not you will excuse me for trespassing upon your attention for a few moments, especially when you learn the occasion. The Church of Pine Ridge, within whose bounds you have a plantation, is now making an effort to give the gospel to every rational being under its care, the *young* as well as the *old*, the *bond* as well as the *free*. In order to do this effectually, it is necessary to adopt the system of *plantation preaching*, which is now acknowledged to possess more advantages than any other. It requires, however, a greater number of preachers than where all can be assembled in one place. One minister can take charge of about nine plantations, giving them instruction, *preaching* and *catechising* every second or third Sabbath; preaching during the week when desired, celebrating marriages, visiting the sick, and burying the dead. There are already two such assistants employed in my parish, and thus far the plan has succeeded admirably.

Nearly all the planters here feel their responsibility for their servants so deeply that they have united to provide *regular* and *frequent religious* instruction for them by good and competent teachers. In this way the servants are made accountable for themselves, and the master is relieved from his most solemn responsibility in this respect.

Nearly every plantation has adopted the plan, and by uniting, the expense is very trifling, about one dollar per head, for all over four years of age. The services of an *educated* man (and none others are so well suited to the work) cannot be obtained for a salary less than $500 or $600.

Some of the smaller plantations, in order to have as frequent services as the others, give rather more than a dollar apiece.

As a Church we are laboring and praying for the conversion of the whole world, and we deem it but reasonable that the good work should commence at home. And masters, when they remember their accountability, and that they are to meet their servants at the judgment bar of God, readily concur with us. They acknowledge their obligation to provide for the *spiritual* as well as the temporal wants of those whom God has intrusted to their care.

I would further add that the teachers employed will be under the constant supervision of the session of the Church, some of whom are themselves planters in this neighborhood.

Hoping to hear from you as soon as convenient, and to learn your views and feelings as regards the subject in general, and also in reference to your own place in particular, I remain

Yours most respectfully and truly,   B. W. WILLIAMS.

"That letter is interesting as detailing: 1. The plan for plantation preaching. 2. The early day when such systematic work was in full operation. 3. The candor and honesty with which ministers talked to masters as to their spiritual obligations to their servants. Of course Methodism, with its *itinerant* system, could most efficiently work the plan of plantation preaching, and soon had the largest negro membership of any Church in the South."

CHAPTER XV.

PLANTATION MISSIONS FROM 1844 TO 1864.

THE division of the Methodist Episcopal Church in 1844 emphasized the work of sending the gospel to the slaves in the South. At various periods the deliverances of the Church had been so threatening in their character, and imprudent men had so often placed the very existence of Methodism in jeopardy, that the doctrine of noninterference with civil institutions by officers of the Church, in their ecclesiastical capacity, removed every obstacle in the way of the Southern Methodist Church. There was no longer any danger that the professed missionary would become an incendiary, and therefore a man indorsed by a Southern Conference was considered by the owners of slaves as trustworthy by virtue of that indorsement alone.

The deposition of Bishop Andrew, because he could not emancipate a slave belonging to his wife, was the occasion of the division of the Church. No sooner was the Methodist Episcopal Church, South, organized than the "Macedonian cry" was heard in every portion of the Southern territory, where large numbers of slaves existed. Increased contributions came to the treasury, and large numbers of the ministry were soon engaged in this labor of love. Within the twenty years comprised between the years 1845 and 1864 more than $1,800,000 was expended, and at the close of the civil war there were over 300 missionaries employed in preaching the gospel to the slaves on the large plantations in the South. As thoroughly organized as any other portion of our Church work, the missions were filled by men competent to teach, men adapted by nature and by grace, as well as by education, to teach and guide the souls committed to their care. Born in the South, thoroughly versed in the negro character, understanding their faults as perfectly as they recognized their virtues, these men of God were welcomed everywhere by the masters and by the slaves. If any exception occurred, it was too insignificant to warrant a record in these pages. So far from entertaining any feeling hostile to the advancement of the slave, common sense taught the slave holder that by as much as his negroes were true Christians by so much were they better servants. If anywhere in the South a model of Mrs. Stowe's slave holder could be found, he was no more a typical specimen of Southern character than Prof. Webster was a type of Boston civilization. Webster murdered his creditor, Dr. Parkman, and burned his body in the stove which heated the professor's room, but all Boston scientists cannot be judged by the standard of this bloody fiend. In like manner, in every age, cruel, ungodly men have dishonored every calling and every community, and the existence of some of these fiends among Southern slave holders was undeniable. But the people of the South detested them, and public opinion was as outspoken against them in the Southern as in the Northern states.

The extraordinary conduct of the slaves during the civil war is an inexplicable feature in the history of that great struggle. Inexplicable, we mean, if this evangelizing work of the missionaries is not taken into the problem. Many writers have believed that Mr. Wesley's followers prevented the uprising of the masses of the English poor at the time of the French Revolution. Religion is the strongest tie that unites man to man in the social constitution. The diffusion of religion " pure and undefiled " is the best safeguard, and the most potent agency for the preservation of civil society. Its operation is uniform. Cultured and uncultured people are alike affected by its precepts. Whether the population be as humble as the hundreds domiciled upon a rice plantation, or as greatly blessed with this world's bounties as the richest and most favored society, precisely to the extent that religion has a place in the hearts of the people to that extent will harmony, love, and peace prevail.

No grander tribute can be paid to the power of the gospel on the one hand, and the sincerity of the poor Africans who professed it on the other than that which is furnished by the state of the negro population of the South in the four years expiring in 1865. Masters in the army, even to the age of threescore in many instances, and coming down to the lad in the midst of his teens in thousands of cases; women left alone upon extensive farms, where an able-bodied man could scarcely be found in a day's ride; negroes taking charge of every interest of their owners, planting, harvesting, selling the crop, and laying in the plantation supplies, tenderly guarding every species of property in danger of waste or loss; careful and faithful stewards of absent owners; these people wept for the slain of the household and rejoiced with the fullness of joy when victory perched upon the banners of their owners, and they kept themselves true to their trust until the last day of their bondage. So few were the heinous offenses against person or property, that the writer does not remember half a dozen instances of assault committed by a negro upon the person of a white woman in all of those terrible years. *That* crime was almost unknown. A symptom of decaying civilization, it was held in such horror that it was scarcely conceivable as a possibility to either race.

Alas! the fearful outbreakings of lawlessness in these latter days are eloquent proofs of the degeneracy of the people, and fearful tokens of dangers to come. But the religious spirit of the Southern slaves was not occasional nor transitory during the war period. Principles, deep-seated and true, held the dark sons of Africa to the gospel of Christ. The Bible was their refuge and their tower of strength, and we shall have occasion to see the types of character developed by the instruction received from the ministry of the missionaries.

If it were necessary to enter into the details of the work on the plantations, we have abundant material. But we have already described the scenes occurring in this mission field, and by the workmen themselves the reader has been thoroughly informed of all of its peculiarities. It is only necessary to state that subsequent to 1844 the plantation mission attracted increased and increasing attention. In 1849 there were fifteen Conferences in whose territory this class of missions was established, and 107 distinct appointments were recognized, with 122 regularly appointed missionaries. In some Conferences, as in South Carolina, Georgia, and Mississippi, there were superintendents whose special work was the right ordering of this important enterprise.

South Carolina kept in the lead, although Mississippi followed very closely. In the latter Conference there was a slave mission district, comprising thirty-five or forty plantations, served by eight or nine missionaries, with a presiding elder at their head. Lake Washington District was created solely for the purpose of giving the greatest efficiency possible to this work. It would be invidious, perhaps, to mention the names of these missionaries, unless we could give place to them all, and to do this would require space equal to the record of a great part of the Conference.

The table which closes this chapter will show the relative strength of the various Conferences, the number of missions, missionaries, Church members, and the amount of money expended for the maintenance of the work. In this table the reader will see the gradual expansion, from year to year, until, in 1860, there were no less than 207,000 African slaves enrolled upon the register of the Methodist Episcopal Church, South.

"The religious sentiment of the whole Southern country was now keenly and zealously aroused in behalf of slave missions. Every effort within the power of her Christian people was put forth to furnish the negro, especially the plantation negro, the light of the gospel. Women, and even little children, contributed to the treasury fund. There is more than one instance on record where the former parted with earrings, breastpins, and other jewelry, that their value in dollars might go to teach the poor negro the way of eternal life. And once—ah! let us forever preserve that incident—a child gave its toys.

"The few planters who had at first opposed the entrance of the missionary, fearing malicious outside influence, had now, with rare exception, acknowledged their error. Indeed, the case of Louisiana was but the case of every Southern state at this time; the call for missionaries far exceeded the supply. Masters and mistresses, even little children, now helped with the work. Many,

many pictures are drawn of Southern maidens, refined and delicately reared, seated under the shade of spreading oak or within some outhouse, teaching the catechism to the little negro children; or again beside the bed of the aged sick, reading from the Bible or hymn book. The mistress, in the absence of her husband, assembled her slaves, morning and evening, reading to them from the most precious of books, while the words of prayer were either from her own lips or those of some earnest, faithful negro.

"On the cold, hard boards of a negro cabin, with only a light wrap covering the night clothes which she had not had time to remove in the haste of her summons, a young girl, delicate herself in health, knelt, hour after hour, repeating the words of Scripture for the last time and singing hymns to the fondly loved old mauma on whose bosom her baby head had been pillowed.

"On a plague-infested island, where death held high carnival and every breeze was a vehicle for his poisoned breath, a man high in social and political position—in short, the Governor of his state —went from cabin to cabin, periling his own life that he might see to the needs and comforts of his stricken people.

"On a bed of pain and sickness, when almost every movement was a torture, a little child—God bless that little child—opened the way of eternal life to the old slave man who attended him.

"On what he thought to be his dying bed Rev.

Charles Wilson still taught his people, night and morning, often with their eyes wet, around him. In the same spirit he and his noble colleague faced the fearful perils of plague-stricken Jehossee. A similar instance of devotion was that of Rev. Mr. Bryan on the islands around Savannah, Ga.

"High and low alike entered into this noble work. There was no phase of it too humble, no duty connected with it too unpleasant to deter the most earnest and painstaking effort. Bishop McTyeire, of the Methodist Episcopal Church, South, declared that during a long ministerial life there was nothing connected with it in which he took more pride and satisfaction than the remembrance of the more than three hundred sermons he had preached to negro congregations. As these words were penned in 1857, he could doubtless have added another three hundred to the number. Bishop Haygood holds as among the most pleasing memories of his maturer life the fact that, as a boy, he endeavored to teach his father's old negro plowman to read.

"Two of the most zealous and untiring friends the negro race ever had at this period, who preached to them, worked for them, and even, on more than one occasion, catechised their children, were Revs. William Capers and James O. Andrew, of South Carolina, both of them at that time bishops of the Methodist Episcopal Church, South.

"The death of Bishop Capers, January 29,

1855, was a sad and heavy blow to the cause that owed its beginning as much to his devoted and zealous effort as to any other source. Even though the first request for a regular missionary to the slaves came from outsiders, it was, nevertheless, the energy and eloquence with which William Capers presented the point before his Conference that secured for the movement its prompt and hearty inauguration. Miss Martin is right when she says that his monument at Columbia bears a grander inscription than that of the greatest soldier or hero of earth:

'Founder of missions to the slaves.'

"As the corpse lay in the chancel of the church at Columbia, one of the most affecting scenes in connection with the day was the large number of negroes who pressed around, each seeking to get a last look at that noble and serenely reposing face. He had been, in the truest sense, their friend, and he was *dead*. Tear after tear fell streaming from their eyes upon his coffin.

"There was scarcely any comparison now between the condition of these plantation negroes and their condition when first the light of evangelization had been kindled among them. Ignorant, superstitious, grossly immoral, it was like seeking to pierce the well-nigh impenetrable darkness locked in the very bowels of the earth. Thousands of them could only speak English in a broken way; hundreds still jabbered unintelligibly in their Gullah and other African dialects.

It was pitiful to hear them trying to address words of petition to God in their broken language.

"'O mausa, I no know dis country talk,'' cried an old woman, with streaming eyes, in the Charleston class meeting. 'I know not'in' but de Africay.'

"'Then, my sister,' said the minister, 'pray to God in the African. He will hear you all the same.'

"When she saw him again, her face was radiant. She said: 'I do as you telle me. I pray God een de Africay. Meh Lord Jesus yerry [hear] me, en now meh soul go *free*.' Her joy grew greater still when she learned to talk to God in the language of the missionaries.

"On an island near Beaufort, S. C., Rev. John R. Coburn found an old negro whose sole religious ideas consisted of crying to the sun and moon when they arose. He soon left him shouting the unspeakable praises of one living and eternal God.

"In the canebrakes of Alabama an old negro named Jack, still clinging to the darkness and superstition of his greegree worship, met a missionary, Rev. E. Mortimer, and after a hard struggle finally opened his soul to the true light. Jack lived to be one hundred and fifteen years old. The light shining so radiantly from his soul found its way to others. For a long while he could only talk in a broken way of his new feeling, but finally the words came clearer and fuller, and he could pray 'fervent, effectual prayers.' The missionary says of Jack's death: 'Old Jack died on his knees while at prayer, without any previous sickness to admonish him of approaching dissolution. His remains were followed to the grave by one of the largest funeral processions ever seen in this village. The citizens and ladies of Greenwood turned out as though to do honor to some worthy citizen.'

"Many of the branches plucked from decay became themselves the source of life to others. Many of those who had caught the seed on fruitful ground became themselves, in turn, sowers of the word. Hundreds of such instances could be given, but I have space for only one: 'At the Plaquemine quarterly meeting,' says a missionary, writing from Louisiana in September of 1857, 'we observed, on Sunday morning, a deeply interested hearer, a black man, on a rear seat. After service he presented himself with a request. He had come with his wife eight miles to have a child baptized, and though sermon and sacrament had been appointed there for colored people in the afternoon, he could not wait so long. His request was attended to. No missionary had ever been on his place, yet he was well instructed and pious; a native of Frederick, Va., and converted there; his wife, he said, was in the gospel before him. On that sugar plantation of Louisiana was seen the leaven principle of religion; he was a witness and evangelist, preaching to his fellow-servants in his own way, and showing them the way of salvation. Said he joyously: "Fourteen of our people turned to the Lord last year."'

"With encouragement and advice he went his way, 'toting' the new Christian. He plunged into the cane fields, there in obscurity to be a witness for the Lord. Some day he will come again, bringing his sheaves with him.

"And thus the work went on and grew year by year, spreading out and striking its rootlets into the soil, occupying, more perseveringly still, the old. The sentiment expressed at this time by Bishop Andrew on behalf of the South Carolina Conference was but the sentiment of the others: 'Whatever becomes of the other mission work, we will *never* abandon our negro missions.' Faithfully were these words kept, even through the storm-rocked period of disastrous war.

"At the close of 1858 there were actively operated 221 distinct slave mission fields, in addition to a full twoscore and more of special colored charges, with a membership in the mission family proper of 53,773 souls. The total colored membership in the Southern Conferences at this period was 155,932, with the additional lists of 32,104 on probation and about 14,000 children under catechetical instruction.

"Presbyterian and Baptist preachers, as well as Methodists, had their regular charges among the slaves. But the greater work done by these was in the congregations of the whites. Preachers and people alike worked faithfully, prayerfully to bring poor sin-darkened Ethiopia into the full noonday of spiritual righteousness. It was not a romantic work by any means. It lacked many of those elements which stir the pulse of enthusiasm, but it was nevertheless the work of hope, of faith, and of pure consecrated effort. It was missionary work in its highest sense, and into this work the Church entered with the full measure of her zeal and liberality. The record of this work should be preserved forever as a glory that cannot be dimmed.

"Though Bishop Capers was dead, the noble and zealous Andrew still lived to push the work with consecrated zeal and vigor. The negro race in America never had a more devoted and sympathetic friend than James O. Andrew, bishop of the Methodist Episcopal Church, South. Wherever he went he talked and worked in their behalf. Neither pen nor tongue was ever silent when a word could be urged for the good of the cause.

"'I remember,' says Dr. C. K. Marshall, of Vicksburg, Miss., 'that when the saintly Bishop Andrew presided over our Conference years ago he emphasized the duty of fidelity to Christ's poor in preaching the gospel, by dwelling at considerable length on the obligation of preaching to the slaves. Said he: "My brethren, our estimates of men differ widely from God's. With him it is not a question of age, condition, or color. He looks alike on master and the servant. *With him souls are souls.* And the soul of the poorest slave, washed in redeeming blood, is dearer to God than the unregenerated spirit of the greatest monarch. For myself I would rather know that some poor slave would cast a flower on my grave when I am gone, in grateful memory of my agency in leading him to Jesus, than to have any honor this poor world could bestow upon me." I quote the bishop's words from memory, but never had the great truth thus announced so fixed itself upon that memory. The pathos, the transparency, the inspiration with which he poured forth that half-hour's appeal filled every attentive ear and feeling heart with a fresh and profound sense of growing obligation to carry the light of divine life into every negro cabin where it was possible to find access.'

"By 1859 the number of slave missions had increased to 290, served by 292 missionaries and covering a field that extended from the Potomac to the Gulf of Mexico, and from the Atlantic seaboard to the Mississippi and beyond. In all this Southern territory few were the plantations that were not now included in the missionary's regular visit or else within access of some church used by both whites and blacks. The number of members exclusively in this mission family throughout the different Conferences was for this year (1859) 56,468. The total colored membership for the Southern Methodist Church at this period was 163,296. Of this number, South Carolina had 41,127; Georgia, 21,455; Alabama, 20,577; North

Carolina, 11,708; and Mississippi, 11,008. The increase of colored membership for this one year was 7,274. The amount paid out for the maintenance of these missions for the one year aggregated $130,076.88. In addition to this there were a number of colored Churches partly supported by the whites. In other cases, where the slaves themselves paid their pastors, they were given the opportunity by their owners to earn the money for themselves.

"It had now become the custom in all the larger cities and in many of the smaller towns for the preachers to devote Sunday afternoon to the religious instruction of the slaves who could not attend the preaching of the whites in the morning. A large amount of missionary work was done in this way. Indeed, the Church was reaching out in every direction to care for and save the souls of the negro population within her bounds. Not for a moment did she slacken in her duty; never once did her prayers grow less or her zeal grow colder; never did she draw her purse strings against any appeal that it lay in her power to answer. Economy in many directions was practiced, that the largest liberality might be possible in this department of Church operations among the blacks. During the thirty-six years of its missionary labors among the slave population of its plantations the South Carolina Conference alone expended a sum closely approaching in round numbers $400,000, or an average of more than $10,000 a year. Next to this came the Alabama Conference, which gave $354,416.67. Following Alabama was the Georgia Conference, giving $302,530.94. This was also an average of more than $10,000 a year for Alabama, and in the neighborhood of $9,500 for Georgia, as the latter was two years and the former five years behind the South Carolina Conference in beginning missionary operations. According to the length of time, putting the calculation upon the basis adopted, the Alabama Conference gave more than any other in the support of this work.

"In 1861, at the beginning of the war, there were in this mission family 77,802 members. This included three colored churches in the cities that were purely mission churches. In the plantation family proper there were 70,301 in full connection in addition to 12,672 probationers, and nearly sixteen thousand children under catechetical instruction. In South Carolina alone there were over two hundred plantations served. The next largest territory occupied was in the Mississippi Valley, and covering ground of both the Mississippi and Louisiana Conferences. For this year Mississippi reported the largest number of slave missions in any Conference—42 in all. While the figures reported in her missionary appropriations are not so large as those of other Conferences occupying like herself much territory, it is doubtless true that much of the revenue expended in the support of these missions was not included in the report of the

Minutes. We have found many instances of Mississippi and Louisiana planters donating bales of cotton and hogsheads of sugar and syrup toward the salaries of the missionaries. There is also more than one instance of planters paying their salaries entire. There is no possible way of getting a correct table of these additional funds. The true amount expended in the evangelization of the slaves, not only by this Conference but by the others of the Southern connection, will never be known until the pages of God's account book lie open in the presence of an assembled world.

"During the year 1862, when the guns of an invading army were thundering at her doors and every sinew of finance was strained to its utmost tension, the South, through the Southern Methodist Church alone, paid out of her treasury for the evangelization of her slaves $93,509.87. What the other Churches paid we cannot tell, but it was probably as much as $57,000, amounting in all to $150,000. For this year (1862) the Methodist Church, South, had in her slave mission family 63,649 members. Several thousand of those in the regular mission family had for various reasons been placed in the work of the regular circuits. Here they were as faithfully cared for as they had been in their own mission. The heroism and the zeal with which the Southern Churches kept their faith in this work of evangelization throughout all this stormy period forms a chapter that must thrill every Southern heart and win the honest admiration and commendation of every fair-minded person, irrespective of creed or section.

"From the year 1862 the numerous breaks in the mission Minutes form insurmountable obstacles in the way of preparing anything like a definite statement. From the beginning of that year to 1865, first one Conference and then another had portions of its territory 'within the enemy's lines.' Sometimes an entire district, maybe two and three, would be thus situated, and were therefore left out of the statistics of the Minutes; or the omission would be that of a whole Conference, with no annual meeting at all. But because there was no report given we must not understand that there was no work done. Far from it. This we know to a certainty: whatever lay within the scope of human power strengthened by divine aid was done that the work might go forward with its full vigor. There were heroes outside the army, moral heroes as well as physical, men who were constantly sacrificing self and the tenderest feelings that this work of salvation to the negro race of the South might not grow stagnant in a single vein through which the life current might be made to penetrate. Physical heroes they were too. The story comes of a brave old missionary out in the Tennessee Valley, who, finding the bridge gone, burned by a retreating army, swam the icy current, that he might preach to his waiting charge on the other side. The negroes made him a fire of pine knots, and as he dried his steaming clothes he preached to them the word of life. Down through a line of pickets, with a shower of bullets following him, rode another of these heroic knights of the cross, that the little band of expectant negroes in the pine woods of Georgia might not be denied the sacrament for which they waited.

"Dr. C. K. Marshall, of Vicksburg, is right when he says of this stormy period as well as of the trying times that preceded it: 'I doubt if more trying conditions ever taxed the power and piety of foreign missionaries, save in a few fields of remarkable embarrassment, than were encountered by the intrepid and faithful workers of those days.' Consecrated women, too, as well as men, struggled to keep the flame of this noble work aglow. Instances innumerable are given of these Christian women, in the absence of their husbands in the army, assembling their slaves, night and morning, for prayer. Often, too, when the missionary was detained, either providentially or by the intervening lines of the enemy, they gathered their slaves for the regular worship, and, reading a selection from the Bible, endeavored to give them a plain and practical sermon from it. This deep and earnest solicitude for the salvation of the negro race had its abiding place deep in the hearts of thousands of the Christian men and women of the South. Born of the Spirit of God, supplied from the fountains of an ever springing humanity, it could not be quenched, even by the angry and turbulent floods of raging war. It was an ever living presence sweetening and purifying, elevating and ennobling. To-day the fair flowers of righteousness that it watered into immortal growth within the hearts of hundreds—nay, thousands—of the old time negro race of the South exhale a sweetness and a fragrance that is unlike that of the later and more exotic growth that surrounds them. We do not intend to demean the younger generation of the negroes of the South. There are many instances of this sweet humility, this deep earnestness of nature, flowing in an unbroken stream from parent to child. Where the religion is pure and deep and fervent, a true, breathing, living religion, the fragrance of gentle purposes, of wholesome endeavors, of elevating instincts, of love, of good-will, and of genuine Christianity will show itself unmistakably.

"Though paralyzed in every nerve by the strain of a three years' war, and having every resource well-nigh exhausted, the South paid out during the year 1864 for the religious instruction of her slaves a sum that would closely approximate, we think, $250,000. Of this amount the Methodist Episcopal Church, South, paid nearly two-thirds, or $158,421.96. During the very last year of the struggle, when poverty and prostration lay on every side, and fully two-thirds of the Southern territory had been swept as though by a cyclone, the sum of $80,000 was raised by the Southern Methodist Church in support of negro evangelization.

"During the thirty-four years of its slave mission period, the Methodist Church, South, paid out upward of $2,000,000 for the Christianizing of the negro race. There is no going behind that sum; to go beyond it—well beyond it—would give the more accurate estimate. I have no doubt whatever, from the careful examination and inquiry that I have given the subject, that a full half million more might safely be counted. What a glorious chain it would form could every 'missing link' be added! And yet there are some people who say that we have done nothing.

"At the setting off, in 1870, from the Methodist Episcopal Church, South, of the Colored Methodist Episcopal Church, the colored membership numbered nearly 80,000. This was a considerable falling off from the membership of over 200,000 it had numbered a few years previous. The question naturally arises: What had become of this membership? The two African Churches of the North had absorbed a large share of it, and the other portion had gone to the Northern Methodist Church.

"Bishop Haygood, in his 'Brother in Black,' estimates that at the close of the war between the states there were nearly half a million negroes who had been brought into the folds of the different Churches through the efforts of the Christian men and women of the South. How many more of this great mass had felt the uplifting influence of the leaven of consecrated effort no man can estimate."

The following table presents a view of the appropriations made by the several Conferences from 1845 to 1864 inclusive, a period of twenty years, disturbed, in the latter part of the time, by the occupation of the Southern territory by the Federal troops. The fidelity of the white people of the South to the religious welfare of the African slaves is one of the most remarkable facts connected with the most remarkable struggle recorded in modern history.

STATISTICS FROM 1844 TO 1864.

Year.	Conference.	Missions.	Members.	Missionaries.	Amount Appropri'ed.
1845	South Carolina...	17	8,314	22	$ 9,720 60
1845	Georgia..........	10	3,106	12	4,343 50
1845	Tennessee	12	3,311	14	2,848 75
1845	Mississippi.......	11	3,022	12	4,152 50
1845	Memphis.........	11	3,383	12	3,254 16
1845	Alabama	11	2,900	12	4,384 35
1845	Virginia..........	3	481	3	1,985 60
1845	North Carolina...	3	187	3	900 00
1845	Arkansas.........	1	113	1	300 00
1845	Florida	3	563	3	1,210 50
1845	East Texas	1	....	1	300 00
1846	South Carolina...	17	9,321	24	9,398 24
1846	Georgia..........	12	3,487	15	5,776 40
1846	Tennessee........	16	3,706	18	3,862 00
1846	Mississippi.......	10	2,397	12	3,600 00
1846	Memphis	13	3,394	16	3,900 00
1846	Alabama	13	3,149	15	4,350 00
1846	Louisiana........	8	2,165	9	3,966 00
1846	Virginia	3	433	3	2,266 00
1846	Florida.	3	465	3	815 02
1846	North Carolina...	2	224	2	1,068 00
1846	Arkansas.........	1	109	1	300 00
1846	Louisville........	1	211	1	300 00
1846	St. Louis.........	1	421	1	300 00
1847	South Carolina...	17	9,439	24	11,870 00
1847	Georgia..........	12	3,176	14	5,110 00
1847	Tennessee........	19	4,716	21	3,221 75
1847	Memphis.........	14	3,567	16	3,286 40
1847	Alabama	14	3,583	16	4,350 60

Statistics from 1844 to 1864 (Continued).

Year.	Conference.	Missions.	Members.	Missionaries.	Amount Appropri'ed.
1847	Mississippi	9	2,357	10	$ 2,700 00
1847	Louisiana	8	2,265	9	1,595 38
1847	Virginia	3	496	3	900 00
1847	Florida	3	465	3	815 00
1847	North Carolina	2	224	2	1,066 00
1847	Arkansas	1	126	1	300 00
1847	Louisville	1	421	1	600 00
1848	South Carolina	16	9,874	23	10,184 00
1848	Georgia	13	4,613	16	5,726 00
1848	Tennessee	15	3,907	17	3,074 34
1848	Alabama	19	3,863	21	4,859 36
1848	Mississippi	15	3,198	17	2,064 60
1848	Louisiana	14	3,292	16	3,424 16
1848	Memphis	14	3,852	15	5,185 32
1848	Virginia	6	1,154	6	1,800 00
1848	Arkansas	4	372	4	1,200 00
1848	North Carolina	3	196	3	1,150 40
1848	Florida	4	603	4	1,200 00
1848	East Texas	2	123	2	600 00
1848	Texas	2	113	2	812 26
1848	Louisville	2	1,498	2	600 00
1848	St. Louis	1	50	1	300 00
1849	St. Louis	1	75	1	300 00
1849	Holston	1	....	1	300 00
1849	Tennessee	12	3,169	13	4,239 28
1849	Virginia	3	520	3	900 00
1849	Arkansas	3	365	3	900 00
1849	Memphis	9	2,451	10	4,514 00
1849	North Carolina	3	563	3	900 00
1849	Mississippi	17	3,348	19	3,358 66
1849	South Carolina	16	9,031	22	10,835 00
1849	East Texas	2	223	2	600 00
1849	Texas	2	188	2	600 00
1849	Louisiana	11	2,215	12	1,912 00
1849	Georgia	12	4,311	14	7,969 76
1849	Alabama	12	2,900	13	5,460 00
1849	Florida	4	458	4	1,207 02
1850	Holston	1	197	1	300 00
1850	Virginia	3	1,297	3	900 00
1850	Arkansas	3	369	3	900 00
1850	Tennessee	5	1,156	4	2,892 00
1850	North Carolina	3	621	3	1,290 20
1850	Memphis	10	2,804	11	5,250 00
1850	East Texas	1	213	1	300 00
1850	Texas	2	217	2	600 00

STATISTICS FROM 1844 TO 1864 (CONTINUED).

Year.	Conference.	Missions.	Members.	Missionaries.	Amount Appropri'ed.
1850	South Carolina...	16	8,326	24	$11,808 16
1850	Georgia	11	3,908	13	8,142 02
1850	Mississippi	16	2,750	18	3,845 32
1850	Alabama	10	3,021	10	6,330 66
1850	Louisiana	4	1,381	5	2,874 00
1850	Florida	5	585	5	1,333 32
1851	Virginia	3	1,098	3	900 00
1851	Tennessee	6	1,284	6	4,316 22
1851	Arkansas	1	220	1	300 00
1851	North Carolina...	4	1,328	4	2,816 70
1851	Memphis	7	1,896	7	6,168 84
1851	South Carolina...	18	8,700	25	12,265 32
1851	Georgia	13	4,039	15	10,184 60
1851	Mississippi	19	4,161	21	3,982 68
1851	Alabama	10	2,475	11	17,220 66
1851	Louisiana	7	1,563	7	2,197 30
1851	Florida	4	751	4	1,903 18
1851	East Texas	2	....	2	600 00
1851	Texas	2	....	2	600 00
1852	Tennessee	7	1,915	7	5,145 86
1852	Arkansas	3	314	3	848 66
1852	North Carolina...	4	1,793	4	3,846 00
1852	Virginia	4	2,141	4	4,896 00
1852	Memphis	10	2,729	11	9,717 76
1852	South Carolina...	20	9,910	27	14,907 66
1852	Georgia	11	3,912	13	11,218 28
1852	Mississippi	23	4,768	26	6,900 00
1852	Alabama	15	3,143	16	13,420 00
1852	Louisiana	12	2,368	14	7,256 96
1852	Florida	4	1,016	4	1,618 00
1852	East Texas	1	109	1	300 00
1852	Texas	6	603	6	2,029 62
1853	Virginia	6	2,218	6	9,069 68
1853	Tennessee	9	2,277	9	2,700 00
1853	Arkansas	2	277	2	600 00
1853	North Carolina...	4	1,713	4	2,400 00
1853	Memphis	11	2,816	12	8,169 76
1853	South Carolina...	22	11,653	28	16,699 40
1853	Georgia	21	6,104	24	11,931 72
1853	Mississippi	26	5,036	28	7,800 00
1853	Alabama	21	4,890	23	15,133 20
1853	Louisiana	11	3,627	12	2,552 66
1853	Florida	6	1,460	6	2,002 60
1853	East Texas	1	340	1	300 00
1853	Texas	9	811	9	2,773 02

Plantation Missions from 1844 to 1864.

Statistics from 1844 to 1864 (Continued).

Year.	Conference.	Missions.	Members.	Missionaries.	Amount Appropri'ed.
1854	Tennessee........	7	2,187	7	$ 4,083 38
1854	Memphis.........	14	3,196	15	7,801 64
1854	Mississippi.......	23	5,886	24	4,385 68
1854	Louisiana........	10	3,606	11	2,923 30
1854	Virginia	5	2,496	5	3,000 00
1854	North Carolina...	5	2,632	5	3,000 00
1854	Georgia..........	28	9,145	31	11,265 86
1854	South Carolina...	26	11,546	32	15,188 06
1854	Alabama.........	20	6,215	21	13,980 50
1854	Florida..........	6	1,324	6	3,082 34
1854	Texas	11	902	10	2,305 80
1854	East Texas.......	2	453	2	600 00
1854	Arkansas.........	3	319	3	600 00
1855	South Carolina...	25	10,523	32	15,375 00
1855	St. Louis.........	1	278	1	300 00
1855	Tennessee	8	2,368	8	5,514 66
1855	Memphis.........	19	4,203	20	8,965 30
1855	Virginia..........	6	2,121	6	3,600 00
1855	Ark. & Wachita..	3	321	3	900 00
1855	Mississippi.......	23	5,426	25	7,821 82
1855	North Carolina...	6	2,981	6	3,600 00
1855	East Texas.......	3	408	3	1,372 56
1855	Alabama.........	21	7,578	21	15,522 74
1855	Florida	6	1,059	6	2,726 72
1855	Louisiana........	13	3,838	14	2,901 54
1855	Texas	13	848	13	1,866 66
1855	Georgia	27	8,031	29	12,636 20
1856	St. Louis.........	2	1,200	2	600 00
1856	Holston..........	1	401	1	300 00
1856	Tennessee........	8	2,621	7	6,138 24
1856	Virginia..........	6	2,120	6	3,600 00
1856	Ark. & Wachita..	6	1,691	5	3,990 02
1856	Memphis.........	20	4,513	18	5,133 32
1856	Mississippi.......	26	5,651	19	7,700 00
1856	North Carolina...	6	2,161	6	3,000 00
1856	South Carolina...	24	9,982	30	18,275 44
1856	Alabama.........	34	8,487	33	20,933 32
1856	Florida..........	11	1,578	9	3,896 40
1856	Louisiana........	9	3,232	9	6,110 98
1856	East Texas.......	2	322	2	600 00
1856	Texas	5	921	5	3,000 00
1856	Georgia	24	8,214	21	14,410 34
1857	St. Louis	2	1,231	2	600 00
1857	Tennessee........	7	2,531	6	5,615 48
1857	Holston..........	1	421	1	300 00

STATISTICS FROM 1844 TO 1864 (CONTINUED).

Year.	Conference.	Missions.	Members.	Missionaries.	Amount Appropri'ed.
1857	Memphis.........	24	4,291	23	$ 8,197 94
1857	Mississippi.......	29	5,984	30	7,137 10
1857	Virginia..........	9	2,857	8	11,666 66
1857	North Carolina...	7	2,431	6	6,400 70
1857	South Carolina...	27	11,026	33	16,023 52
1857	Georgia..........	23	7,891	22	12,396 26
1857	Alabama.........	32	8,301	30	18,144 74
1857	Florida	8	1,384	7	4,100 36
1857	Texas	15	897	14	3,821 92
1857	East Texas.......	4	760	3	2,524 78
1857	Arkansas.........	5	934	5	2,368 62
1857	Wachita..........	5	581	5	2,732 82
1857	Louisiana........	10	3,512	10	5,331 84
1858	South Carolina...	28	12,102	34	18,755 34
1858	St. Louis.........	1	275	1	300 00
1858	Tennessee........	8	2,678	8	5,474 42
1858	Holston..........	2	324	2	600 00
1858	Memphis.........	18	4,579	20	7,551 26
1858	Mississippi.......	32	6,061	34	9,491 20
1858	Louisiana........	10	1,928	9	5,142 06
1858	Virginia..........	13	1,483	11	14,294 18
1858	North Carolina...	9	2,298	8	5,418 76
1858	Georgia	28	8,364	29	15,430 02
1858	Alabama.........	35	7,583	32	22,486 46
1858	Florida	7	1,624	6	4,029 44
1858	Texas	14	960	12	5,173 86
1858	East Texas.......	7	694	6	2,003 32
1858	Arkansas.........	4	391	4	1,628 12
1858	Wachita	5	434	4	3,333 32
1859	St. Louis.........	2	334	2	600 00
1859	Tennessee........	10	2,618	10	4,626 90
1859	Holston	3	408	3	900 00
1859	Memphis.........	19	4,057	18	7,683 78
1859	Mississippi.......	35	6,289	36	10,200 00
1859	Louisiana........	14	2,012	14	4,534 58
1859	Virginia.........	16	3,539	15	14,588 44
1859	North Carolina...	10	2,127	10	7,058 44
1859	Georgia..........	40	10,734	43	16,420 66
1859	Alabama.........	38	8,381	39	25,849 10
1859	Florida	12	2,878	13	3,332 80
1859	Texas	27	1,658	25	6,451 80
1859	East Texas.......	9	781	7	4,133 20
1859	Arkansas	7	626	6	1,568 80
1859	Wachita..........	14	922	12	4,000 00
1859	South Carolina...	31	9,104	37	18,128 38

Plantation Missions from 1844 to 1864. 323

STATISTICS FROM 1844 TO 1864 (CONTINUED).

Year.	Conference.	Missions.	Members.	Missionaries.	Amount Appropri'ed.
1860	St. Louis	2	431	2	$ 600 00
1860	Louisville	5	983	5	2,500 00
1860	Tennessee	13	3,417	12	5,140 86
1860	Holston	4	593	4	1,200 00
1860	Memphis	24	4,093	23	7,023 06
1860	Mississippi	46	7,659	48	14,400 00
1860	Louisiana	16	2,957	18	6,333 30
1860	Virginia	20	4,587	20	13,558 44
1860	North Carolina	12	3,259	12	6,558 44
1860	South Carolina	33	10,231	38	16,309 02
1860	Georgia	38	11,071	41	19,292 04
1860	Alabama	40	9,208	40	27,091 66
1860	Florida	11	2,913	10	3,490 46
1860	Texas	29	1,761	29	8,702 62
1860	East Texas	8	824	8	2,400 00
1860	Arkansas	8	674	7	2,400 00
1860	Wachita	20	1,226	18	2,545 32
1861	South Carolina	38	10,928	42	9,692 62
1861	Louisville	4	928	4	1,200 00
1861	Tennessee	16	3,557	14	4,800 00
1861	Holston	4	674	4	1,200 00
1861	Memphis	22	4,124	21	6,300 00
1861	Mississippi	42	8,061	43	8,733 50
1861	Louisiana	13	2,633	13	3,900 00
1861	Virginia	20	4,492	20	6,000 00
1861	North Carolina	14	3,264	13	3,318 14
1861	Georgia	39	11,125	41	11,838 52
1861	Florida	10	2,821	9	2,966 28
1861	Alabama *	40	9,208	40	27,091 66
1861	Texas	32	2,045	30	4,429 32
1861	East Texas *	8	824	8	2,400 00
1861	Arkansas	7	654	7	2,100 00
1861	Wachita	20	1,221	18	2,540 02
1862	Louisville *	4	928	4	1,200 00
1862	Tennessee	15	3,451	13	4,500 00
1862	Holston	5	711	5	2,691 48
1862	Memphis	20	4,110	18	6,000 00
1862	Mississippi	39	7,432	40	11,700 00
1862	Louisiana	14	2,433	14	4,200 00
1862	Virginia	18	4,362	18	4,200 00
1862	North Carolina	16	4,166	15	4,424 75
1862	South Carolina	26	8,737	32	10,285 44
1862	Georgia	38	10,931	39	13,798 20

* Figures for this year not given. These are the figures for preceding year.

STATISTICS FROM 1844 TO 1864 (CONTINUED).

Year.	Conference.	Missions.	Members.	Missionaries.	Amount Appropri'ed.
1862	Alabama	36	8,962	35	$10,800 00
1862	Florida	8	2,652	7	2,400 00
1862	Texas	28	2,011	27	8,400 00
1862	East Texas	9	868	9	2,700 00
1862	Arkansas	7	654	7	2,100 00
1862	Wachita	21	1,241	18	5,400 00
1863	Tennessee	15	1,351	13	3,900 00
1863	Holston	4	684	4	1,200 00
1863	Memphis	22	3,912	20	6,648 46
1863	Mississippi	36	7,302	36	10,800 00
1863	Louisiana	12	2,332	12	3,600 00
1863	Virginia	12	3,124	11	3,300 00
1863	North Carolina	14	3,821	14	4,200 00
1863	South Carolina	25	....	29	27,000 18
1863	Georgia	39	11,611	39	45,460 34
1863	Alabama	37	9,020	37	31,311 50
1863	Florida	10	2,804	9	2,700 00
1863	Texas	28	2,011	27	8,400 00
1863	East Texas	9	868	9	2,700 00
1863	Arkansas	7	654	7	2,100 00
1864	Louisville	2	613	2	600 00
1864	Holston	3	694	3	900 00
1864	Virginia	14	3,226	14	8,400 00
1864	North Carolina	13	3,654	13	3,900 00
1864	South Carolina	29	*13,373	32	42,475 80
1864	Georgia	37	11,421	36	11,700 00
1864	Montgomery	22	5,153	22	24,508 00
1864	Mobile	23	5,684	33	26,938 16
1864	Florida	9	2,703	9	2,700 00
1864	Texas	29	2,213	27	8,100 00
1864	East Texas	10	963	9	2,700 00
1864	Arkansas	8	684	8	2,400 00
1864	Wachita	18	1,172	16	4,800 00

*This includes the newly established mission in Charleston, which numbered 3,842.

In the foregoing table we have placed the Conferences in the order in which plantation missions were established. The collections taken for the purpose extended in some few instances to the year 1864, but the last year of the civil war afforded no opportunity for missionary operations of any kind. In 1864 the Alabama Conference appears in the divided territory, forming "Mobile" and "Montgomery" Conferences, and the aggregate contributions of these bodies are included under "Alabama."

It will be seen by this table that the highest figures were recorded in 1861, the first year of the civil war. At that time there were 329 missions, 327 missionaries, 66,559 members, and $86,359.20 appropriated for the "plantation" missions to the slaves in the South. As increasing operations of the Federal army reduced the territory of these Conferences, the work of the missionaries was suspended, and ultimately it was destroyed by the results of the war.

It must be remembered also that many of the Conferences had no extensive communities of African slaves, and therefore the "plantation mission" was not in existence. The gospel was preached to the negroes in common with the whites everywhere throughout the South, and in many places, smaller stations especially, a negro mission was attached to the work of the pastor, and once a month or oftener the pastor gave a part of the Sabbath to the "colored charge." In regular stations of the larger classes the afternoon was usually a special time allotted to the negroes, and the only exception to this rule was in the large cities, where the negroes were sufficiently numerous to form pastoral charges of their own. To those experienced and often able ministers were regularly appointed.

The reader will be interested in the table which follows. We have taken the appropriations made by each Conference from 1829 to 1864, and by dividing the time into two periods we are able to see the work accomplished prior to and subsequent to 1844. As in the table of details, the Conferences appear in the list in the order in which plantation missions were established.

AMOUNTS APPROPRIATED FOR PLANTATION MISSIONS FROM 1829 TO 1864.

CONFERENCE.	1829 to 1844.	1844 to 1864.	Total.
South Carolina....	$ 58,879 81	$ 315,197 18	$ 374,076 99
Georgia...........	41,980 80	255,050 72	297,030 52
Tennessee.........	14,524 56	83,094 14	97,618 70
Mississippi	19,302 79	130,773 06	150,075 85
Memphis	8,683 45	120,751 00	129,434 45
Alabama	17,366 36	340,166 67	357,533 03
Virginia	2,400 00	109,825 00	112,225 00
North Carolina....	2,110 70	66,316 53	68,427 23
Arkansas..........	1,104 50	27,804 22	28,908 72
Florida...........	905 90	46,416 42	47,322 32
East Texas........	....	26,133 86	26,133 86
Louisiana.........	....	70,769 06	70,769 06
St. Louis	....	3,900 00	3,900 00
Louisville.........	....	6,700 00	6,700 00
Texas.............	....	68,066 88	68,066 88
Holston	....	9,891 48	9,891 48
Wachita..........	....	25,351 48	25,351 48
Total	$167,258 87	$1,706,207 70	$1,873,466 27

CHAPTER XVI.

Traits of Christian Character.

IN no land, east or west, has the gospel won a greater number of conquests than those recorded by the missionaries to the slaves in the South. The character of the negro in his savage state we have seen described by thoughtful and impartial observers. His removal from his native country to the United States, accomplished by the basest of treachery and the cruelest of means in the great majority of instances, only transferred him from a heathen to a Christian country. In the nature of the case it was impossible for many of the direct blessings of civilization to reach him as a slave on a large plantation, cut off from all means of improvement and from all associations likely to elevate his moral character.

It was in this relation to American society, that of a transplanted heathen, that the negro became a subject of philanthropic labor and self-sacrificing toil. Unlike the stolid Chinaman, the negro has a temperament eminently adapted to religious emotions. Forms and ceremonies go for little, because to whatever extent these sons of Africa are capable of appreciating them, to that extent do they relegate them to the fetichism and voodoo worship of their native land.

But the religion that one can *feel* and enjoy and that cripples no sense of enjoyment by the rigid enforcement of an iron-bound decorum is the religion that captures the African. When St. Paul said "we are saved by hope," he uttered a sentiment that touches the lowly sons of toil at every point of their pilgrimage. "There's a better day a coming" are the words of an old refrain that have girded up the loins of millions who were just about to faint by the wayside.

When the Methodist preachers came with stirring songs and earnest exhortations, and, above all, when they followed St. Paul's example and told a thrilling experience, the dusky children of Africa surrendered all they had to surrender and became Christians of the best type that they knew. Shall any man call in question the genuineness and sincerity of their profession? Let us listen to the testimony recorded in the amazing history of four millions of peaceable, quiet, and obedient slaves, exercising the most sacred trusts for four years while a war was waged for their emancipation from bondage to their masters. Let us hear the testimony of wise and good men, thorough judges of human character, who have described the virtues of these humble followers of Christ, and have acknowledged themselves debtors even to the poor slave whose faithfulness enlarged the blessings of God conferred upon their religious instructors.

From the notable persons whose memorial cannot perish from the earth, we shall select a few as examples of great numbers for whom we can find no space in these pages.

First among the witnesses to the fidelity of the converted African we shall introduce Bishop Capers. A man of large heart, sympathizing with the poor, the lowly, and the distressed everywhere, his philanthropy had a practical turn, and he did more than any other man of his time for the religious welfare of the slaves. From his pen we take the following sketch of

CASTILE SELBY.

"I can call to mind no other person of our colored society of that early day, who, of nearly Castile's age, was estimated as much as he, though there were some very worthy men among them. The weight and force of his character were made up of humility, sincerity, simplicity, integrity, and consistency; for all of which he was remarkable not only among his fellows of the colored society in Charleston, but I might say among all whom I have ever known. He was one of those honest men who need no proof of it. . . . Just what he seemed to be he invariably was—neither more nor less. Add to this a thorough piety which, indeed, was the root and stock of all his virtues, and you will find elements for the character of no common man; and such was Castile Selby. . . . Love of order was a ruling passion with Daddy Castile. Not only was the house he lived in and the few inferior articles of furniture it contained kept in order—that is, clean and to rights—but there was order in that old tarpaulin hat and well-patched linsey-woolsey coat, which marked the old cartman as he trudged the streets from day to day with his old bay horse and well-worn cart hauling wood. And then there was order in that clean, unpatched, but still linsey-woolsey coat, and that blue-striped handkerchief tied about his head, in which he was to be seen at the house of God, morning, afternoon, and evening, on the Sabbath day.

"If I ever knew a man who was so completely satisfied with his condition as to prefer no change whatever, that man was Castile Selby. His dwelling might have been better, his apparel better, and he might have relieved himself of much fatigue and exposure, but he deemed it unbecoming. On these and kindred subjects I knew his feelings well, having had much conversation with him, and telling him plainly I thought him wrong. But I could not convince him, while he satisfied me he was governed by a sense of duty, the fitness and force of which he was better prepared to judge than perhaps I was. For example: Noticing the meanness of his clothing, and expressing a fear that it might not be comfortable, 'No, master,' he said, 'these old clothes make me quite comfortable. They just suit my business, and so they just suit me.' Remarking on his Sunday clothes, that he might improve them a little, 'Ah, sir,' he answered, 'don't you see how our colored people are turning fools after dress and fashion, just as if they were white. They want somebody to hold them back. I dress for my color. Besides that, sir, how can I take what the Lord is pleased to give me to do some little good with and put it on my back?'

"But it was his indefatigable industry, not allowing of a reasonable suspension of his labors in bad weather, which most frequently induced our most friendly disputes. . . . .

"'Well, well, Father Castile,' I would say, 'out again in the rain with that old coat! Why in the world will you expose yourself so? And are not your legs swelled even now?'

"'Ah, sir, I thought you would scold if you happened to meet me. But no matter, master. The rain won't hurt me: I am used to it.'

"'But it *will* hurt you; it *must* hurt you. And I dare say those swelled legs came by just such exposure as this. You ought to be at home; and do, pray, now go home and keep yourself comfortable.'

"'For your sake, sir, I would go home, but several families are looking for me to haul them wood to-day, and I must not disappoint them.'

"'And who will haul them wood after you have killed yourself?'

"'I won't kill myself, sir. I have been used to this all my life, and use, you know, is second nature. I never find myself any better for lying up. But, master, aren't you out too?'

"'Yes, I am; but it is only for a little time, and I am fully protected; but here you are regularly at it for a day's work, with no protection from the weather but your hat and that threadbare blanket overcoat. You really ought to go home. . . . You can't stand it, Father Castile, and you ought not to try to stand it. Do, pray, go home.'

"'Ah, master, they say, "better wear out than rust out." There are too many lazy people rusting out for me to lie up because it rains a little. . . . I can't help working, sir, and I don't want to help it. It is the lot it has pleased God to give me, and it suits me best.'

"As the infirmities of age increased on my old friend, and while his habits of continual industry seemed indomitable, I became anxious about him; and after conversing with several of our brethren, and finding them of my own mind with respect to him, I determined to adopt a course which I supposed must prove effectual. I told him that while his long course of holy living had made him friends of the principal members of the Church, who shared with me the kindest feelings for him, and were more than willing to provide for all his wants, it placed him in a position with respect to the colored society which we thought required both for himself and them that his time should be differently employed from what it had been. We were fully persuaded that it was our duty to rescue him from his cart, and put it in his power to employ all his time in a way which we believed would prove more to the glory of God; and that was (while he should be able to go about), to visit the sick, aged, and infirm, and look after the flock generally, praying with them, and doing them all the spiritual good in his power. For his comfortable support during the remainder of his life, such and such reliable gentlemen would pledge themselves, I would pledge myself, and the stewards of the Church would see that he lacked nothing.

"'Now, my old friend,' said I, 'we want you to sell your horse and cart immediately and use the money as you think proper. You shall want for nothing. And let it be your only business to help all the souls you can to heaven.'

"He received this proposition with profound sensibility and many thanks, but could be induced only to add that he would think of it. It was just before my journey to attend the General Conference, and on my return to Charleston I had scarcely reached my door before I saw Castile Selby, just as aforetime, seated on his throne, the old cart.

"'Ah, master,' said he, 'the very thing you would do for me to make me useful would hinder more than it would help me. It would make some envious, some would call me parson and say the white people had spoiled me; and nobody would take me to be the same Castile I have always been. There is nothing better for me than this same old cart.'"

Thus far Bishop Capers wrote. Castile died in 1849. Of his death the *Southern Christian Advocate* says:

About the time Mr. Polk, ex-President of the United States, breathed his last, there was to be seen in this city [Charleston] a venerable patriarch among the colored members of the M. E. Church, South, lying on his dying bed, extensively known as "Father Castile." He has been for fifty-seven years an upright, consistent, and useful professor of religion. . . . He has been honored with the respect and confidence of every minister of the South Carolina Conference who has been stationed in this city during the lapse of half a century. Bishop Capers, in particular, has ever felt for him a warm personal attachment, well deserved on the part of the patriarchal class leader.

We remember a scene we witnessed some twenty-eight years ago, in what was supposed to be at the time the dying chamber of Dr. Capers. Given over by his accomplished physician, Dr. S. H. Dickson, surrounded by his weeping family and nurses, the Doctor had spoken, as he thought, his farewell words. At that moment Father Castile entered the room. "I am glad to see you," said his sick friend, "you find me near my end; but kneel down and turn your face to the wall and pray for me." Many a tear fell during the solemn moments of that prayer. By what the philosopher would call a singular coincidence, but what the Christian resolves by the first principles of his religion into an *answer to prayer*, the Doctor passed the crisis while the good old man was on his knees. In a few moments he said: "I feel better." . . . .

Father Castile died in perfect peace after little or no illness, and with no apparent suffering, in the eighty-eighth year of his age. A funeral sermon was preached in Bethel Church over his remains by the presiding elder of the Charleston District, and all that was mortal of the good man was followed to the grave by a large assemblage of his friends.

In the city of Charleston there were many faithful negro men and women whose lives were conformed to the principles of the doctrine of Christ. Prominent among these was one who was popularly called "Maum Rachel." Of her and other noteworthy members of the Church, Dr. A. M. Chreitzberg furnishes the following notes:

Her name was Rachel Wells. She lived in Anson Street, Charleston, and was a member of Trinity Church. She happened to a severe accident while coming down the steps of the gallery, which laid her upon a bed of agonizing pain at the very time that a number of the ablest of Methodist ministers were in the city and a great revival was in progress at the Church. Bishop Capers, knowing what a great deprivation it must be to her to stay away from the exercises, called to see her. He said to her: "Sorry I am, very sorry for you, Maum Rachel; and the more, that this sad accident should have happened just now, when we have such good meetings every night at Trinity. You would be so happy if you could be with us there."

"I hear ob de meetin', sir," she answered, "an' t'ank God fur 'em fur you' sake; but as fur me, I hab no need o' dem. I couldn' do widout Trin'ty Chu'ch 'fo'e, an' while I well I neber off my seat dar, day nur night, but since dis t'ing come 'pon me you call bad acciden', I hab no need ob Trin'ty Chu'ch. All he do fur me wid de meetin' befo'-time, he do fur me now widout de meetin', an' mo'e too, bless de Lo'd!"

"Could a synod of divines," says Bishop Wightman, in speaking of these words, "have set forth more strikingly the true doctrine in regard to the 'means of grace' than Maum Rachel did? They were necessary for her in ordinary circumstances, but providentially precluded from them, the blessed Jesus had a shorter way to her than by Trinity Church. What a depth of divine philosophy is unfolded in the thought, so clearly conceived, though uttered in broken English!"

Maum Rachel was, at the time of her death, the oldest member of the Charleston Methodist Church, white or colored. She was the first colored member who joined the Society, at the time when the first regular meetings were held at the house of her master, Mr. Edgar Wells. She saw the foundation laid of the First Cumberland Street Church, a year or two after the close of the Revolution. She outlived two generations of Methodists—"a beautiful example of the power of religion to make a servant upright and happy."

Another of these saintly old colored women who adorned Charleston Methodism was "Maum Mary Ann Berry." Dr. Capers gives us the picture of her, clear, beautiful, strong, a picture before which the best of us feel like uncovering: "I never knew a female, of any circumstance in life, who better deserved the appellation of deaconess than Mary Ann Berry; one who seemed to live only to be useful, and who, to the utmost of her ability, and beyond her ability, served the Church and poor. And I might say, too, that what she did was always exceedingly well done, directed by an intelligent mind as well as a sanctified spirit; so that, humble as was her position in common society, she was really a mother in Israel. Her meekness, her humility, and a peculiar gentleness and softness of spirit, which distinguished her at all times, might have done honor to a Christian lady of any rank."

And here again he gives us the picture—pen painted, it is true, yet how vivid and touching—of Maum Nanny Coates. What an example to inspire zeal in welldoing! "Did I mention Maum Nanny Coates? Bless old Maum Nanny! If I had been a painter going to represent meekness personified, I should have gotten her to sit for the picture. It was shortly after I had been appointed Secretary for the Missions, that, being in Charleston at the house of my brother, as we were sitting together in the parlor one evening, Maum Nanny entered. I wish I could show her to you just as she presented herself, in her long-eared white cap kerchief and apron of the olden time, with her eyes on the floor, her arms slightly folded before her, stepping softly toward me. She held between her finger and thumb a dollar bill, and, courtesying as she approached, she extended her hand with the money. 'Will you please, sir,' she said in subdued accents and a happy countenance, 'take this little mite for the blessed missionaries?' I took it, pronounced that it was a dollar, and said: 'Maum Nanny, can you afford to give as much as this?' 'O yes, sir,' she replied, lifting her eyes, which until then had been upon the floor, 'it is only a trifle, sir. I could afford to give a great deal more, if I—I had it.'"

These three women were all freed by their owners for their faithfulness and virtue.

And while Dr. Capers was writing of his "friends" in Charleston, Bishop Andrew, too, was paying many feeling and beautiful tributes to his friends in Wilmington. Writing from that same Conference—the North Carolina at Washington—where he had made so noble an effort in their behalf, he says: "And then among the blacks there was our faithful old chorister, Roger Hazle, who used to set the tunes for us. I have his image before me now as I used to see him when I gave out the hymn, rise in his place in the gallery, hymn book in hand, and set the tunes for the whole congregation. And I remember, too, how I used to stand in the pulpit, weary and hoarse at the close of my third sermon, and when I gave out the last hymn how the colored people used to sing with so much sweetness and power that it seemed almost enough to raise the shingles from the roof. And who that knew Wilmington in days of yore would fail to remember in this connection old Will Campbell, venerable for his years and greatly beloved for his consistent piety? His record was on high—he was an honest, guileless, simple-hearted Christian, a man of sterling integrity and unblemished reputation. And with these were associated many others of great worth who filled up their humble stations in society and passed quietly away from earth to heaven."

One of the most pious and devoted of these colored members at Wilmington was one Bishop Andrew does not mention in this letter, but who is often referred to by Bishop Capers and by Mrs. Margaret M. Martin, of Columbia, S. C., in her religious writings. This was Uncle Harry Merrick, a figure as prominent in the Church circles of that place sixty years ago as any in it, black or white. He occupied a front seat in the gallery, and that seat, from the time of the erection of the church building almost to the day of the old saint's death, was scarcely ever vacant at any of the meetings, day or night. He could pray and sing. O how he *could* sing! "I've come to see Jesus," and "Band of Music," could ever any one sing them as Harry Merrick did? Mrs. Martin speaks of hearing him after he had grown very old and his voice was quavering. She says: "We have a delightful choir in Wilmington, one of the finest I know anywhere, and generally it swells in its full tide of song even above the music of the congregation; but at that time you could catch it but at intervals of one single note of silvery sweetness. Much as I love fine music, I confess there and then I did not regret that old Harry Merrick's dear old cracked voice from the gallery was heard above all the rest. Nobody listened to it but felt there were notes there that had gone right up to make up the heavenly diapason. To the Christian's heart, at least, it was 'harmony, it was heavenly harmony.'"

Harry Merrick was a power in prayer as well as in song. Often, while the white mourners were at the altar, he was called on to pray for them; and there, kneeling at his place in the gallery, he sent forth mighty supplications to the throne of grace. He has long since gone to mingle his buglelike notes with the choir celestial.

Dr. John W. Hanner, a veteran of the Tennessee Conference, still lingering along the shores of time, furnishes us with some pleasant notes of "Aunt Joycie" and others among the African contingent in Tennessee and Alabama. The manner of preaching, peculiar to some of these sable orators, is thus described by Dr. Hanner:

In 1843 the Tennessee Conference included Huntsville, Ala. Here we had a large colored membership to whom we regularly preached and administered all the rites of the Church. Some of these negroes were very intelligent, and many of them far advanced in the spiritual life. They had a chapel built specially for their use, and it was always crowded on the Sunday afternoons of the regular appointment.

On one of these occasions, going to preach to them, I found the house packed and running over. As I advanced toward the pulpit I saw a colored preacher sitting in it. He met me and asked permission to preach that time. I readily consented, for I thought it advisable for them to hear one of their own race occasionally.

After singing and prayer the preacher began:

"I don't know why de Lord called dis unwordy sarvant to preach dis fun'ral; but I's got it to do. My tex' is in de Riverlation, 'Behol', I stan' at de doo' an' knock; if any man open de doo', I will come in an' sup wid him, an' he wid me.'

"I'm gwine to preach de fun'ral o' Tom Cook. You all knowed Tom Cook, how weeked he war. He played cards, an' de fiddle, an' danced, an' tole lies, an' cheated, an' took t'ings w'at didn't b'long to him, an' drunk whisky. Poo' Tom! he's dead an' gone to hell; an' his wife's dar too! I'm gwine ter preach boff dere fun'rals to wonct." And preach them he did, with a startling candor few would have had the courage to imitate.

"I'll tell you how de Lord knocks," he concluded. "One day I was gwine to mill, an' a voice spoke to me from de sky: 'George! George Purdom!' I looked up to see whar de voice come from, an' dar I seed twelve angels standin' roun' de sun. Ebery one had a watch in his han', an' ebery one say: 'Twelve o'clock.' Den de divine power come down an' knock me cross de full lengt' o' de big road; an' I saw all my sins go down into hell like a gallon pot o' black dye. You sinner man, laughin' at me out dere, I tell you de day's gwine to come when your laughin'll be turned into mournin'.

"In ole Virginny when de rich ladies ride out in de car'age dey take 'long a book fur to read. So de young lady open de book an' a voice spoke to her fum de book: 'Your gole is cankered, your silber is turned to dross, but de lub o' God shall stan' forever!' She shut de book an' begun to cry. She war mighty rich. She says: 'Driber, turn de car'age roun' an' dribe me home.' Her fader come out an' seed her cryin' an' he axed: 'O my daughter, w'at is de matter wid you? If you'll quit dis 'ligion, I'll gib you a bar'l o' gole an' a bar'l o' silber.' An' she said: 'Fader, de book says, "Your gole is cankered, an' your silber is turned to dross; but de lub o' God shall stan' foreber."' An' he begin to cry, too; so dey boff got 'ligion. Dat's de way dey do t'ings in ole Virginny, whar I come from, an' dat's de way dey's got to do it eberywhar dey gits it.

"Now, sinners, you hear me; if you don't repent an' git dis 'ligion, you's gwine to hab a ram-shack-lin time o' it when deff comes fur you."

His utterance of the last paragraph was vehemently fervid, rapid, and loud, emphasizing the right words. The effect was amazing. Like the trees of the forest when moved by the sweeping winds, his congregation swayed to and fro, their heads moving from side to side; then a wild, ringing shout burst from the throats of fully one-half of them. Evidently there were many who had the religion referred to, and didn't need to fear the coming of the pale-horse rider.

This sermon is not given by way of caricature, but as an illustration of the deep and intense fervor that so often swayed many of these exhorting sons of Ham.

Rev. Elisha Carr, for a long time a member of the Tennessse Conference, spent the last years of his life doing little else save preaching to the negroes and catechising their children. Great is the debt owed him by this race. He was untiring in his efforts to bring them to the knowledge that is in Christ Jesus.

In the days of the old time camp meetings, seats were provided for the negroes back of the stand. One night, the sermon preached and mourners called, Brother Carr went to his work around the altar bearing a lighted candle. Seeing a young, spruce-looking negro looking on with apparently little concern, Brother Carr said to him: "Have you got religion?"

"No, sir."

"Are you trying to get it?"

"No, sir."

"Do you wish to try?"

"Not now, sir."

"Then hold this candle while I sing and pray with those who do wish it." And he held it, sweating freely. The place grew too warm for him; next night he was a mourner.

When catechising, Brother Carr placed the little darkies in line and spoke to each one by name. After the usual questions of the catechism, he often put questions not in the book. He was catechising on one of these occasions when he suddenly put the question: "What's your name?"

"Little Ben, sir."

"Who made you?"

"God, sir."

"What did he make you out of?"

"Biscuit, sir."

"What did he make you for?"

"To eat biscuit an' 'lasses an' wait on de white folks."

It is needless to add that Brother Carr soon corrected Little Ben's notions of existence and duty.

Sometimes Brother Carr would ask questions and seem to know things that would startle his dusky audience considerably. It was this apparent knowledge of their various misdoings that caused them to regard him with a kind of superstitious awe, and to declare frequently that he was "kin to God."

Rev. N. A. D. Bryant, formerly of the Tennessee Conference, but in later years a resident of Texas, gives a number of anecdotes and reminiscences of his ministerial labors among the slaves. Although he was a slave holder, there was no prejudice against him on that account, and his course as a missionary to the slaves on large plantations was highly beneficial to the humble parishioners, and to their owners.

"In my rounds as a missionary," says Mr. Bryant, "I met with many negroes who were constantly giving me striking evidences of more than ordinary character and ability. Some of them have since made their mark in the world, noticeably Bishop Lane, of the Colored Methodist Church. More than one of those on my missions afterward made preachers, and by no means mere commonplace ones. One of the best negroes I ever knew was Emanuel Mask. I became acquainted with him in 1855 at his master's house in Fayette County, Tenn., when he was a slave. He was then authorized to preach the gospel among his people. His master, who was a noble man and a Christian, and who had for years evinced the deepest interest in the salvation of the negro race, gave Emanuel a written permit to go around the country and preach to his race. This he did to the great pleasure of the people everywhere, white as well as black, for Emanuel was an earnest and forcible speaker, and even the whites listened to him with profit. I frequently invited Emanuel to my house to preach to my slaves. Some members of my own family were always present on such occasions, and most heartily did they bear testimony to his wonderful ability to arrange and make clear his subject, and to the aptness and fitness with which he quoted passages of scripture.

"Another remarkable negro of my acquaintance was Silas Philips. I did not know him, however, until after the war. He came to La Grange, Tenn., soon after freedom. He had enjoyed both moral and religious advantages in his old home, and was an eloquent illustration of what the gospel could do for his race and of the earnest efforts of those who had sought to shed the light upon his way. When he came to La Grange, he had a modest sum of money, with which he purchased a home, and at once entered upon his course as a moral and useful citizen. His fine, manly conduct soon won the confidence and respect of all. He had been taught to read, and though comparatively illiterate, could, nevertheless, expound the scriptures with great clearness and force. He soon became a prophet among his people.

"Simon Hunt was another one of his race who deserves more than a passing notice. Simon had been born a slave, though he was only a youth during the war. Still he was large enough to remember the earnest catechising he had received from the missionary. Many words, too, of the sermons to which he had listened had taken deep root in his heart. Simon was born within sight of my house, and I knew him from a youth up. He was a model in every way. Soon after freedom came he made the right start on the new road by joining the Church. Shortly thereafter he was licensed to preach. He became a power among his people, for few preachers, white or black, surpassed Simon in native eloquence. Some of his illustrations were truly astonishing. He could sweep an audience as the wind of the forest sweeps the leaves that bestrew its track. He had a fine presence, a remarkably fine head and face, but what was more attractive still, he deported himself with manly dignity, an inbred gentleness of manner that none could help but admire. Wherever Simon is to-day, may the Lord continue to bless him and make him as a second Moses to his people!

"My pen is upon a subject in which it finds something more than a mere pleasure. Cheerfully, heartily does it bear witness to the many fine traits of character, the real nobility of soul that distinguished so many of those who were once in so lowly a position among us. Tenderly, too, does it linger over that old time affectionate relation that existed between so many masters and their slaves. I do not speak at random, but from experience; not for the sentiment of the thing, but on the part of truth. By inheritance and purchase I owned quite a number of slaves. When told, in 1863, that they were free, only ten or fifteen of my servants left, the rest remaining and working as usual. Considering the state of affairs then existing, the excitement of the war, the commotion of social affairs, it was a wonder that many more did not go. The conduct of those who remained only stands out more forcibly. When the war came to an end and freedom was universally established, these negroes who had remained faithfully by me through every trial, came to me and said: 'We do not want to leave you. You have been a good master to us, and we desire still to serve you. Furnish us with land and mules, and we will work for you and for ourselves.' This was done, and well and faithfully for twenty-two years did they carry out every requirement of the new relation. It was only broken by my removal to Texas."

From the pen of Rev. A. P. McFerrin, brother of Dr. John B. McFerrin, we have the following anecdotes of the family altar and the religious associations of the slaves in Christian families. No one acquainted with the Southern people forty years ago can fail to indorse the sentiments of one whose testimony is valuable from whatever point of view it may be considered:

> Another means of grace outside the preaching in the white churches and the evangelical work on the plantations was in the family prayer meeting. There were many religious masters who, night and morning, regularly assembled their fami-

lies and also summoned their slaves to prayer. And this brings to mind an interesting incident of my boyhood days.

Old Uncle Dick was a native African, brought to this country when a boy. He was a true and earnest Christian. My father, Rev. James McFerrin, who was a member of the Tennessee Conference, had, on a certain morning when out quite early, occasion to speak some special words to Uncle Dick concerning some matter that had not gone well. It was not a serious matter, anyway, but Uncle Dick was very sensitive, and had become highly wrought up in his feelings. Just at that moment the summons went forth: "Come in to prayer." Father read the scripture lesson, followed by a hymn, which was always in the order of family service, and then prayed a fervent prayer. Uncle Dick was so deeply moved that when the prayer ended he arose weeping and almost shouting. Forgotten now were his wounded feelings of the moment before, and in his deep joy he almost embraced my father. The incident reached every heart and brought the utmost peace between the two principals of the morning scene.

The sounding of the horn, morning and evening, was the signal for all to come to prayer, big and little. Such a family life as this was sure to bring about the most beneficial results, especially where both master and mistress took a direct interest in the welfare of every soul, which was often the case.

Mentioning the morning and evening horn blowing calls up another touching incident of an old slave. At the death of my father, when the estate was divided, an aged negro by the name of Charles fell to the share of my brother, the late William M. McFerrin, of the Memphis Conference. In time, through age, Charles became superannuated, spending the evening of life in and around his quiet cabin. One afternoon, about the going down of the sun of a serene and beautiful day, Uncle Charles stood near his gate, leaning against the fence, a few feet from his cabin door, earnestly gazing upon the heavens. Suddenly, on looking up, he cried out: "Hear! hear! de ho'n is blowin'!" He then turned slowly toward his cabin, lay down on his bed, and in a few moments gently breathed away his life. Had the "horn" called him from earthly prayers to eternal praises in his heavenly Master's kingdom?

There can be no just conception of Southern slavery with its many modifying and qualifying influences, without its qualifying adjective of *domestication*, making it what it really was, *domestic slavery*, with rare exceptions.

A native of the South, with a lifetime lengthened out to the allotment of man's earthly pilgrimage, and with fair opportunity of forming a judgment from many standpoints, the writer is free to express the opinion that the people of the South, taken as a whole, white and black, were, prior to the war, the best to do people morally, socially, and religiously that the world has ever beheld. No people of equal extent of population and like ample surroundings ever lived so free from want, starvation, inhuman oppression, and those grosser iniquities that degrade and brutalize humanity.

Next to wife and children the slave owner's sympathy and concern were for the welfare of the colored members of his family. Never has the ownership of slaves, as held by Southern masters, been so sadly misunderstood as by those unfamiliar with its true import. No intelligent owner of slaves, as held in the South, ever conceived the idea of being possessed of an absolute property in the life and soul of his slave, as represented by some whose opinions were formed simply on the vague representations of such as really never had a true conception of the reality of the situation. The owner held proprietorship in the product of his slaves' labor, and was accountable to the laws of the land and public sentiment for the perpetration of wrongs inconsistent therewith. Duty and self-interest alike created a felt concern in behalf of the slaves' welfare, while this limited ownership was the surest protection of the negro, since the value of the anticipated services depended on the health and prolongation of life. Hence healthful and comfortable conditions were specially looked after, and prompt and careful nursing afforded in cases of sickness. Multiplied thousands of negro children were brought safely through the critical periods of childhood and youth by the attentive carefulness and tender nursing of the mistress of the household.

Much of the special work of the missionaries of our Church was in behalf of the slaves of the large plantations, the pastors of the regular work being used to subserve the purpose of looking after the religious welfare of the domestic portion remaining in their midst. But in this respect, as well-nigh all others, the civil war made an end of the old *régime;* and no thoughtful Southerner would, if in his power, restore the old order of things. That has passed away, and with trust and hopefulness we look forward to the new; for the appearing of those better things to come, which in due time will be manifested under the guiding hand of Him who makes all things to work together for good to his trusting ones. Already the signs of the horizon point to the coming of a betterment that far surpasses anything that could have been imagined by the most fervent enthusiast. The good seed sown in the past, amid the most discouraging surroundings, will ultimately show their fruits. Sown in prayers and watered with tears, as they were, such sowing cannot fail of its harvest, rich and sure. The old system of domestic slavery, so harshly criticized and so widely blamed by the outside world, has this one indisputable sequence, a fact evident to God, to man, and to angels—namely, that the slaves of the South, thus developed in our midst, are the best and most hopeful specimens of the African race which the world has ever beheld, and that whatever elevation the African world may ever attain unto will be brought about by the instrumentality of these same once enslaved but now enfranchised people, developed and still dwelling in our midst. The question naturally presents itself to every thoughtful mind: May not these Christianized freedmen of the South yet prove the indispensable factor in working out the redemption of the great continent whence sprang their forefathers? "By their fruits ye shall know them," saith Jesus, and behold! here are the fruits.

Rev. S. M. Cherry, of the Tennessee Conference, contributes some interesting notes relating to the missionary labors of Elisha Carr, the venerable man whom the negroes were accustomed to say was "kin to God."

"Sometimes Brother Carr catechized a whole congregation of negroes," says Mr. Cherry. "On one of these occasions, after preaching, he propounded this question: 'What was the name of the first bird that Noah sent out of the ark?'

"A gawky boy on the front bench answered: 'I b'lieves hit war a jay bird, sir.'

"'Wrong,' said Brother Carr; 'again.'

"'I thinks hit *mout* er bin a blue heron,' ventured another.

"'I see,' said Brother Carr, frowning his disapprobation, 'that you are guessing. Now I want some one to answer who knows what he is talking about.'

"Just at this point an old negro in the back of the church whispered to his neighbor: 'I thinks I knows.'

"Brother Carr, overhearing him, demanded an answer; whereupon the old darky, straightening himself with a great deal of consequence, boldly asserted: 'Dat bird war a turkey buzzard, sir.'

"This so disgusted Brother Carr that he brought the examination to a close at once."

Dr. T. L. Boswell, a man of commanding influence in the Memphis Conference, furnishes a sketch from which we select two paragraphs, regretting that the limits assigned to this work will not allow a publication in full.

"I have witnessed many affecting scenes," says Dr. Boswell, "between Christian masters and their slaves in the old slavery times in the South. One case that I specially recall was that of Ned Davis and his body servant, Dennis. Dennis was a true Christian, pious and faithful. He had been the close attendant of his master in the latter's wild days in North Carolina and other places, and had had to follow him into many places where a Christian man would not *voluntarily* go. But Dennis was a bondman and must obey, though he maintained his Christian integrity at all times. When I knew master and servant together at La Grange, Tenn., in 1840, Ned had become religious, and I often saw the two happy together, shaking hands and rejoicing on their way to the better land. Ned often spoke of the sinful ways into which he had compelled his servant to go, while tears of regret filled his eyes. It was indeed a goodly sight to see them together praising God.

"The good done among the slaves by the gospel was manifest in many ways and on many occasions, but in none more conspicuously and beneficially than during the war. Here the old men, women, and children were left without any human protection in their midst and at their mercy. And in this exposed and helpless condition I do not remember a single instance in all this country wherein they laid hands on them to hurt them. And when the Yankee armies came, carrying away many of the less civilly disposed of the blacks with them, the better class remained to work for the support and protection of old master and mistress and the children till freedom came."

Rev. T. J. B. Neely relates the following affecting incident:

Gambro was an old slave owned by my father. He was one of the noblest of his race. In his hands were placed great responsibilities, and in no case was he ever unfaithful. Religion was his theme, the enthusing current of his life. At night he sung and prayed in his cabin, and exhorted his fellow-servants to righteousness. All knew Uncle Gambro, and all, wherever he went, honored and respected him. As my father stood beside his dying bed old Gambro said to him: "Master, you have been merciful and good to me and Nancy, and I want to thank you for it before I go. You've preached to us a long time, sir, and we've seen some mighty good times together, but now they say I must die. I feel that I shall soon be gone. I've been talkin' to the Lord a long time about this matter. I have now come right up to the river and the next step—O, my Lord, *where* shall I land? On the other bank? on the *glorious* bank? Yes, thank the Lord! As you prayed last night, sir, he *will* raise me up at the last day, and I will be satisfied when I wake up in his likeness."

The next morning he lay stretched upon the plank cold and stiff in death. The neighbors came in, both white and black, to pay the last tribute to the grand old man they had truly honored. He had fought a good fight; he had kept the faith. My father gave him a Christian burial, and with loving hands we covered him in the clods of the valley. Dear Uncle Gambro! peace to thy ashes, and a blissful immortality when we shall all be raised up at the last day!

Rev. W. A. Parks furnishes the following pleasing account of the religious influence exercised by the white pastors over their colored charges. Mr. Parks was stationed in Athens, Ga., in 1857, serving a large and flourishing "colored charge."

"During the first revival in the Athens Mission," says Mr. Parks, "about one hundred were converted and joined the Church. Among the number was a sprightly lad some twelve years of age, the slave of Prof. Johnson, of Franklin University. Lucius Holsey—for such was the lad's name—was house servant, waiter in the dining room, and errand boy. He was of a bright color, rather small for his age, quick of movement, and with a clear, penetrating eye.

"Thirty years had come and gone since the conversion of that boy when the North Georgia Conference was in session in Augusta. I was appointed to preach on Sunday at 11 o'clock in Trinity Colored Methodist Church. I was greeted by a large audience of the most intelligent of the colored population. Seated in the pulpit was Holsey, then bishop of the C. M. E. Church. He gave me a cordial welcome to the pulpit, for he had been pastor of that church. He was to me a stranger; but I was not a stranger to him, and he greeted me as though he had been a lifelong friend. He closed the services for me. After the prayer he arose and addressed the congregation in about these words:

"'I must be pardoned for detaining you, but I must relate to you a bit of my experience. I was converted at Athens when a boy about twelve years old. There was a great revival in the Church, and many were converted. The gentleman who has just preached to you was the pastor. He preached a sermon on Sunday morning that sent conviction to my heart, and brought me to see that I was a sinner and lost without salvation. I went away from the church with a heart burdened with sin. I found no comfort in the company of my former associates. I could do nothing but pray. I prayed as I waited in the dining room; I prayed as I went to and from the post office; I prayed all the week, and thought of little else but my sins, with a yearning for deliverance I cannot express.

"'On the next Sunday morning my duties were such I could not go to church, but I went at night. I answered the first call to the altar, and there I wrestled with God in prayer. I had gone to the altar to find salvation, and I was not willing to leave it till the burden was rolled from my heart. Finally all others had left the altar, the congregation had been dismissed, and I alone remained, crouched down in front of the altar in an agony too great to describe. All but a few had left the church. Mr. Parks said: 'Brethren, I think this boy will be converted to-night. Let us get around him and pray for him.' They knelt around me, the pastor and my colored friends. Mr. Parks led the prayer, and while he was pleading with God for my salvation the Lord rolled the burden of sin from my heart and heaven's light came shining in. O what a happy boy I was! I have had many ups and downs since then, but in all my sorrows and toils in the ministry the Lord has been with me. I still have that same light and joy that came into my heart as I knelt at the altar of the Athens church.'

"Then turning to me, his forefinger pointing to heaven, the tears coursing down his cheeks, he said to me: 'Brother, when you get to heaven, and the blessed Lord places a crown on your head,

I will be one star in that crown!' Then with a heart too full for utterance, and in a tremulous voice, he dismissed an audience nearly all of whom were suffused in tears."

The Rev. Leonard Rush, of the Georgia Conference, relates an incident that illustrates the liberality and fraternal feeling of these sons of Africa:

"One of the plantations I served on the Chattahoochee Mission belonged to ex-Governor Hamilton, of South Carolina. When I took charge of this place, I found two leaders, a Methodist and a Baptist. The Methodist leader was a low man in stature and the Baptist a tall one. The name of each was Billy. They called one 'Short Billy' and the other 'Long Billy.' There were four hundred slaves on this plantation. Long Billy and his flock held a certificate of membership from the Baptist Church in Savannah. When I had been preaching at this place two years, 'Long Billy' came to see me one day and said: 'Master Rush, I have heard you preach two years, and you preach just what I believe, and I and all my members will join your Church, provided you will immerse us when we wish to be baptized.' I promised to do so, and he and all his charge—I think about thirty in all—became members of our Church.

"They had some customs on this plantation that I very much admired. When a child was born, as soon as the mother was able to carry the child to the place of worship, they had a day of thanksgiving to God for the preservation of the mother, and that another human being had been brought into existence. They then presented the child before the congregation and offered it to God with many prayers for its safe passage through the world, and for its eternal welfare in the world to come. When any one became a seeker of salvation, if it was a woman, they committed her to the care of two or three of their most pious women, who advised her, prayed for her, and led her on until she came through the Spirit. By coming through the Spirit they meant what we call conversion. If the seeker was a man, two or three of the brethren took charge of him in the like manner.

"About the close of my fourth year on this mission we had a wonderful work of revival, and between forty and fifty came through the Spirit. I examined each of them carefully, and I believe they were truly born of the Spirit. The day I appointed to baptize them turned out to be one of the coldest I had ever known. We had to march a mile to the Chattahoochee, where the ordinance was to be administered. On leaving their cabins they formed a procession two deep, the leaders in front, next some of the principal members, then the candidates for baptism. Behind them came the other Church members, with the worldings in the rear. As they started they raised a song, and how they did sing! They sung all the way to the river.

"The day was beautiful, the sky was clear, and the water as clear as the sky. The sun shone with noonday splendor. When we entered the bed of the river, we had to pass over a bed of clean white sand before we got to the edge of the water. Here Short Billy presented his candidates for baptism, and then Long Billy presented his. The latter said: 'Master Rush, here are seventeen that I wish you to immerse, but here are three sickly ones, and it would be unsafe for them to go into the water, so I only want you to sprinkle them.' I went through our baptismal formula, and then arranged all to be baptized by affusion in a line facing the water, leaving room for me to pass between them and the water. They then all knelt down, facing the water, and I dipped the water in my mission-horn and baptized them according to the rites of the Methodist Church.

"Long Billy then waded out into the water to where it was of sufficient depth for immersion, and, standing with his face upstream, offered a very devout prayer. I then, with his assistance, immersed his subjects. When I entered the water, I felt like I was on fire until I lost all feeling. I then had to ride a mile before I could change my clothes. I very narrowly escaped an attack of pneumonia from that day's work."

From the pen of Dr. H. S. Thrall, of Texas, we have these pen-portraits of remarkable negro Methodists in Texas.

"In 1842," says Dr. Thrall, "Austin, Tex.,

was depopulated by Indian raids. The government returned to the city in 1844, and in the fall of that year the writer of this was sent there to reorganize the Methodist Church.

"When I arrived in the city, one of the first acquaintances formed was that of Rowan Hardin, a lawyer, belonging to a celebrated Kentucky family of Methodists. Mr. Hardin informed me that the only religious services held in the city, of which he had heard, were those by a colored preacher named Nace Duval, a slave of the Duval family.

"Nace was an excellent Christian, with considerable preaching ability. He had collected a large class of colored Methodists, and was active in visiting, exhorting, and holding meetings. I found him efficient help in my work among his race. He had considerable influence with the whites, and, with his assistance, we built a small house of worship for the negroes. It was located on the hill where the colored congregation of the M. E. Church now worships in that city.

"After freedom, Brother Nace removed to San Antonio, and organized a Church for the colored people in that city in connection with the African M. E. Church. That congregation now has a resident bishop. Their church is on the west side of the San Pedro Creek in that city. Their patriarch, Nace, died in the faith at a good old age, universally loved and respected.

"In 1848 the writer traveled what was then

known as the Washington Circuit. At Independence he found one of the most able and influential preachers he has ever met. He was universally known as 'Uncle Mark.' The planters paid his master for his time, and he traveled extensively, preaching, organizing churches, and doing an excellent work for his people. About that time the owner of Uncle Mark removed to the West, and the planters, unwilling to lose his labors and influence among their slaves, raised the money among themselves, and purchased him; but as our laws did not allow of emancipation, he was deeded to three Methodist preachers in trust for the Methodist Episcopal Church, South.

"In 1853 the Texas Conference elected Uncle Mark to deacon's orders as a local preacher, and Bishop Paine ordained him at the Conference at Bastrop. After the war he united with the A. M. E. Church, and lived to a good old age, loved and respected by white and black.

"I once heard Uncle Mark illustrate the conduct of unstable Christians. 'You,' said he, 'are in and out, joining the Church and backsliding. Bless your souls, the Lord don't count you in the crop! You belong to the "Drop Shot Gang!"'" (a gang composed of feeble women and children, not counted as hands in the crop).

"On another occasion he was preaching against pride. He said: 'You think a poor negro has nothing to be proud of; but on Sunday afternoon give one of these boys a red bandanna handkerchief and white cotton gloves, and he's as proud as Lucifer.'

"There was a singular depth and pathos in the good man's voice, and he had a wonderful facility in illustrations. At that early period there was less prejudice against colored preachers than now appears in some places. Uncle Mark often attended our camp meetings, and certain hours at the preaching-stand were given to the negroes. When he arose in the pulpit to address his fellow-slaves, numbers of the whites would gather near and listen with profound attention to the old man's eloquent appeals.

"In 1850 and 1851 I was stationed at Galveston. We then had but one church building, and on Sunday afternoon Ryland Chapel, as our church was named, was occupied by the colored people, the pastor conducting the services, which usually consisted of preaching, catechising, etc. I found here an excellent colored society, among them some truly gifted speakers. Their names have escaped me, but the record is on high. One of them was a barber who hired his own time and who kept one of the most fashionable shops in the city. He managed to have a good deal of leisure, and was a great help in doing pastoral work among the negroes.

"We soon found it necessary to have a separate place of worship, and with the help of the white congregation, and such assistance as the negroes could give, we secured a lot on Broadway and built a small church. Some of the happiest meetings I had during my Galveston pastorate was with the colored brethren in the Broadway Church. After the war that congregation and property went into the possession of the African M. E. Church. There is now a commodious building on that Broadway lot, belonging to the A. M. E. Church."

From the pen of Rev. Whiteford Smith, D.D., of the South Carolina Conference, we have the following account of a famous character among the colored people in South Carolina:

"I first knew Sancho Cooper while I was in college at Columbia, S. C.—1826 to 1830. He was then the trusted servant of Dr. Thomas Cooper, the noted skeptic, President of the college.

"As our first recitation in the morning was held at sunrise, the students were in the habit of employing some of the servants who resided in the campus, or its immediate vicinity, to bring them water and make fires at or about daylight. Sancho Cooper was one of these, as it did not interfere with his duties at home. Of his early life the tradition, as I have heard it, was that his former owner had had no objection to him except on the score of his religion. He was bitterly opposed to his holding meetings and praying with the negroes on the plantation; and inasmuch as Sancho could not be persuaded to give up his conscientious convictions of duty in this respect, he was threatened and afterward cruelly punished to make him stop praying, and finally sold for no other fault but this.

"I have heard that when Dr. Cooper purchased Sancho he told him he had no objection to his praying, so that he faithfully discharged his duties to him. I have heard Dr. Cooper speak in terms of warm approval of Sancho's character, and express a wish that all the negroes were like him. As far as I ever heard, he had the confidence and respect of the Doctor's family and the community at large. It is related that on one occasion an aged negro woman lay dying in the kitchen. The family was greatly attached to her and had gathered about her bed, smitten with deep emotion. While Sancho was praying with and for her she became very happy, shouting the praises of God, whereupon Sancho, turning to them, called upon them to witness how happy were the effects of religion on an old negro.

"Sancho was class leader among the colored members of our Church in Columbia for many years, and held in high respect by his pastors and by the white membership of the Church generally. His honesty and truthfulness I never heard questioned. At one time he was at the head of a society, composed of the colored members of the Church, who had banded together for the purpose of mutual improvement, and also for charitable purposes. They met once a week and regularly contributed to a fund called "the poor fund," the surplus of which went to the sick and aged.

"In 1832 I entered upon the work of the ministry. In 1841–42 I was stationed in Columbia.

Dr. Cooper was then dead. I found Sancho still one of the faithful leaders among the colored people. Gaining his confidence, he spoke to me freely of his master's death. One day during the Doctor's last illness he called Sancho into his room and directed him to shut and lock the door. He then pointed to a large quarto Bible upon a shelf and bade him take it down. Sancho did so, when the Doctor told him to keep it for his sake. He then spoke to Sancho very feelingly of the religion that faithful old servant had so long professed—told him it was right and to hold on to it, that he had known what it was himself when he was young, but that the people in public life and high positions, with whom he had been called to associate, had been the means of leading him away from it. Sancho went on to say that Dr. Cooper had told him that he wished him to kneel down and pray for him. To this Sancho objected, on the ground of his unlettered ignorance and incapacity to pray for so learned a man, saying, ' I am not fit, master, to pray for so great a man as you,' and urged him to send for one of the ministers then stationed in the city, who would be far more able to talk and pray with him. But the Doctor told him he was good enough to pray for him, and insisted on it until Sancho complied with his wishes to the best of his ability. Upon Sancho further urging him, he asked what minister would come to see him. Sancho told him that he knew Rev. William M. Kennedy would come. He said the Doctor finally consented, but objections were interposed, and thus Mr. Kennedy was never sent for. Thus we have evidence that the hard and unbelieving heart of this noted skeptic was indeed melted at the last, and there is no doubt that the consistent life of this faithful old negro had much to do with it, else why did his master so cling to him when the dark waves of death's river were beating about his feet?

"Sancho brought the Bible his master had given him to the parsonage to show to me, and left it in my possession some days. He treasured it highly and had determined that at his death it should be given to the library of Wofford College. But in the destruction of Columbia during the late war it could never be found, and is supposed to have been consumed in the conflagration of that city. This Bible was said to have belonged to Dr. Cooper's father, who was a minister of the gospel and a great friend of John Wesley. I heard Dr. Cooper say that he had known Mr. Wesley very well and often been dandled on his knee when he stopped over at his father's house on his travels.

"As an instance of Dr. Cooper's kind consideration of Sancho's religious feelings and devotion to duty, I have heard it said that on one occasion, when the Doctor had company on the evening of Sancho's class meeting, finding that Sancho remained to attend on the house, he reminded him that this was the evening for his meeting, when Sancho replied that the Doctor had company.

The Doctor answered him, 'No, no!' and insisted on his not allowing that to detain him from his meeting, and bade him go.

"Sancho lived to a ripe old age, well provided for by his master, who had left him an annuity in his will."

CHAPTER XVII.

Memorials of Faithful Slaves.

MRS. SUSAN S. McPHERSON, of Fayetteville, Ala., records some reminiscences of a Southern plantation.

"I used regularly to read the Bible," says Mrs. McPherson, "to all such as came to hear. I had stated seasons set apart for this. After reading the texts I would explain them as well as I could, and then give a little talk touching religion carried into the daily life. Three of our men became preachers, powers for untold good among their people. All three of these men could read. They had been taught on the plantation. One could consult Dr. Clarke's 'Commentary' on any subject he desired. He could write also. When set free, he supported himself by teaching school. I also encouraged my children to teach the young negroes how to spell and read. Sometimes we had regular schools on the place, at which the young instructors did something else besides merely *play* at teaching.

"We had many trusted family servants, who were treated like anything else but servants, and who, in turn, were devoted to us. I must tell of one of these. Her name was Amanda. She had been born in our home and raised up there. We never thought of Amanda as a servant, much less as a slave. Hers was one of the most beautiful characters I have ever known, black or white. If ever she exhibited even the least inclination to bad temper, I never knew it. In her disposition she was most gentle and docile, with plenty of spirit, yet yielding obedience with a sweet and hearty readiness that was sure to win all who saw her. Amanda came as near being a perfect human being as I have ever known. She was positively without fault, save a little shortcoming here and there that could not be said to amount to a fault. She was coal black, not a particle of mixed blood in her, a truly noble specimen of her race. She is still living, a courteous, gentle old woman that it is a real pleasure to know. Around her has grown up a family of children whose polite manners and good behavior is the remark of all. Such negroes as these are a blessing to any community.

"Among my husband's slaves was one that had been brought direct from Africa. He had been taken from there when fifteen years of age. It took him a long while to learn to talk so that we could understand him. When he heard of the good world where he might meet his friends, old Jack was one of the happiest negroes on the earth. After he was converted his cup of joy seemed running over. His religion shone in his face and spoke in every tone of his voice. Daily he praised God for having sent him to America, where he had learned of things so precious to him. When old Jack got happy, he would hug his master and bless God for having placed them together. Jack had unusual intelligence, was quick to understand, and as quick at retort. Once, just after he had been publicly shouting and proclaiming how precious he had found Jesus to his soul, a young man looking on said to him: 'Jack, don't be so certain about having Jesus with you. You only *hope* you have him, I guess.'

"'Mr. Thomson, you *hopes* you have your hat on your head?'

"'Hope, Jack? why I *know* I have it on.'

"'But you can't *see* it: it's on the back of your head.'

"'But I can *feel* it,' returned Mr. Thomson, a little out of patience with Jack's questioning.

"'Yes, that's jus' so. You *feels* it. Well, Mr. Thomson, that's jus' de way wid Jack. I *knows* I's got my Jesus in my heart. I can't see him, but I *feels* him. O *how* I feels him! Bress de Lord! bress de Lord!' And Jack went to shouting again.

"In 1850 Jack expressed a desire to go to Africa and preach to his people there. That he might have the wish of his heart, my husband set him free. He also began the preparations to send him over; but when the time came, Jack's heart failed him. He couldn't leave his family. Of course we could not think of sending his family with him, for Jack was quite a patriarch, having a wife and twenty children. All his children who grew up made good and useful men and women. Several of them are living now in this place. They stand well in the community. His grandchildren and great-grandchildren still serve my family. They do all my house work and attend to other calls. The tie that exists between us is strong. Only death can sever it.

"As to Jack, he died in great peace, still shouting forth the praises of his Jesus. His master had him buried in the family burial ground. There he sleeps beside the generations of those he loved and served so well. The attachment of these old family servants to the old plantation home was touching. It was always hard for them to leave it; and when fortune or chance drifted them back again, they were the most overjoyed of creatures.

"Some time after freedom one of our old servunts who was at a distance was attacked with a lingering sickness. She constantly begged to be carried back to the old home, pathetically protesting that she could not die away from it. At length her desire was granted. Her happiness was touching to see. The last words on her lips were: 'I have a home in glory.'"

We could fill many pages with the records of faithful servants who preserved after their emancipation their affection for their former masters and mistresses, proving the reality of their attachment by testimony that cannot be doubted. Within the knowledge of the editor of this volume there are more than a score of instances in which emancipated slaves, or "freedmen" and "freedwomen," as they are called, have labored for years as hired servants, taking their monthly wages to eke out the small income of their former owners. Denying themselves of all the luxuries and many of the conveniences of life, these faithful negroes have ministered to those who were in other days their masters and mistresses, recognizing the debt of gratitude that was due to those who were, under Providence, their benefactors in the days of slavery.

Many instances similar to the one recorded by Col. J. J. Stockwell, of California, might be inserted. This one is of a peculiar character, and we give it in full:

In the year 1873, owing to the prevalence of yellow fever, we fled from Shreveport, La. Every one had lost his head on account of the dire scourge. Friends were deserting friends, and even among the members of the same family cases of cold-hearted desertion were known to have occurred. Against so unprepossessing a background the example of faithfulness I am about to relate stands forth the more luminous.

In our flight we came near to the house of a former slave of my father, Mary Ann by name, who was then, with other hired hands, working on a farm in the vicinity. She had lived with us on the old home plantation; had been kindly treated and brought up in the light and knowledge of the gospel. In return her heart was filled with gratitude and affection. Few white people would have proven it with the heroism she did.

It soon became known all through the neighborhood that we had been exposed to the fever. In consequence we were shunned as though the dread plague had broken out among us. No white person would come near us, not within a hundred yards of our dwelling place. But this faithful old woman, this former servant, came regularly to administer to our wants, and this, too, in the face of the strongest opposition. She came daily to bring us milk, vegetables, and other necessities. But for her and the supplies with which she furnished us, we must have suffered sorely.

When the man for whom she was working heard of her coming to us, he harshly forbade her to do so again, threatening to discharge her if she persisted. But Mary Ann's faithfulness was far above any worldly consideration. She continued her visits to us, but now chiefly at night, bringing her small tokens of care and affection.

But this was not the only instance of Mary Ann's faithfulness. Several years before this, during my father's illness, she left her home and came to nurse him, remaining with him to his death. I have known Mary Ann on several occasions to walk twenty miles to visit us, and to bring us such little presents as she could afford. Through the varying changes of life her heart still clung faithfully about those who had been connected with her and who had been good to her in the old plantation home.

The following article, from the pen of Mrs. Mary Winans Wall, of Louisiana, makes worthy mention of a nobleman of nature, whose name will be perpetuated as long as goodness and generosity are esteemed among men. As this record embodies the subject of this chapter as well as the purpose of this book, we give it in full:

I speak from experience when I say that Southerners—many of them—were warmly zealous in their endeavors to promote religious instruction among their slaves.

It was always a matter that lay near the hearts of Methodist preachers. Being a preacher's daughter, and wife, I can speak from knowledge. In my childhood days negro servants were considered as part of the family, and treated very much as the children were, being cared for and directed in their duties. In families where I was intimate the servants were regularly called in to prayers. In my own family, during the absence of my father, my mother would read a chapter, we would all sing a hymn, and then often she would ask "Uncle Winter" to lead us in prayer.

Judge McGhee, who owned hundreds of slaves, was very careful to have them regularly preached to. His son's (Capt. George McGhee's) earliest recollection is of sitting in his nurse's lap and hearing preaching to the slaves in a large room on his father's plantation. I will not be positive, but I think that it was a bishop who preached to them that night. I was visiting at the house, and I remember that Conference was sitting at Woodville.

In the Mississippi Conference there were always missionaries appointed to preach to the blacks. As a general thing they were favorably received and encouraged in their labors. Some of the planters, however, did not want their negroes preached to, fearing abolition teaching.

At old Midway Church, in Wilkinson County, Miss., there was a part of the building that was especially set apart for the negroes, and they often outnumbered the whites. They heard just the same gospel, and had the same sacraments that the whites had. This was from 1818 to 1840. Slowly things changed. The abolition excitement, then at white heat, combined with other things, began to tell, and the patriarchal system of domestic slavery reached its decline. Yet the missionaries, despite the cold shoulder often turned upon them, went from plantation to plantation preaching and teaching. Nobler and grander soldiers of the cross were never found. They counted no sacrifice too great in their Godlike efforts to advance this lowly work. Let the Church honor their memory, and keep it green forever.

A gentleman in West Feliciana, La., who was not a Christian, asked for a preacher for his slaves. He said: "I do not wish to see my negroes die without religious training." He voiced the sentiment of many who were nonreligious themselves.

At Clinton, La., where I moved after marriage, there was a large congregation and membership of colored people. They were regularly preached to on Sunday afternoon. They met at 2:30 o'clock, and were a neatly dressed, good-looking, and contented people. Sometimes a white minister preached to them, and again one of their own color. The law was then that a white person must be present during the services I have often sat and listened to their exercises, when my husband was away.

I always tried to teach the colored children, as my mother had done before me. After I came to Clinton I established a Sunday school for them that was always well attended. It was at that time not a very popular thing to do, but I persevered. I could afford to do so, as I had influential friends to defend my course. I had one lady to say to me, "I can't help believing you are an abolitionist," and all because I was simply making an effort for the souls of these black creatures. Even my own sons were against me, or that is against the work. One of them used to say, nearly every Sunday: "Mother, let those negroes alone." But I kept resolutely on my way, despite all dissuasion or opposition. I had blessed help in the work. Sometimes Mrs. Judge McVea and Mrs. Lucy Barton helped me. One sweet young girl helped me for awhile, but her uncle made her quit it.

There are two colored ministers who claim me as their theological instructress. As they are exceptionally intelligent and pious, it is no small credit that they reflect. One of these is Blind William Nailor. He learned every word of Capers's "Smaller Catechism" from me and nearly all the larger one, together with the Creed, many hymns, and a great deal of the Bible. He is now a minister in the A. M. E. Church. He comes to see me at intervals, and gratefully thanks me for the care I bestowed upon him. Often when traveling about the parish I come upon those, now grown men and women, who joyfully recognize me, and speak to me as their former Sunday school teacher. It warms my heart to think that many of these have gone right. But there are some who have not. That worries me, but then I remember that it is the way of the world ever: *all* who are taught, never mind how conscientiously or well, do not do right.

I have seen consistent lives among some colored people who did not join the Church. One of the most faithful people I ever knew was "Uncle Toney." He could not be induced to join the Church, and yet he was in every way to be trusted. His father was an African, surrounded by all the dark superstitions of his race, and I have often wondered if he were not the cause of his son's refusal to come into the Church. But I think Toney tried to live right. When dying he made this answer to those who were endeavoring to get him to acknowledge himself a follower of Christ: "I've always tried to keep up my plantation." Rev. J. C. Burruss, to whom it was repeated, said that was as good a confession of faith as we need wish—for Toney.

Some of these old time slaves were a pleasure to all and a blessing to their owners. Judge McGhee owned a man named Charles. He had manners as courtly as Henry Clay—my model of manners. He had a nice white frame cottage, rode a horse, and enjoyed the confidence and favor of the white people, yet he was just as deferential as the humblest field hand. He was worthy both of love and esteem. Always on his return from New Orleans or the North, Judge McGhee brought a quantity of supplies not only for his family, but for his servants. Once, as they were spread out before him, he said to Charles: "Charles, what do you want of those things?" "Well, master," returned Charles, "I would like some of that furniture checks." I have forgotten whether he said he wanted the checks for a spread, or some bed curtains, but think it was for curtains. If Charles had said, "Master, I would *love* to have a silver mug, or a carpet," I do not doubt that Charles's wish would have been gratified, so highly did his master esteem him. But Charles was the humblest of creatures; he never once thought of such things as being suitable to him. He was, too, one of the most faithful. No one ever seemed to him to equal his own folks.

When Gen. Taylor, after the Mexican war, had a reception in Woodville, Charles was in attendance on his white people. Next day some one said: "Charles, what do you think of the General?" Well," returned Charles, "he was well enough, but I did not see *any* gentleman who came up to *the Judge.*"

I kept faithfully to my class in the Sunday school till freedom came. Twenty years in all had I faithfully devoted to them, and it pained me to see the readiness with which they left me, until only seven were left. William Nailor stood steadfastly by the Church into which I had brought him, until that Church made separate provision for its colored members, when he entered the A. M. E. Church.

Not unfrequently the missionary to the slaves was called upon to follow the example of St. Paul in returning a runaway slave to his master. One instance of this kind Mrs. Lizzie T. Gulick, of Texas, relates. She was the daughter of Rev. John W. Talley, of the Georgia Conference, who was for many years distinguished for his labors among the negroes.

"One morning," says Mrs. Gulick, "our old nurse came in and told brother and me that there was a runaway negro in the kitchen. With fear and trembling we went out to see him. His clothes were in rags and his head and feet were bare. He sent a message by us to father. He was engaged, but returned a message to the negro that he would see him after awhile. In the meantime, he told us to see that the cook gave the poor fellow some hot coffee and a good breakfast.

"I saw tears on the negro's black face, but his eyes brightened as soon as my father appeared. He had heard my father preach, and many times he had been kindly talked to and encouraged to make a brave and faithful man of himself. His story was soon told. When angry with another negro, he had been insolent to his master, and in his passion and fright had fled from the field to the woods, where he had remained hidden ever since, living as best he could. Now he wanted to go home to his master, but he was afraid to go alone. In his loneliness his heart turned to the good, kind preacher. He had no other friend who could go with him to his master, and help in the task of telling how sorry he was for the wrong he had done.

"My father's heart was touched. Soon all was arranged, and in a little while he, with the ragged runaway negro in the buggy with him, was on his way to the master. With a little intercession, the master was soon ready to forgive and forget. The old negro loved my father to the end of his life with a deep and idolatrous affection."

Rev. A. D. Betts, of the North Carolina Conference, furnishes the following:

In the later days of slavery the laws of North Carolina did not allow negroes to hold religious meetings without the presence of some white person, so the pastor appointed a white class leader for the negroes in each church.

At Zion Church, in Brunswick County, we had a large number of negro members. They requested me to appoint Brother W. H. Walker their class leader. At that time he owned a small farm, had a nice family of children, and owned a few slaves. Some years before he had been overseer on the largest plantation in the neighborhood. What a tribute was this! these slaves choosing for their spiritual guide the man who had for years governed them on the farm!

About the middle of the year I preached on Missions at 11 A.M. and took up a collection. It was a fine one. Among other contributions, four persons paid twenty dollars to have their pastor made a life member. There was the usual number of negroes present, and I noticed them paying very close attention.

That afternoon, as was my custom, I preached specially to the negroes at 3 o'clock. At its close I took up a collection for Missions. I was taken greatly by surprise when the negroes began at once, and in fine spirit, to raise twenty dollars to make their class leader a life member of the society. In a few minutes it was done. Brother Walker was deeply moved, as he had need to be. Never have I known a heartier or a more honest compliment paid.

Afterward we rode to Wilmington and had our certificates framed. I do not know which was the prouder, he or I. His hung in an honored place on his parlor wall through life. The incident related needs no further comment.

CHAPTER XVIII.

Testimony of Prominent Freedmen.

THAT the missions to the slaves on the large plantations involved greater risks than other stations of itinerant ministers will be conceded by all persons acquainted with the facts. The rice plantations especially were centers of malarial influence. Large bodies of water kept stagnant upon the level rice fields, permeating the soil to a great depth, filling crevices and subterranean lakelets, just deep enough to be within reach of atmospheric changes, and the recession of the pent-up mass of water leaving these pools and lakelets to welter and boil in the summer sun with myriads of decaying vegetable germs of disease-producing quality—these were the conditions out of which periodical attacks of fever could not fail to come. The blacks, accustomed for generations and for ages to similar conditions in the tropics and on the seacoast of Africa, were hardened against these fevers, but the whites were almost universally attacked whenever they came within range of the deadly miasma. How many soldiers of the cross died as martyrs to these fevers we will never know. The yellow fever has its times of visitation, and thousands fall while the world looks on, pities, sympathizes, or mourns the destruction of human life. Heroes on these occasions are immortalized. They die in the glare of newspapers and telegraphs, throwing a halo of glory upon such deathbeds. But from year to year, one by one, the patient itinerant died by the wayside, and the people of his own state scarcely heard of it. He alone knew the risks in venturing upon the work, and he alone knew the reward of the faithful messenger who died in carrying the Lord's message.

An illustration, which is one of more than a score that might be given, will be found in the following paper from the pen of Rev. John W. Talley, of the Georgia Conference:

In 1836 I was made presiding elder of the Savannah District, and for four years combined the duties of this position with that of superintendent of the slave missions on the Savannah River: Skidaway, Whitemarsh, Burnside, Islands below Savannah, Back River, S. C., Ogeechee, etc. This work was regarded by some as the forlorn hope, by others the field of honor, and the best men of the Conference were willing to be sent there. I knew and loved two promising young men who were appointed to this dangerous work, and there died in young manhood. One, Alfred Beatty, of handsome form and face, of fine intellect, educated at West Point, gave himself up for this work. The first year in it he fell by the country fever and left his widowed mother and a devoted wife. The other was a young brother by the name of Rawls. He was a remarkably saintly youth, and devoted to the work of the Master. The day before his attack he, Rev. James E. Godfrey, and myself went from the wharf at Savannah in a boat to the plantation on Back River and north end of Hutchison Island. On many rice fields the flood gates had been opened to the putrid water that had stagnated under a burning sun. I, Brothers Rawls and Godfrey, in a four-oared boat, rowed, that Sunday morning, over the putrid water from the rice fields to Mr. Smith's plantation, and returned to Savannah Sunday night. That young missionary's work was accomplished; the Master said it was enough. He had nothing more to do but to lay himself down and die. Monday morning revealed the fearful truth. The physician kept his own counsel, and the young, saintly Rawls suffered. All day and all night Brother Godfrey and I, assisted by our good wives, sat by his bed and soothed and ministered to him as best we could. One short week he suffered; black vomit ensued and his death was imminent. We never left him. Young, promising, talented, devotedly pious, another martyr had fallen in his zeal to rescue the negro's soul from the thraldom of sin.

Who will write of the dangers and sufferings and death Southern Methodist preachers endured in preaching the gospel of the Son of God to the negroes of the rice and cotton fields?

Brother Samuel J. Bryan was an angel of mercy to the negroes on many of these plantations. He traveled on the rice dams from plantation to plantation, and at all hours of the day and night to mitigate the sufferings of the negroes prostrated by the cholera. The owners were at a distance, in many instances the overseer dead, and agents and physicians too frightened to risk spending one night in the house occupied by the cholera patients. But Samuel Bryan, with his trust in God, knew no fear. He could be seen stooping over their prostrate forms, ministering to their wants, and helping to load the boats with the sick and frightened negroes whom their masters were sending to high pine lands, where they could be better nursed. Again he was seen disbursing the provisions the affrighted owners had ordered for the relief of their suffering slaves. The owners would not risk their own lives on the infected plantations, though the loss of slaves and property amounted to a loss of thousands. But Samuel Bryan and the other missionaries for the love of God and the hope of saving souls were happy in their work of love to the poorest and most ignorant.

Afterward Rev. Andrew Hammell was superintendent of this mission field, visiting it often in company with the regular missionaries: Brothers John Davis, Quillen, John W. Remshart, and others.

Then Dr. Lovick Pierce, in his time, was visiting and catechising, from plantation to plantation, and preaching at the various places. Can the world or the Church produce such an array of men, heroes as well as servants? There are others, many others, I have not named, but their names are written in heaven.

That the negroes of this generation should cherish the kindliest feelings toward the whites, and especially their old masters, is perfectly natural, and we should not be surprised to find utterance given to this sentiment. Bishop Henry M. Turner, probably the foremost man in the African Methodist Episcopal Church, of which he is now a bishop, was born free; but his wife was a slave, and his first introduction to the people of Athens, Ga., was in 1858, when he was soliciting money to purchase his wife's freedom. Rev. W. A. Parks, of the North Georgia Conference, who gives us this information, could not state whether success attended the efforts of the preacher, but he testifies to the deep interest kindled among the white people by Turner's preaching.

The Rev. Samuel Leard, one of the most useful missionaries in the South Carolina Conference, received a letter from Bishop Turner, of which the following is a copy:

To Rev. Samuel Leard.

Dear Father in God: Language is inadequate to express my pleasure at a reception of the letter from one to whom I owe so much; who when I was a wild, reckless boy, in 1851, at the camp meeting just beyond Abbeville Court House S. C., opened to me my sad condition, in one of your masterly sermons, and as a mighty instrument in God's hands led me to the feet of a pardoning Jesus.

From 1851 up to this moment I have carried in my breast a

grateful heart that God ever gave you to the ministry. I love you while living, will love you when dead, and will love you in heaven.

A short sketch of my life would run as follows:

I was born near Newberry Court House in 1833-34, possibly 1834; went to Abbeville with my parents when a boy, and was bound to Mr. Thomas Jackson (carriage maker) to learn the trade. I joined the Church under Rev. Mr. Crowell, on probation, at Abbeville, in the latter part of 1848, but soon went to cursing and getting drunk whenever I could get whisky, and was the worst boy at Abbeville Court House until you, at Sharon Camp Ground, in 1851, so stunned me by your powerful preaching that I fell upon the ground, rolled in the dirt, foamed at the mouth, and agonized under conviction till Christ relieved me by his atoning blood. I was licensed to exhort shortly afterward by Dr. Boyd, now sleeping in the cemetery at Marion, S. C., and from that time to the present I have been in the Master's service.

I went to St. Louis, Mo., in 1858, was admitted into the itinerant service of the African Methodist Episcopal Church, and went to Baltimore and spent four years at Trinity College, with a view of going to Africa as a missionary. But the war being in full blast disarranged my plans. . . . I have preached and worked for God in every position held, from the day I gave you my hand up to the present. I am a poor sinner living upon the mercies of God, and would be thankful to be remembered by you at a throne of grace. God, however, has honored me far beyond my merits.

God bless you, and may your earthly career terminate amid blessings innumerable!

Your humble servant,   HENRY M. TURNER.

Bishop J. A. Beebe, one of the bishops of the Colored Methodist Episcopal Church, says:

I was born in Fayetteville, N. C., June 25, 1832. My parents were both slaves. I belonged to the family of the Beebes, whence I get my name. I remained a slave until I was about twenty-seven years of age; at which time, my owners giving me the opportunity, I bought my freedom. I was a boot maker by trade, at which trade I made the money to buy my freedom.

I joined the Methodist Episcopal Church, South, in 1849, under the Rev. Mr. Conner, of South Carolina. I was made fully satisfied of my spiritual change under the preaching of Rev. Mr. Samuel Frost, in 1850. In 1851 I was blessed to have the pleasure of listening to a number of sermons on the subject of sanctification by the Rev. A. C. Adams, and by the aid of the Rev. Mr. Bobbit and the Holy Ghost I was led into the blessed light of the indwelling of the Spirit of the Lord, during which time I was moved to preach the Gospel of Christ. But owing to the condition of things at that time in the State of North Carolina, I could not then do so.

In 1865, immediately after the late war, I received license to preach from the African Methodist Episcopal Zion Church. In November of the same year I joined the traveling connection of that Church, and was ordained deacon by Bishop J. J. Clinton, and in 1866 elder by the same bishop. In 1871 I severed my connection with the Zion Church, and joined the Colored Methodist Episcopal Church under Bishop Miles. In 1873 I was elected a delegate to the General Conference of that Church, held at Augusta, Ga., and was there elected a bishop.

While a member of the Methodist Church, South, before the war, I had constant opportunity of hearing the gospel preached. We had regular preaching from the ministers who were appointed from the Conference to labor among the colored people. In addition to this we had the opportunity of hearing the regular preacher to the whites. On every Sunday evening occurred the special preaching to the colored people. Then the church would be crowded with those seeking to hear the promises of the gospel of Jesus. The conversion of hundreds of my people resulted from this preaching. As to myself, I hold in dear remembrance the blessings of those days.

Bishop Lane, of the Colored Methodist Episcopal Church, writes:

I began to seek religion at the age of twelve years. My owners were pious and religious people. My old master held his family prayers night and morning. He was a Methodist of the purest type. He had been a class leader for fifty-eight years in succession I heard preaching from the time I can remember. The missionaries came regularly on their visits, and my master made every opportunity for his people to hear them. He was a good, true man, faithful to God and his obligations, and I pay this tribute to him from my heart.

In the year 1854, on the 11th day of September, I embraced

REV. ISAAC LANE,
Bishop of the Colored M. E. Church.

a hope in Christ. On Monday morning, while in the field at my work, I was made happy in a Saviour's love, and joined the Church soon after. I carried joy and comfort in my soul for several days. I felt and wished that my poor mother could enjoy the gift of saving grace. I at once began to pray for mother and wife. But the prayer offered was to myself when alone. At night I would hold family prayer with my wife and mother. And in those prayers the good Lord blessed my labors and brought them all into the Church. After my old master's plan, I wanted to be alone at noonday; so one day as I was seeking a secret place to pray I was overcome with the feeling that I ought to preach. I strove for months to get rid of it, but all in vain. I went to my old master and made known to him my struggle and the feeling that was then strong upon me. He gave me his sympathy, and directed me to a certain preacher for counsel and aid. But this man did not believe in a negro preaching, and he gave me no aid at all, and so my trouble fell heavier than ever. I next went to an old colored preacher whom the Methodists had helped and were friendly to his exhorting. He was a pure Christian, and he told me that if God had really called me, he surely knew his own business better than man, and for me not to trouble myself, but to trust in God. I did trust him, and the inspiration soon came to send in to the Southern Methodists my petition to preach. I did so at one of their Conferences. They did not refuse me. Indeed, they held out a hand of help and encouragement. Rev. George Harris was the presiding elder, and Rev. A. R. Wilson the preacher in charge. I thought then that he was the best man in the world. My mind has not suffered much change yet, as he is now living in the same town in which I live, and he is the presiding elder of the Jackson District.

I was licensed to exhort in the year 1856, by the Southern Methodist Church at the fourth Quarterly Conference on the Jackson Circuit. I was called on often after that by the white preachers to preach to my people on the Sabbath evenings. The white preachers all respected me and helped me in every way they could. Still it was very embarrassing to me, without any education as I was, to preach before the white preachers. But they were kind to me, and seemed not to notice my mistakes. So I got so after awhile that I could preach before them without much embarrassment, such preaching as it was. But God helped me, and wonderfully blessed my work.

From that date to 1865 the white preachers and I held meetings for my people. We had glorious meetings and many converts, which soon made our country famous for Methodism during the war. But we had stormy times at some places. The old days of the beginnings of the Wesleyan movement in England, in Ireland, and Wales had their reflex in these. Many times my life was in danger, and my white brethren were constantly persecuted for allowing me to preach. The persecutors even went so far as to burn down church after church because I had preached to my people in them. But my white brethren upheld me. And not only the Methodists, but Christians of other denominations. One good old Presbyterian brother said to me after I had preached in his church: "Brother Lane, keep on preaching to your people, and we will keep on building churches until the trumpet blows. Let them burn down. We will build, and you *shall* preach."

That was the spirit in which the Christian whites met me, and that is the spirit in which they would do the same thing to-day did the opportunity offer. I pay this tribute to my noble white brethren with a heart warm and grateful toward them. I want to see my race in unity and harmony with the whites. I want to see peace and love and the spirit of Christianity prevail, and not the vicious doctrines of bad men, of corrupt politicians, who have only their own ends to serve, and in serving them care naught for the negro's welfare nor for his soul.

Among the excellent men elected bishops of the Colored Methodist Episcopal Church, set apart in 1870 as an organization distinct from the Methodist Episcopal Church, South, Bishop Lewis H. Holsey occupies a prominent position. He contributes to these pages the following interesting paper:

I was born in 1842 near Columbus, Ga., and mainly reared in Sparta, Hancock County, Ga. In 1858 my owners moved to Athens, Ga. During the first months of this year (1858) I made up my mind that I would learn to read, so that I could read the Bible. To accomplish this coveted end I stopped going visiting at night, and devoted all my spare time to my spelling book. In those days "the old Webster blue-back speller" was the only spelling book used, so far as my knowledge goes. I bought two of these little books, one of which I tore into leaves. Each day while engaged in my work I studied from a single leaf taken from my speller, so folding the leaf that a lesson or two was on the outside of the fold. When night came on, and I had fin-

REV. LEWIS H. HOLSEY,
Bishop of the Colored M. E. Church.

ished my labor about the house and yard, I went to my sleeping apartment, and there on my back, with head toward the fireplace, I took down my whole speller, going over and reviewing the lessons that I had studied during the day from the folded leaf. My light was made by burning fat pine wood chipped from old roots and stumps that stood in the yard and garden.

I learned the alphabet by hearing the white children repeat it. Being in earnest and industrious along this line, I learned to read the Old and New Testaments in six months, besides learning to write and commit to memory many passages of the blessed word of God. From reading the word of God, and hearing it expounded by the preacher, I made up my mind to be a Christian. That year (1858) Rev. W. A. Parks was sent to Athens as pastor to the colored people. It was during the months of April and May that he had a revival meeting in which one hundred colored persons were converted and added to the Church, many of whom lived exemplary lives, demonstrating the power of a vital Christianity.

I had been praying some time before this meeting, but with no firm and decided conviction that I would seek religion in earnest. I went to church one Sunday, and Brother Parks preached from the text: "Friend, how cometh thou in hither, not having on the wedding garment?" As the glowing words fell from his mouth they seemed as arrows piercing my heart and soul, and my frame quivered with fear. I felt as if the Jesus of whom he spake was talking to me with his own thrilling accents. At the close of his sermon he invited seekers to the altar for prayer. My feeling was indescribable. Must I go or must I stay? was the momentous question that my spirit seemed to propound to me. At any rate, when I found myself I was upon my knees at the altar. This was on Sunday. While on my knees I promised the Lord that if my life was spared I would seek him day and night until I should find him. When I went home, I went to the barn and prayed for many hours, and nearly all night I continued in deep humility and earnest prayer to God for the pardoning of my sins, which appeared to me to be as the stars of heaven and as the sands of the seashore for multitude. For one dreary, long, dark seven days, whether at work or otherwise engaged, my prayer like smoke on a calm day ascended in earnest words to God in the name of his dear Son who loved me and gave himself for me. During that week I attended church every night, going to the altar each night for prayer. Sometimes our faithful and loving pastor would preach, and then some others; but no matter who preached, he closed up the meeting by a few words of instruction to "the mourners."

Sunday came; the day passed. It was a day of sorrow, agony, and prayer with me. I began to fear that I had committed the unpardonable sin against the Holy Ghost. What that sin was I did not know, but I was afraid of it. But another Sunday came, and as usual during the past week I went to the altar, with a determination that if I went to hell I would go praying. After prayer I remained at the altar. Brother Parks rose up and laid his hand on my head and said: "Brethren, I believe God will convert this boy right now." When he said this, I felt that all my sins and condemnation left me, and lightness of heart and a thrill of joy ran through my frame, and I wanted to sing and cry out, but by great effort I subdued my feeling. The meeting continued some days after, and I felt like a new man—yea, I was new. Never, to my latest day on earth, can I forget the time, place, and the experience. As Brother Parks was not an elder, his uncle, H. H. Parks, who was then pastor of the white Methodist Church, did the baptizing. I was baptized by him, and taken into the Church.

Never shall I forget the zeal, earnest, and honest work of Brother W. A. Parks and his uncle Harwell. They could have done no more for the salvation of their own people than they did for the colored. They prayed, preached, and worked with a devotion for the good of the colored people in their charge that seemed not only heroic, but angelic. I am a brand plucked from the fire by their heroic and splendid efforts. All over this Southland many, if they would, can bear the same testimony, because they came out of the bondage of sin into his blessed light by or through the preaching and labors of other noble white men who, like Brother Parks, toiled faithfully for the redemption of their souls. Indeed, the colored Methodists of this country may go into other divisions of the Methodist Church, and associate with whom they please, but let us and them remember that the brethren of the M. E. Church, South, begat them unto a lively hope in Jesus Christ.

The course of this brother has been eminently conservative, and in every difficult position he has proved himself an able and trustworthy counselor of his race.

Hon. Charles H. J. Taylor, late Minister to Liberia, writes:

I am one of those who incline to the opinion that American African slavery was the way intended by an all-wise and omnipotent Creator to bring the negro race to civilization and Christianity, who, with their fathers during the prosperous days of prehistoric Africa, had turned their backs upon God and gone off after idols. "The soul that sinneth it shall die." For every crime there must be punishment. It is right, it is natural that it should be so. Let no one think for a moment that I seek to paint in mild color the cruel and unchristianlike treatment meted out to slaves by some who served as masters only to afflict the decent, sober, and God-fearing element—by far the larger part—of the slave-holding states. There are two sides to the slavery question; the one should be told with as much pleasure to cause joy, as the other is related to occasion pain and irritate old sores left by fratricidal conflict. To tell the worst feature and leave the best unsaid would not only be wrong, but a crime.

To say that there were hundreds of masters who owned slaves who desired continually their spiritual and temporal welfare is to say what every informed person knows. I know now an old slave owner—God bless him!—who takes pleasure in relating how glad he was to own slaves, that he might constrain—yes, compel—them (for they were, in their untutored state, but children) to walk in the paths of industry, morality, and Christianity. He had often said to me that no food came into his house that did not enter for all alike, the bond and the free. When he purchased clothing or presents for his family, they were counted a part and got their share. Another picture: Sunday morning when he started to the old church in Perry County, Ala., they accompanied him. He was, indeed, a candle set upon a hill, a light which was not and could not be hid. So he lived during those days when responsibility and anxiety rested entirely with one class, while obedience, and with that obedience happiness, belonged to the other. The habits of the slaves so reared served them well as slaves and have made them successful as freemen.

Only last night I was conversing with a gentleman who is engaged in business in front of my office, and we happened to begin talking about the agitation and the general unsettled condition of "these times;" and then, by way of contrast, of the old times when there was, in so many, many instances, the most tender relation between black and white, owner and slave. How different then from now, when everything is in a ferment through the poisonous words and baneful influence of those who have no real interest in the negro himself, but simply desire to use him as a tool in furtherance of their own selfish ends! He talked about a certain old family black man with whom he was raised; how his father never bought him anything without purchasing the same thing for the black. Freedom came, and with freedom the sower of evil, and dissatisfied the old family servant with his surroundings. He left the home bought by his former master, which belonged as much to him as though he had a deed from his master for it. He had in his possession when he left a good supply of clothes, some money, and other property. Years after he returned in rags and tatters. He had gone wrong; never having to care for himself, being always provided for, the faculty of "self-preservation" was undeveloped. This gentleman told me that his father was dead when the old servant returned, and the thought of how the servant looked when he left home and his appearance when he returned hurt him so much and made him feel so sad that he could not restrain his tears. He said that he would rather have lost one thousand dollars than to have seen the sight.

A distinguished citizen of this place (Atlanta, Ga.), and an office holder, a few days ago was telling me about the returning to him of a woman he used to own. She had been gone ever since the war, and he believed her dead. He said that he was as proud to see her as he could possibly have been to see his natural mother. She is now at his house, and can live there until she dies if she desires.

Hundreds of the negroes who own their little homes in the South can and are glad to testify how their former owners helped them to acquire these places.

Every morning of my life when I visit the Recorder's court

room and the City Court, about the first thing I observe is a white man whispering in the ear of Judge James Anderson, or seeking Hon. Howard Van Epps in his room, on behalf of some unfortunate darky, said darky having been at one time the old family servant. This is not all: the interested white man waits, and if the colored man is fined, he pays the fine for him.

This article cannot be closed until I have performed my duty by a class of whites who, although not yet commented upon, stand entitled to the longest robe, the brightest crown, and a higher seat than any that has yet been mentioned. I speak of that class who are entitled to the noble honor of having been the first to enkindle the glowing light of evangelization in the darkened soul of the negro. Good men and women they were, with the spirit of their divine Master aflame in their hearts, and made of such material as asked only to wear out in that service toward which the noblest impulses of their Christianity had directed them.

I have talked with numbers of negro men and women who gladly tell me that they first felt the heaviness of their sins, and how wretched and lost was their condition without the application of the blood of Jesus, by attendance upon the meetings held by these saintly men and women I have named. No one knows, except those who have passed through the difficulties they encountered, just what their afflictions often were. Many were the cruel "cuts in words" they received for having faith in their ability to make the negro an intelligent Christian worshiper. But being full of the divine unction from above, and being strong of purpose, they continued, never halting, never fainting, never daunted, ever ready, ever waiting, and always willing, until now those of them who still live can rejoice in the God of their salvation at knowing that the seed they sowed years ago—though by many thought to have been in barren soil and lost—has quickened and sprung up into living trees of giant usefulness for the service of the Lord. God grant their eyes may not close in death until they see another picture, that of the American African brought to Christ through their efforts, taking passage for his former benighted land, there to evangelize that great continent, bringing its people to a knowledge of the truth they themselves found in the bonds of slavery! Yes, God grant that those who worked while others slept (at a time when my poor race was owned as property in this country), to teach them the doctrine of true liberty—the freedom of religion—may be spared, many of them, to gaze upon the good result of their noble, Christian labors!

When these Christian pioneers die—that is, when they go into another house, for die they will *not*—let no negro, if seats are scarce in that celestial city, sit down while one of them is standing. In other words, let my race make haste to act up to the noble principles so early instilled into them by these evangels of light, these Christian men and women who went about, and who still go about, doing good—yea, make them glad that they ever formed our acquaintance and taught us what a good thing it was to know God in the pardon of our sins.

The feeling of affinity that binds these two races together can never be destroyed, let bad men say what and do what they will. The time is ripe for the springing seeds of love—Christian love—good will and unity. The Lord send the harvest!

The Rev. A. J. Stinson, presiding elder of the Columbia, S. C., District, in the Colored Methodist Episcopal Church, writes:

I was born in Crawford County, Ga., January 13, 1847. My father and mother, then slaves, were converted before my birth under the ministry of the Methodist Church, South. At the age of three or four years I moved with them to Floyd County, nine miles west of Rome. Here in the neighborhood the white people had a schoolhouse in which meetings were held on Sundays for the colored people. We were preached to alternately by the Revs. Kitchens and Newton. Mr. Oliver McClennan was our class leader. They were all of the Methodist Episcopal Church, South, and all labored nobly among us. I remember vividly, though then a child, the gracious times of those days.

At the age of five I was baptized by the Rev. Mr. Newton. I then felt my first and lasting impression of religion and realized deeply my obligation as a baptized believer, both to God and to his Church. The keen remembrances of that hour to this day electrify my soul, and I see in my mind that old man as he took me in his arms and, looking toward heaven, said: "God bless this child!" Here a flood of holy fire sweeps over my soul, but I must not let my emotions overcome me.

At the age of fifteen I felt assuredly the call to preach, though I had not as yet made an open profession of religion. Then the terrible clash of war, which demoralized our civilized country, came on, and for four years cannons roared, musketry rattled, and sabers clashed, while the brave bled and died. Yet the fire of God's holy spirit, as a living volcano, burned on in my heart, and in the hearts of others of my race, where the sacred flame of evangelization had been enkindled by the noble efforts of the white Christians.

At the close of the war I moved to Waters District, a few miles east of Rome. Here, at Rush's Chapel, Thursday, August, 1866, while Revs. Thomas Pledger, William Hickey, and A. M. Thigpen—the latter then pastor in Rome—were conducting a revival meeting for the white people, but which any of us who wished were allowed to attend, my soul, while Rev. Mr. Pledger preached, was revived as into a burning flame. Thinking, however, that it would appear rude to give vent to my feelings there—though the whole congregation was shouting—I made for the door, then outside to the woods, where I praised God alone for four hours. On the Sunday following Rev. Mr. Pledger preached for the colored people in the same church, and thirty-five of us became members. Rev. William Hickey, our pastor, was present and appointed me the same day as class leader and exhorter.

But I must not conclude ere telling how I came to be at that Thursday meeting, where Rev. Mr. Pledger aroused such a fire in my heart. It was through Mr. Branchfield, father of Rev. William Branchfield, of the Georgia Conference. God bless him! Passing me on his way to church, he said to me: "Come, my boy, and go to church with me." I told him I would be on soon, but I had no idea as I spoke of keeping my promise. After the good man had gone, however, his words, his face, and his manner all came back to me so forcibly, seeming to speak to me even then, that I could resist no longer, and so I went on after him to the house of God, and was there and then gloriously converted. Thank God that I can say, like David: "I was glad when they said to me, Let us go into the house of the Lord."

Rev. Washington Phillips, with his sons, occupies a prominent place in the Colored Methodist Episcopal Church. Rev. J. T. Phillips writes:

I was born at Newnan, in Coweta, Ga., June 24, 1837. I am the oldest son of Rev. Washington Phillips, of Milledgeville, Ga. My father joined the Methodist Church at the age of fifteen; he has been a member sixty years. My mother was converted when I was four weeks old, and joined the Methodist Church shortly afterwards. She has been a member fifty-three years

I joined the Methodist Episcopal Church, South, under the preaching of the Rev. Mr. Knox, who was then pastor of the Church at Milledgeville. It was during the time of a revival; white and black were alike powerfully impressed. The preacher preached to both white and colored, as faithfully to one as to the other. Milledgeville was a station. The pastor preached once a month also in the country to white and colored. I was converted May 8, 1859. That date remains engraven upon my memory. I at once commenced talking, going from house to house, telling my people of the blessed Saviour I had found. The church at Milledgeville was very large. The colored members were given full use of the gallery. They crowded it day and night.

I was licensed to preach by Elder Josiah Lewis in 1867, and joined the Conference in 1869. I preached four years in Milledgeville, was five years presiding elder, and eleven years on circuits. While I was presiding my white brethren were ever kind to me. They helped me gladly in many ways. They gave me money and they gave me encouragement. I cannot tell how many of them gave me lots on which to build churches. I have never bought a single lot on which to build a church; all have been given through the kindness of my white brethren. I gratefully give this testimony to their kindness, help, and liberality. They treated me as a Christian and a brother. May it return to them a hundredfold.

My owners, too, were kind. They allowed their children to teach my father's children to read. I will be fifty-three years old in June. I have three brothers, and all four of us are Methodist preachers. By God's grace we hope to meet in heaven.

I have seen many ups and downs in life, but through them all the star of light, kindled through the noble Christian efforts of the white ministry, has shown over the way, lighting me along the path that leads to my Father's house of many mansions.

I long to see harmony, good will, and brotherly charity between the two races that it seems God's will shall live together. I want the sentiments and teachings of Christian men and women to prevail and not the plots and vile intrigues of scheming politicians. As a general thing, the negro loves the white man. He looks up to him and trusts him, and it is a great mistake when the white man fails to meet this trust with the kindliness and grace he knows so well how to use.

I say to my colored brethren to trust the white man whose noble concern is for their immortal souls, whose hand is fearless to help in time of trouble, whose souls is knit to them by the old kindly ties of days of yore, whose ancestors through pains and noble toils brought spiritual light to the negro's soul. These are the men—and thank God there are many of them throughout the South to-day!—who have sincerely at heart the negro's best interest, who treat him as a fellow-human being, who are glad to see him succeed in life, who deal justly with him, are considerate of his claims, and who meet him as a brother, a brother in Christ, on the broad plane of Christianity.

With these testimonies of gratitude from the members of a race formerly held in bondage we close the record of toil, hardship, and self-denial on the part of the missionaries of the cross. That they have not been exposed to every danger incurred by pioneers in heathen lands is true, but they encountered difficulties peculiar to their times and to the nature of their work. Most of these workmen have gone forward to the meeting of the "General Assembly and Church of the Firstborn" in heaven, and those who remain must follow soon. To each will come in due season the welcome plaudit: "Well done, good and faithful servant, enter thou into the joy of thy Lord."

www.ingramcontent.com/pod-product-compliance
Lightning Source LLC
Chambersburg PA
CBHW051745300426
44115CB00007B/690